身心障礙學生的轉銜教育與服務

Transition Education and Service for Students
with Special Education Needs

台灣學障學會　策劃

林素貞、趙本強、黃秋霞　主編

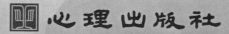
心理出版社

目次（Contents）

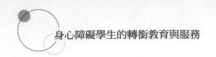

作者簡介（About the Author）

林素貞（**Su-jan Lin**）

職稱：國立高雄師範大學特殊教育學系教授

學歷：美國奧瑞崗大學（University of Oregon）特殊教育學系博士

專長：身心障礙學生轉銜教育、學習障礙者教育、個別化教育計畫、身心
　　　障礙學生課程與教學、特殊教育行政與法規

Charlotte Y. Alverson

職稱：美國奧瑞崗大學（University of Oregon）副教授研究員、美國「國立
　　　轉銜技術協助中心」（National Technical Assistance Center on Transi-
　　　tion, NTACT）諮詢委員

學歷：美國奧瑞崗大學（University of Oregon）特殊教育學系博士（主修中
　　　學階段特殊教育與轉銜）

專長：中學階段身心障礙學生的轉銜方案、身心障礙學生高中畢業後成果
　　　之究、特殊教育的決策分析

劉馨君（**Kimy Liu**）

職稱：美國加利福尼亞州立大學斯坦尼斯洛斯分校（California State Univer-
　　　sity, Stanislaus）特殊教育師資培育副教授

學歷：美國奧瑞崗大學（University of Oregon）特殊教育學系博士

專長：閱讀教學與評量、師資培育研究、美國特殊教育法規

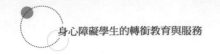

Michael L. Wehmeyer

職稱：美國堪薩斯大學（University of Kansas）特殊教育學系教授、堪薩斯大學 Beach Center on Disability 中心主任

學歷：美國德州大學達拉斯校區（University of Texas at Dallas）人類發展與溝通科學以及發展心理學雙博士

專長：自我決策、生涯轉銜、智能及發展障礙青少年與成年之教育與輔導、課程教學

趙本強（Pen-Chiang Chao）

職稱：中原大學特殊教育學系副教授

學歷：美國亞歷桑納州立大學（Arizona State University）課程與教學系博士（主修特殊教育）

專長：身心障礙學生轉銜教育、自我決策、測驗評量、輕度障礙

張大倫（Dalun Zhang）

職稱：美國德克薩斯州農工大學（Texas A&M University）特殊教育學系教授

學歷：美國紐奧良大學（University of New Orleans）特殊教育暨復健服務系博士

專長：身心障礙學生轉銜教育與服務、自我決策

李依帆（Yi-Fan Li）

學歷：現為美國德克薩斯州農工大學（Texas A&M University）教育心理學系博士班學生（主修特殊教育）

專長：身心障礙學生轉銜教育、身心障礙學生就讀大專校院議題

Leena Jo Landmark

職稱：美國聖豪斯頓州立大學教與學學院（School of Teaching and Learning at Sam Houston State University）副教授、Eleanor and Charles Garrett 轉銜和障礙研究中心（Center on Transition and Disability Studies）主任

學歷：美國德克薩斯州農工大學（Texas A&M University）教育心理學系博士（主修特殊教育）

專長：身心障礙中學生的轉銜與教學、自我決策、轉銜計畫、家庭參與、身心障礙學生在大專校院的教育實務

Kendra Williams-Diehm

職稱：美國奧克拉荷馬州大學（University of Oklahoma）教育心理學系特殊教育組副教授

學歷：美國德克薩斯州農工大學（Texas A&M University）教育心理學系博士（主修特殊教育）

專長：身心障礙學生轉銜服務、自我決策、身心障礙學生高中畢業後成果之研究、認知與發展障礙

周宇琪（Yu-Chi Chou）

職稱：中原大學特殊教育學系助理教授

學歷：美國堪薩斯大學（University of Kansas）特殊教育學系博士

專長：自我決策、自閉症教育、社交技巧訓練、課程調整

鄭淑芬（Shu-Fen Cheng）

職稱：中原大學特殊教育學系副教授

學歷：美國明尼蘇達大學雙城分校（University of Minnesota, Twin Cities）教育心理學系博士（主修特殊教育）

專長：輕度障礙、測驗評量、智能障礙、聽語障教育

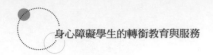
鞠頌（Song Ju）

職稱：美國辛辛那提大學（University of Cincinnati）教育學院特殊教育組副
　　　教授

學歷：美國德克薩斯州農工大學（Texas A&M University）教育心理學系博
　　　士（主修特殊教育）

專長：中學階段身心障礙學生轉銜教育、身心障礙學生就讀大學與就業議
　　　題、身心障礙青少年犯罪議題、身心障礙學生的自我決策。

余昌儒（Jimmy Yu）

學生，就讀臺北某科技大學

林靜如（Ching-Ju Lin）

臺北某科技大學助理教授

王小語（Lisa Wong）

學生，就讀臺北某科技大學

前言（Preface）

　　台灣學障學會成立於 2005 年，至 2020 年剛好屆滿 15 年，也歷經了五屆的理監事會。學會的設立宗旨為促進臺灣學習障礙的研究、教育和福祉發展，多年來透過年會、研討會、電子報、粉絲專頁，以及參與各項活動完成各項任務和使命，而出版專書也一直是學會發揮學術影響力的重要方式，同時也是學會的優良傳統。過去四屆的理監事會皆策劃出版過學習障礙相關主題的學術專書：《突破學習困難：評量與因應之探討》、《突破閱讀困難：理念與實務》、《帶好每一個學生：有效的補救教學》、《突破數學學習困難：理論與實務》，此四本專書探討學習障礙學生聽、說、讀、寫、算的主要學科學習問題，也涵蓋從學習障礙的鑑定、課程與教學的介入到學習的評量探討，對臺灣學習障礙教育的實務教學與研究注入了一股強大且深厚的正向影響。

　　臺灣學術界長期對特殊教育都非常積極的投入，學習障礙學生近年來也一直是身心障礙學生中出現率最高的一群，也因此學習障礙學生的相關教育議題一直受到許多的關注；但當我們投入這麼多的特殊教育資源，身心障礙學生接受了十幾年的特殊教育服務之後，我們應該自問一個問題：**學習障礙學生在高中或大學畢業以後的發展如何？我們所提供的特殊教育服務是否可以更有效地協助學習障礙學生成功地邁向他們的成人生活？**而這些議題正是轉銜教育與服務的核心價值。因此，在出版上述特殊教育課程與教學的教育輸入議題之後，學會的第五本專書：《身心障礙學生的轉銜教育與服務》，是想要從轉銜的學理、研究、實務到學習障礙學生的個案經驗分享，探討特殊教育最後一哩路的教育輸出議題：我們在高中階段如何協助身心障礙學生後續能順利進入升學（大專校院）、就業與成人獨立生活之生命階段。

　　長久以來，我們都非常關注學習障礙學生的鑑定安置、課程教學、評量等歷程議題，在這些議題上也有了豐富的教學實務和研究成就；相對

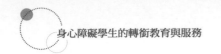
地，學生在高中期間的轉銜教育與連結到高中畢業以後的成果與流向，在政策、教學實務和研究上，過去都較少涉及這個議題。基於臺灣在轉銜的實施和研究尚呈起步階段，故本書的編輯乃向美國的轉銜實務與研究學者邀稿尋求支援，也因此內容較多取材借重於美國的豐富經驗，亦由美國與臺灣的學者攜手合著，所以本書實為具有跨國文化經驗整合特色的一本學術專書。

本書共有八章，主要作者都是專研轉銜教育與服務的主題，部分資料會以中文和英文並列，主要是讓美國作者了解本書的重要訊息。第一章和第三章是由美國和臺灣學者共同合寫，第二章、第三章、第四章和第六章則是美國學者以英文撰寫，因此這四章都設計有「中文重點摘錄」，以幫助中文讀者閱讀。以下說明各章的內容概況。

本書第一章為概論，全面性介紹轉銜的定義、歷史發展到現今的實施概況，由林素貞教授設計大綱，說明臺灣目前在轉銜政策和實施上的現況，而兩位任教於美國的 Charlotte Y. Alverson 教授和 Kimy Liu 教授則以英文撰寫，敘述美國的轉銜政策、實施和研究成果，最後再由林素貞教授翻譯成中文並整合加入臺灣的內容。

第二章是說明近二十幾年來美國如何研發出轉銜的實證本位教學與實證本位預測指標，以作為實施轉銜服務的發展方向。本章作者 Charlotte Y. Alverson 教授是長期參與此研發計畫的研究人員之一，本書內容可謂是第一手資料。

第三章由美國的 Michael L. Wehmeyer 教授和臺灣的趙本強教授以英文合寫，論述美國和臺灣如何教導身心障礙學生的自我決策能力。教導身心障礙學生自我決策能力是轉銜教育與服務的關鍵重點，而兩位學者皆是美國和臺灣研究自我決策能力發展的翹楚學者。

第四章呈現美國身心障礙學生升學高等教育及就業轉銜的歷程，此歷程乃是特殊教育最後一階段的學校教育介入，所以更形重要。本章由美國學者張大倫教授領導他的研究團隊完成，成員之一的李依帆也是在臺灣訓練的特殊教育教師，目前正在美國攻讀博士學位。

第五章係由趙本強教授的研究團隊，針對臺灣身心障礙學生轉銜至大

專校院的實證資料，提出研究分析結果，能夠客觀呈現目前臺灣身心障礙學生在高等教育的轉銜後現況，此章亦可以對照比較第四章的美國經驗。

第六章是由張大倫教授的研究團隊合著，介紹美國實施轉銜評量的定義和教師可以運用的工具。轉銜評量的發展在臺灣仍屬方興未艾，希望藉由此章的內容，可以激發我們對轉銜評量的了解與未來發展。

第七章是介紹由一項研究成果所提出的臺灣高中階段學校本位的轉銜教育輔導歷程，其中的轉銜評量實施有使用第六章所介紹的轉銜評量工具。本章由林素貞教授所著，以兩校為例說明資源班和特教班的轉銜相關教學活動的規劃，也呈現兩校身心障礙學生高中畢業後的成果。

第八章是透過兩位學習障礙學生的重要關係人：父親與輔導教師，協助兩位學習障礙學生陳述他們的生涯轉銜故事，從學習障礙學生從小在學習與生活的困難，導引出他們如何面對學習上的挑戰及衍生的生活問題，他們又將會如何走出自己未來的希望人生。

本書從擬訂篇章主題、邀稿到最後的稿件編修，都非常感謝編輯小組的趙本強教授和黃秋霞教授不畏辛苦和通力合作，尤其涉及國外學者的邀稿和編修到中文重點摘錄工作，更是需要許許多多的溝通與時間投入，台灣學障學會致以最高謝意。台灣學障學會的四本學術專書一直都由心理出版社協助出版，第五本亦一承傳統由心理出版社協助發行，在此非常感謝林敬堯總編輯願意耐心指導與專業協助，本書方能在台灣學障學會 2020 年的年會時間同時出版，在年會中也將邀請本書作者之一的張大倫教授作轉銜議題的專題演講。期待本書能對臺灣身心障礙學生的轉銜教育政策、實務和研究產生促動的激勵，能帶動我們關注身心障礙學生的高中轉銜教育以及高中畢業後的發展，尤其是學習障礙青少年在升學、就業和獨立生活準備的學校轉銜教育與服務，乃是目前我們特殊教育需要急起直追和奮力向前的課題。

台灣學障學會第五屆理事長

林素貞 教授　謹誌

第一章　轉銜教育與服務概論
Introduction of Transition Education and Service

林素貞（Su-jan Lin）、Charlotte Y. Alverson、
劉馨君（Kimy Liu）

　　對於絕大多數的身心障礙者和他們的家人而言，身心障礙是終身的議題；美國和臺灣的特殊教育之設立宗旨，都是用以提供身心障礙學生適性的特殊教育和相關專業服務，以協助身心障礙學生可以發揮其生命之最大潛能。誠如美國《身心障礙者教育法》（Individuals with Disabilities Education Act, IDEA）的立法目的，乃是「確保所有身心障礙兒童都有機會接受免費、適當的公立教育，強調以特殊教育和相關服務，以滿足身心障礙兒童的獨特需要，並為他們下一階段的教育、就業和獨立生活做好準備」（IDEA, 2004, 34 CFR §300.1(a)）。臺灣《特殊教育法》的立法目的也是特殊教育的目標，乃為「為使身心障礙及資賦優異之國民，均有接受適性教育之權利，充分發展身心潛能，培養健全人格，增進服務社會能力」（教育部，2009），臺灣和美國的特殊教育法立法精神亦揭櫫了國家提供特殊教育的終極目的。

　　從我國和美國的特殊教育立法精神可以得知，我們皆期待身心障礙學生在完成義務教育之後，仍可以和其他非身心障礙學生一樣繼續升學、就業和獨立生活，期盼身心障礙學生也能和其他人一樣，依循著年齡的漸長與成熟，一步一步成功地邁向社會化的成人生活。依據我國《108 年度特殊教育統計年報》（教育部，2019b）的資料顯示，107 學年度的身心障礙學生從學前到大專校院共有 12 萬 6,464 人；而此一年度的特殊教育經費預算為 111 億 7,380 萬元，占教育部主管總預算的 4.55%，已達《特殊教育法》所訂定之 4.5%的標準，其中身心障礙教育的預算為 107 億 8,894 萬 9,000 元，占特殊教育經費預算的 96.56%；同時地方政府之直轄市和各縣市的特殊教育

總預算經費約為 303 億元，占全國地方縣市教育預算總額的 7.34%，亦達《特殊教育法》規定之地方的法定標準 5%。如此高額比例的教育經費投入於身心障礙學生的特殊教育，我們確實應該了解特殊教育的成效究竟為何？經過長期的特殊教育協助，身心障礙學生是否可以充分發展身心潛能、培養健全人格、增進服務社會能力？亦即是身心障礙學生，是否可以為他們下一階段的繼續教育、就業和獨立生活作好準備，邁向成功的成人生活？這些議題就是轉銜教育與服務議題，轉銜是一段長時間的教育需求的整合規劃，轉銜教育與服務的實施如同特殊教育的最後一哩路，終點是特殊教育的目的：協助身心障礙學生順利銜接高中或大學畢業後的升學、就業和成人獨立生活之人生進程。

　　美國的《身心障礙者教育法》強調，身心障礙學生最終能具有自給自足的經濟能力、繼續教育和獨立生活的目標，這些目標的設立乃是來自於早期的轉銜政策和長期實證研究的發現，這些長期研究都提出身心障礙學生高中畢業後的成效表現不佳。我們很難說明轉銜政策或是教育長期實證研究何者為先，導引出特殊教育的設立目標，應該是兩者相互呼應、相輔相成，締造出對美國身心障礙教育宗旨、具體目標和影響。本章將先從時間序介紹美國一百多年來轉銜服務的政策與模式的發展，再論及美國轉銜相關研究，以及聯邦政府資助的研究計畫之成果，後續說明美國各州教育部門如何執行以身心障礙學生高中畢業後的成效，評估州政府所屬學區和學校執行特殊教育的成效，此外亦說明學校轉銜教育實施的重要向度，以及學校應如何與職業復健機構合作；相較於美國轉銜政策與服務的實施，本章亦針對臺灣目前轉銜的現行法規和政策提出說明與討論。

壹、美國轉銜教育與服務的政策和模式發展

　　美國轉銜教育與服務的政策和運作模式乃相互影響，引領著今日轉銜教育與服務的定位，轉銜的發展從 1910 年代至今，若以時期區分可以成為三個主要階段：1910～1980 年代、1990～2000 年代，以及 2004 年至今，分述如下。

一、1910～1980 年代

從 1917 年的《史密斯—休斯法案》（Smith-Hughes Act）開始，一百多年來美國聯邦政策一直關注教育要為學生高中畢業以後的生活預做準備這個議題，此法規後來也成為《國家職業法》（National Vocational Act），這是第一個美國聯邦政府向各州提供配套教育經費的聯邦政策，這個政策可以提供支援給教導職業領域的教師，以促進農業、貿易和工業方面高中教育的實施，目前這些領域也包括在職業和技術教育的方案中（Poppen & Alverson, 2018）。1965 年所通過的《小學和中等教育法》（The Elementary and Secondary Education Act of 1965, ESEA），乃以國家立法來培養下一代國民的工作力，以作為消除貧窮的手段，後來《小學和中等教育法》修正案更特別為身心障礙學生提供職業教育的支援（Poppen & Alverson, 2018）。

1960 年代，美國的學校和職業復健機構簽署了一項正式協定，創立了跨機構合作的「工作／學習合作方案」（cooperative work/study programs），此即為 Halpern 所提出美國轉銜教育與服務之三個重要社會運動的第一階段，此方案試圖減少或減輕青少年高中畢業後最初幾年的掙扎期，因為他們必須開始面對在其社區中承擔的各種成人角色（Halpern, 1992）。

此由公立學校和地區性州政府的職業復健機構一起建置的合作計畫，主要提供輕度身心障礙學生學科學習、社會技能、職業訓練課程，由公立學校指定一位教師擔任高中的職業輔導員，此教師將利用其在學校的部分時間，協助學生找到職業工作安置方案，此職業安置方案可以列入這些學生的高中部分課程學習，此外由教師擔任的職業輔導員同時也會轉介學生給各州政府的職業復健機構，進行職業復健服務。

然而，此合作計畫到 1970 年代就中止了，因為執行運作上發生了兩個主要問題。問題一是此教師額外擔任職業安置的工作薪資，乃由職業復健機構支付，因此職業復健機構也要負責督導此教師的工作表現，此跨機構共同評估人員考績的狀況，讓許多高中校長對於執行這樣的合作關係感到困擾。問題二是 1973 年美國修訂的《復健法》（Rehabilitation Act of 1973）規定職業復健機構不得支付費用給其他機關，如果那是機構本身應該執行

的工作，然而當時因為學校教育並沒有特別執行職業安置的相關課程，所以那時的職業復健機構尚可以支援公立學校的此計畫。但在 1975 年美國公告了《全體障礙兒童教育法》（Education for All Handicapped Children Act, EHA, 1975），此法案規定學校提供給學生的工作經驗方案，可以算是學校必須提供給身心障礙學生的適性教育，亦即是從此學校必須提供有職業學習經驗的課程給學生，因此《全體障礙兒童教育法》的內容和《復健法》的規定相牴觸，職業復健機構從此不可再付薪資給學校兼任此職業輔導工作的教師，所以工作／學習合作計畫於是宣告結束（Test, Aspel, & Everson, 2006）。

　　Halpern（1992）所稱轉銜教育與服務三個重要社會運動的第二階段是「生涯教育」時期。生涯教育萌芽於 1970 年代，乃是由當時的美國教育部長 Sidney P. Marland 所提出，他將生涯教育視為當時美國教育部在普通教育的最優先執行政策（Hoyt, 1982），從國小、國中到高中的各級學校都要提供所有學生的生涯教育課程，生涯教育強調在所有教育階段都要實施學生的生涯覺知、生涯探索、生涯決策和生涯規劃（Halpern, 1992; Test et al., 2006）。1974 年，美國教育部成立了生涯教育處（Office of Career Education），1977 年，美國通過了《生涯教育實施獎勵辦法》（Career Education Implementation Incentive Act, P. L. 95-207），該辦法亦特別提到所有學生包含身心障礙學生，都必須接受生涯教育課程，當時該法案撥款 4 千 5 百萬美元用於執行該政策。然而在 1983 年，美國國會撤銷了《生涯教育實施獎勵辦法》的經費補助，從此生涯教育政策只剩下協助輕度身心障礙學生從高中到職場的就業服務（Hoyt, 1982）。同一時期，1976 年美國的特殊教育專業組織「特殊兒童協會」（Council of Exceptional Children）也正式成立「生涯發展分會」（The Division on Career Development），專注於身心障礙學生的生涯教育發展

　　Halpern（1992）所提出美國的轉銜教育與服務三個重要社會運動的第三階段，乃是 1980 至 1990 年代的「轉銜」時期。「轉銜」理念的萌發，乃始於 1983 年美國教育部特殊教育和康復服務辦公室（Office of Special Education and Rehabilitation Services, OSERS）所公告的一份政策文件，這份聲明

強調服務與支援學生的重要性，以幫助學生在高中畢業後能順利進入成人的角色。Will（1983）的宣言與《職業教育實施獎勵法》（Career Education Implementation Incentive Act）中的用詞相呼應，聲稱「讓學生具備就業的資格是美國教育的一項默示承諾」（p. 2）。在此政策文件中，轉銜被定義為：「……注重結果的過程，包括廣泛的服務和經驗，以導引出學生未來的就業。轉銜是一個長時間階段期的概念，它包含高中階段、高中畢業時、後續的高中畢業後教育或成人服務，以及剛開始就業的最初幾年，轉銜是介於安全和結構化的學校環境與機會多和風險高的成人生活之間的橋梁」（Will, 1983）。此份政策聲明亦將高中和就業描述為兩個獨立的個體；而連接這兩個個體的是三座「橋梁」，以供學生選擇使用，幫助學生從高中移轉到就業，稱為「從學校到工作生活的橋梁模式」（bridges model-from school to working life）（如圖 1-1 所示）。該政策宣稱，從高中到工作和成人生活需要「在中學做好充分準備，在離開學校時提供充分支援，並在成人的情況下提供所需要得機會和服務」（Will, 1983, p. 2）。

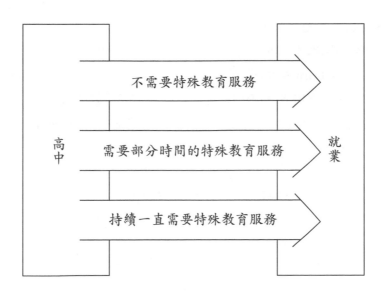

圖 1-1　從學校到就業的橋梁模式

　　Will（1983）在美國教育部特殊教育和康復服務辦公室（OSERS）的政策上提出，就業是身心障礙學生高中畢業後的主要目標，「注重就業是有效轉銜的核心結果，也是衡量轉銜是否成功的客觀評估標準」（p. 4）。「從學校到工作的橋梁模式」（bridges model-from school to working life）的特點是學生轉銜時通常需要的服務類型，此三個橋梁通道分別是：(1)不需要特殊教育服務（no special service）：學校裡所有人都可以運用的資源，不特定指身心障礙者；(2)需要部分時間的特殊教育服務（time-limited services）：身心障礙者才可以使用的，有時期限制的資源，例如：社區中的職業復健機構，通常會要求身心障礙申請者必須具備高中的畢業證書；(3)持續一直需要特殊教育服務（ongoing service）：身心障礙者終身都可以使用的永續資源（Will, 1983）。

　　橋梁模式推出後，相關學者乃批評 OSERS 的「從學校到工作的橋梁模式」只關注於學生的就業，似乎過於狹隘。Halpern（1985）則提出了一個修訂的轉銜模型，以擴展 OSERS 的橋梁模型，此即為三個支柱的「社區適應模式」（community adjustment model），如圖 1-2 所示，希望大家能夠更關注身心障礙學生離校後的整體社區生活適應問題（林素貞，1995）。Halpern 於此模式中提出成功轉銜的三個重要支柱：社區環境、就業，以及社交人際網絡。Halpern（1985）的模型將就業放在三個支柱最前端和最中心的位置，此乃與 OSERS 的橋梁模式保持一致，因為就業包含求職網絡、求職技能、最低工資水準、雇主的獎勵措施、工作歧視和結構性的失業等。第二支柱是社區環境，除了個人住家的滿意以外，人們還必須考慮所在社區鄰居的品質和安全，以及居家附近的社區服務和休閒娛樂的使用機會。第三個支柱是社交人際網絡，此包括人際關係的主要層面，例如日常溝通、自尊、家庭支援、情感的成熟、友誼和親密關係（Halpern, 1985, p. 481）。

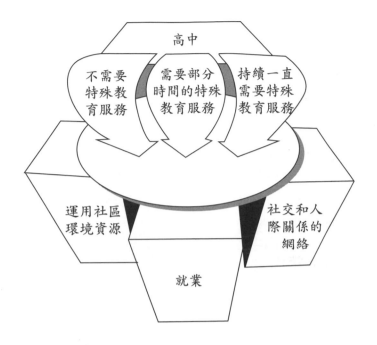

圖 1-2　社區適應轉銜模式

資料來源：Halpern（1985, p. 481）

　　Halpern 於 1980 年代所提出的社區適應轉銜模式並未包含高中畢業之後的繼續教育的支柱，事實上在 21 世紀之後，短期的培訓方案、二年制和四年制大學，或是專業級的職業訓練等，都是學生高中畢業後常見的繼續教育。Carnevale、Smith 與 Strohl（2013）估計，在 2020 年，65%的工作職缺都需要在高中之後的某種持續進修。以今日觀點論之，1980 年代提出的社區適應轉銜模式，若在今日社會的發展趨勢，則需要增加「繼續教育」的支柱，因此擴大此模式確實有其時代的必要性，不僅從目前對工作所需的基本教育水準要求，或是從過去二十年來接受高等教育機會的身心障礙學生人數的增加中可見一斑。1990 年，美國有 26%的身心障礙學生在高中畢業後接受繼續教育，2005 年時此一比例已經增加到 44%（Cameto, 2007）。美國國家教育統計中心（National Center for Education Statistics, 2006）發現，2004 年有 10%的新生進入大學時具有身心障礙學生的身分，2015～2016

年，19%的大學部學生乃具有身心障礙學生的資格（National Center for Education Statistics, 2019）。此外，進入大專校院就讀的機會並不限於輕度或高出現率的身心障礙學生，例如：聽力障礙或特定學習障礙，美國思想學院（thinkcollege.net）和認知障礙學生轉銜與中學後方案（TPSID, thinkcollege.net/tpsid）等專案，正在為認知障礙者和其他發展障礙者（如自閉症）提供繼續就讀高等教育的機會，Think College 在「大學搜索」中列出了 270 個身心障礙學生可以參與的課程（參見 thinkcollege.net/tpsid），對於在 21 世紀的大多數身心障礙青年而言，高中畢業後轉銜繼續教育，顯然已經是一項主要的選擇。

二、1990～2000 年代

1990 年美國《全體障礙兒童教育法》（Education for All Handicapped Children Act）重新修改內容且更名為《身心障礙者教育 1990 年修正法》（Individuals with Disabilities Education Act Amendments of 1990, IDEA），此法案又被稱為美國的轉銜法案，因為這是「轉銜」一詞與其定義第一次出現在美國的特殊教育法規當中，並且載明轉銜服務的內容，以及針對 16 歲的學生制定個別化轉銜計畫（individualized transition plan, ITP），開始提供轉銜服務。此時，轉銜服務被定義為「一套整合性的學生活動，強化以學生的學習結果導向之歷程，統整學生從學校到畢業後離校的活動，包括高中畢業後的高等教育、職業訓練、整合性就業（包括支持性就業）、繼續教育和成人教育、成人服務、獨立生活或社區參與。整合性的學生活動應基於學生個人的需要，考慮到學生的偏好和興趣，並應包括教學、社區經驗、就業發展和其他成人生活目標，並適學生需求提供日常生活技能和功能性職業評估」（IDEA, 1990, 20 U.S.C. 1401(a)）。

美國於 1997 年又重新公告《身心障礙者教育 1997 年修正法》（Individuals with Disabilities Education Act Amendments of 1997），此法案對轉銜教育有更具體的規範，以強調提升身心障礙學生可以獲得教育的機會和「……使他們為就業和獨立生活做好準備」（IDEA, 1997, 34 CFR =300.1

(a)），同時下降開始實施轉銜教育與服務的時程為 14 歲。此外，1990 年美國《身心障礙兒童之教育法案》（Education for All Handicapped Children Act）尚未論及實際執行轉銜評估和成年的年齡定義，而這兩個議題也都納入了 1997 年的法案規範（Flexer, Simmons, Luft, & Baer, 2001）

三、2004 年至今

2004 年，美國《身心障礙者教育 2004 年修正法》針對轉銜又提出更多具體的修改；首先，修訂了該法的目的：「確保所有身心障礙兒童都有機會接受免費、適當的公立教育，強調特殊教育和相關服務，需滿足身心障礙兒童的獨特需要，並為他們未來的繼續教育、就業和獨立生活做好準備」（IDEA, 2004, 20 U.S.C. 1401(d)(1)(A)）。此法案對「未來的繼續教育」一詞乃明確指出，特殊教育應該為身心障礙學生的繼續高等教育做好準備。 第二，修改了轉銜服務的定義：(1)「為身心障礙兒童開展的一套整合性的學生活動，旨在建立達成教育成果的歷程，重點是提高身心障礙兒童學科能力和功能性能力，統整學生從學校到畢業後離校的活動，包括高中畢業後的高等教育、職業訓練、整合性就業（包括支持性就業）、繼續教育和成人教育、成人服務、獨立生活和社區參與」；(2)基於孩子的個人需要，考慮孩子的優勢、偏好和興趣；(3)「包括教學、相關專業服務、社區經驗、就業發展和其他成人生活目標，並視學生需求提供日常生活技能和功能性職業評估」（IDEA, 2004,20 U.S.C.1401(34)）。 這些變化進一步強調了特殊教育應該為身心障礙兒童高中後的生活一高中後繼續教育、就業和獨立生活一做好準備，同時學校的教育應該從學生的優勢能力考量學生的學科能力和生活技能的發展。第三個變化是轉銜服務的啟動年齡，該法規定，轉銜服務不可遲於身心障礙學生年滿 16 歲時生效的第一個個別化教育計畫，此後依隨個別化教育計畫每年要修定一次，此扭轉了 1997 年「轉銜服務從 14 歲開始」的規定。第四個變化是轉銜計畫的內容乃載於個別化教育計畫之內，轉銜計畫包含適齡的轉銜評量、轉銜服務、學習課程，以規劃出可評量的學生高中畢業後的教育目標，包含就業、教育、職業訓練和

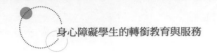

獨立生活能力。

美國《身心障礙者教育 2004 年修正法》的轉銜相關規定反映了特殊教育的基礎典範的轉變——即是從轉銜的觀點導入身心障礙兒童的教育重點，以及個別化教育計畫的擬定（Kohler, 1996; Kohler, Gothberg, & Coyle, 2017）。基於長期性投入和關注學生高中畢業後的成效，《身心障礙者教育 2004 年修正法》對於轉銜的相關變革，乃要求學生的個別化教育計畫團隊所設計的計畫，需要協助學生避免從高中畢業到成人的掙扎困難時期，順利轉換到成人的生活和角色。

貳、美國轉銜研究和聯邦政府的研究計畫

1970 和 1980 年代，早期轉銜議題的研究人員對身心障礙者接受教育後的結果展現出濃厚的興趣（deJung & Reed, 1978; Liebert & Weissman, 1982）。1980 年代，大量的研究人員（Edgar, 1985, 1987, 1988; Hasazi, Gordon, & Roe, 1985; Kranstover, Thurlow, & Bruininks, 1989; Mithaug, Horiuchi, & Fanning, 1984; Schalock, Wolzen, Ross, Elliott, Werbel, & Peterson, 1986）提出類似的相同問題：「接受特殊教育的身心障礙學生畢業離開學校後發展為何？接受特殊教育服務的學生之就業狀況為何？特殊教育的目的是什麼？」最後這些研究結果和其他長期追蹤研究的結果一致，即是接受特殊教育的學生在高中畢業後的就業、教育或獨立生活的比率，都比非身心障礙學生為低，例如：(1)身心障礙青年主要會從事低技能和低工資的工作；24%的人沒有工作，36%的人離職的主要原因是被解雇（Mithaug et al., 1984）；(2)有工作的身心障礙青年中，63%的平均每週工作時數是 22 小時；(3)78%的身心障礙者生活在需要督導協助支援的居住環境中（Schalock et al., 1986）。

1985 年至 1990 年期間，美國教育部進行了第一次的「全國長期縱貫性轉銜研究」（National Longitudinal Transition Study, NLTS），1985～1986 學年約有 10,370 位 13 至 21 歲的身心障礙學生開始參與此計畫。NLTS 的目的是調查高中畢業後身心障礙學生的流向，內容包含就業、薪資、繼續教育

和獨立居住狀況。NLTS 的調查結果將研究對象統稱為「全國身心障礙青年和各州接受特殊教育的青年」（Newman, Wagner, Cameto, Knokey, & Shaver, 2010）。Wagner、Blackorby、Cameto 與 Newman（1993）指出，NLTS 的調查結果為：(1)高中畢業後，感官障礙學生比學習障礙學生有較高比率進入 2 年制或 4 年制的大學；(2)學生高中畢業後的流向受到個人的障礙類別、學校（不佳的教育方案）和家庭條件（如單親家庭、貧困）的影響；(3)輕度身心障礙青年在高中期間有持續參加職業教育或特定職業的概論課程，將比沒有接受類似職業教育課程的學生，多出20～40%獲得競爭型就業的機會；(4)身心障礙青年的就業率是 57%，顯著低於非身心障礙青年的 69%（Blackorby & Wagner, 1996）。

　　第一次「全國長期縱貫性轉銜研究」結案後的第 15 年，2005 年美國教育部又啟動了「第二次全國長期縱貫性轉銜研究」（National Longitudinal Transition Study-2 ,NLTS2），此研究與第一次縱貫性研究一樣，NLTS2 使用多階段抽樣方式建立具有代表性的青年樣本，樣本依據學區和特殊學校的地區、規模（學生人數）和社區的經濟狀況進行分層抽樣（Newman et al., 2010），研究時期為 2001 至 2009 年，於 2000 年 12 月 1 日建立總共約 11,270 名，13 至 16 歲或七年級以上的身心障礙學生資料。此研究的調查結果發現：(1)19%的身心障礙學生就讀於四年制學院和大學，而非身心障礙學生則為 40%；(2)與四年制大學相比，身心障礙學生較高比例就讀於二年制學院或職業學校；(3)身心障礙學生進入四年制大學且接受校內身心障礙服務，35%的身心障礙學生可以畢業，而同時非身心障礙學生則有 55%的畢業率；(4)身心障礙學生的就業率繼續低於非身心障礙學生（如每週有較少的工時、工資較低和福利較差）（Newman et al., 2011）；(5)與非身心障礙的青年相比，較多的身心障礙青年在高中畢業後與父母、親屬或法定監護人生活在一起（Newman et al., 2011）；(6)身心障礙青年在經營家庭責任和獲得駕駛執照等生活技能方面，落後於非身心障礙的同齡者（Newman, Wagner, Cameto, & Knokey, 2009; Wagner, Newman, Cameto, & Levine, 2005）。

　　「全國長期縱貫性轉銜研究 2012」（National Longitudinal Transition Study 2012, NLTS 2012）是第三次的全國縱貫性轉銜研究，約有 13,000 名身心

障礙學生參加這次研究。2012 年 NLTS 的研究乃新增兩組研究樣本，包括符合《復健法》具有 504 計畫（504 plan）身分的學生和非身心障礙學生，這兩組新樣本的加入，乃用於比較比較符合《身心障礙者教育法》的身心障礙學生和其他兩組非身心障礙學生的關鍵經驗和結果。當 NLTS 和 NLTS2 已經有存在資料可以進行比較時，NLTS 2012 還可以加入進行不同時間下的差異比較，例如：在 Liu、Lacoe、Lipscomb、Haimson、Johnson 與 Thurlow（2018）的比較研究中發現：(1)接受特殊教育的青年之父母報告他們是失業者的人數，從 2003 年的 15%增加到 2012 年的 20%，比例增加將近 5%；(2)17 歲和 18 歲青年在過去兩年中持續報告有參加自己的個別化教育計畫會議，2003 年有 74%，2012 年則有 81%，但是報告曾與學校人員開會討論自己高中畢業後轉銜計畫的比例，卻從 79%降至 70%；(3)進步最多的是情緒障礙和認知障礙的青年，包括參與更多課外活動和利用學校的服務，這兩類學生在高中畢業後的關鍵經驗中也表現出上升趨勢。從 2003 至 2012 年，有情緒障礙的青少年在學校參與體育活動和社團的人數，從 40%增長到 56%。情緒障礙青少年的父母也報告，這一群學生接受教學助教、閱讀或翻譯服務的比例，也從 15%增加到 29%；(4)與他們的同年齡者相比（即是符合《復健法》具有 504 計畫的學生和非身心障礙學生），符合《特殊教育法》的身心障礙學生更有可能在社會經濟上處於不利地位，例如：他們生活在低收入家庭的可能性要高出 12%，以 58%相對於其他同年齡者的 46%，而其父母有工作或是受過大學教育的比例也較小（Lipcomb, Haimson, Liu Berghardt, Johnson, & Thurlow, 2017）；(5)符合《復健法》具有 504 計畫的學生和非身心障礙學生都對於學校都感到樂觀，而符合《特殊教育法》的身心障礙學生則較容易遭受霸凌或被休學，並且較少參與學校和社區的活動（Lipcomb et al., 2017）；(6)身心障礙青年（94%）比他們的非身心障礙同儕（76%）更期待在高中畢業後能參加繼續教育或高等教育（Lipcomb et al., 2017）

　　整體而言，美國在三十多年來所進行的全國長期縱貫轉銜研究，乃為了解和處理身心障礙學生就學和高中畢業後離校的經驗，建立了實務運作和決策的學理基礎，而這些研究資料也影響了美國特殊教育的介入，此些

研究也為檢驗有效教學策略和預測身心障礙學生高中畢業後的成果，奠下良好的實證研究基礎（Haber et al., 2016）。2016 年僅依據 NLTS2 系列的資料進行二次分析，研究者就出版了六十多篇稿件（Test & Fowler, 2018），若再加入 NLTS 2012 的資料，這一系列的稿件報告將會繼續增加。美國政府對一系列全國長期縱貫性轉銜研究的投入，大大促進了特殊教育和中學轉銜領域的發展，因為這些研究提供了有代表性的國家整體發展之結論，在各州和其學區所收集的資料，也可做為各地區檢視自己的身心障礙學生高中畢業後成效的良機。

參、臺灣轉銜服務的相關法規

反觀臺灣轉銜服務的相關法規，2009 年修訂公告的《特殊教育法》，應該是臺灣特殊教育正式揭櫫轉銜服務的元年，此法第 31 條：「為使各教育階段身心障礙學生服務需求得以銜接，各級學校應提供整體性與持續性轉銜輔導及服務；其轉銜輔導及服務之辦法，由中央主管機關定之」（教育部，2019b）。因應此母法，教育部乃於 2010 公告《各教育階段身心障礙學生轉銜輔導及服務辦法》，此辦法便成為我國實施身心障礙學生轉銜的最主要法源。

《各教育階段身心障礙學生轉銜輔導及服務辦法》第 2 條揭示了臺灣轉銜服務的目的：「為使身心障礙學生（以下簡稱學生）服務需求得以銜接，各級學校及其他實施特殊教育之場所應評估學生個別能力與轉銜需求，依本辦法規定訂定適切之生涯轉銜計畫，並協調社政、勞工及衛生主管機關，提供學生整體性與持續性轉銜輔導及服務」（教育部，2010）。

臺灣各教育階段身心障礙學生轉銜輔導及服務的具體實施，乃載於該辦法的第 3 條：「學校辦理學生轉銜輔導及服務工作，高級中等以下學校應將生涯轉銜計畫納入學生個別化教育計畫，專科以上學校應納入學生特殊教育方案，協助學生達成獨立生活、社會適應與參與、升學或就業等轉銜目標」（教育部，2010）。第 4 條則是各教育階段身心障礙學生轉銜輔導及服務的內容：「跨教育階段及離開學校教育階段之轉銜，學生原安置場所

或就讀學校應召開轉銜會議，討論訂定生涯轉銜計畫與依個案需求建議提供學習、生活必要之教育輔助器材及相關支持服務，並依會議決議內容至教育部特殊教育通報網（以下簡稱通報網）填寫轉銜服務資料。前項轉銜服務資料包括學生基本資料、目前能力分析、學生學習紀錄摘要、評量資料、學生與家庭輔導紀錄、專業服務紀錄、福利服務紀錄及未來進路所需協助與輔導建議等項；轉銜服務資料得依家長需求提供家長參考」（教育部，2010）。

第8條則規範轉銜輔導及服務的實施時程規範：「學生升學高級中等學校或特殊教育學校高職部之轉銜，學生原就讀學校應依第四條規定於畢業前一學期召開轉銜會議，邀請家長及相關人員參加，依會議決議內容至通報網填寫轉銜服務資料，並於安置或錄取確定後二星期內填寫安置（錄取）學校，完成通報。高級中等學校及特殊教育學校高職部應於學生報到後二星期內至通報網接收轉銜服務資料，應於開學後一個月內，召開訂定個別化教育計畫會議，邀請學校相關人員及家長參加，並視需要邀請學生原就讀學校相關人員參加」（教育部，2010）。

轉銜會議的實施載於第9條：「學生升學專科以上學校之轉銜，學生原就讀學校應依第四條規定於畢業前一學期召開轉銜會議，邀請家長及相關人員參加，依會議決議內容至通報網填寫轉銜服務資料，並於錄取確定後二星期內填寫錄取學校，完成通報。專科以上學校應於學生報到後二星期內至通報網接收轉銜服務資料，於開學後一個月內召開訂定特殊教育方案會議，邀請學校相關人員參加，並視需要邀請學生原就讀學校相關人員及家長參加」（教育部，2010）。

針對高職階段身心障礙學生可實施職能評估，第10條說明如下：「設有職業類科之高級中等學校及特殊教育學校高職部，應於學生就讀第一年辦理職能評估。前項學生於畢業前二年，學校應結合勞工主管機關，加強其職業教育、就業技能養成及未來擬就業職場實習。第一項學生於畢業前一年仍無法依其學習紀錄、行為觀察與晤談結果，判斷其職業方向及適合之職場者，應由學校轉介至勞工主管機關辦理職業輔導評量」（教育部，2010）。

第 11 條要求學校必須對身心障礙學生的跨階段轉銜做資料通報:「國民中學以上學校學生,表達畢業後無升學意願者,學校應依第四條規定於學生畢業前一學期召開轉銜會議,邀請學生本人、家長及相關人員參加,並於會議結束後二星期內依會議決議內容至通報網填寫轉銜服務資料,完成通報。學生因故離校者,除法律另有規定外,學校得視需要召開轉銜會議,並至通報網填寫轉銜服務資料,完成通報。前二項學生離校後一個月內,應由通報網將轉銜服務資料通報至社政、勞工或其他相關主管機關銜接提供福利服務、職業重建、醫療或復健等服務,並由學生原就讀學校追蹤輔導六個月」(教育部,2010)。

《各教育階段身心障礙學生轉銜輔導及服務辦法》乃對現階段臺灣的轉銜服務作了詳明規範,類似於美國的《身心障礙者教育法》對身心障礙學生轉銜服務的要求。然而,目前此主要法規乃有下列四個議題值得探討,包括:正名、釐清內容定義、跨法規之結合,以及簡化行政作業,分述如下。

一、正名

專科以上學生轉銜輔導及服務應納入學生的個別化教育計畫,名稱宜修訂之。《各教育階段身心障礙學生轉銜輔導及服務辦法》第 3 條規定:「學校辦理學生轉銜輔導及服務工作,高級中等以下學校應將生涯轉銜計畫納入學生個別化教育計畫,專科以上學校應納入學生特殊教育方案……」(教育部,2010)。然而,依據 2013 年修訂的《特殊教育法》中第30-1 條:「高等教育階段學校為協助身心障礙學生學習及發展,應訂定特殊教育方案實施,……高等教育階段之身心障礙教育,應符合學生需求,訂定個別化支持計畫,協助學生學習及發展……」(教育部,2013),亦即是呼應《特殊教育法》的規定,學生轉銜輔導及服務工作,專科以上學校應納入學生的個別化支持計畫(individualized support plan),而非學生的特殊教育方案(individualized education program)。此不對應的錯置現象之產生,源自於《各教育階段身心障礙學生轉銜輔導及服務辦法》於 2010 年公告實施,訂定辦法之際乃依循 2009 年公告的《特殊教育法》第 30 條舊條

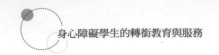

文內容設計，但是《特殊教育法》中第 30-1 條已於 2013 年增訂公告之；也因此，《各教育階段身心障礙學生轉銜輔導及服務辦法》第 3 條所述及專科以上學生的轉銜輔導工作宜納入的學生個別化教育計畫名稱，宜因應《特殊教育法》的修訂內容，儘速修法更正之。

二、釐清內容定義

　　「生涯轉銜計畫」的內容宜明確說明。《各教育階段身心障礙學生轉銜輔導及服務辦法》第 4 條規定：「……學生原安置場所或就讀學校應召開轉銜會議，討論訂定生涯轉銜計畫與依個案需求建議提供學習、生活必要之教育輔助器材及相關支持服務，並依會議決議內容至教育部特殊教育通報網（以下簡稱通報網）填寫轉銜服務資料。前項轉銜服務資料包括學生基本資料、目前能力分析、學生學習紀錄摘要、評量資料、學生與家庭輔導紀錄、專業服務紀錄、福利服務紀錄及未來進路所需協助與輔導建議等項……」（教育部，2010）。此條文的重點應源自第 3 條所述身心障礙學生的「生涯轉銜計畫」，方有後續此第 4 條之轉銜會議的召開和在特殊教育通報網填寫轉銜服務資料。然而在此辦法中，「生涯轉銜計畫」應包含哪些內容？如何評估身心障礙學生個別能力與轉銜需求？目前本辦法中都未有具體明確的說明，所以目前我國各教育階段學校教育人員對於「生涯轉銜計畫」的內容和實施，仍然視為極具挑戰的任務，教育實務界的說法和做法也都不盡相同。

三、跨法規之結合

　　「生涯轉銜計畫」與《特殊教育法》的個別化教育計畫和個別化支持計畫之規範宜作明確連結。依據 2012 年我國修訂之《特殊教育法施行細則》第 9 條，個別化教育計畫內容之第 5 款，乃有指出學生之轉銜輔導及服務內容包括升學、輔導、生活、就業、心理輔導、福利服務及其他相關專業服務等項目，但是未有其他更詳細的定義說明；而《特殊教育法施行細則》第 12 條針對大專以上學生的個別化支持計畫內容，也僅提到學生之轉

衛輔導及服務內容，並未做內容說明。亦即是學校在進行身心障礙學生生涯轉銜輔導的歷程時，「生涯轉銜計畫」與「個別化教育計畫」內容第 5 款和「個別化支持計畫」內容第 3 款應如何結合運作，《特殊教育法施行細則》和《各教育階段身心障礙學生轉銜輔導及服務辦法》宜有明確界定與說明，以利學校相關人員的實施。

四、簡化行政作業

特殊教育通報網的轉銜服務資料應與生涯轉銜計畫內容等同化。《各教育階段身心障礙學生轉銜輔導及服務辦法》第 4 條規定：「……學生原安置場所或就讀學校應召開轉銜會議，……並依會議決議內容至教育部特殊教育通報網（以下簡稱通報網）填寫轉銜服務資料。前項轉銜服務資料包括學生基本資料、目前能力分析、學生學習紀錄摘要、評量資料、學生與家庭輔導紀錄、專業服務紀錄、福利服務紀錄及未來進路所需協助與輔導建議等項……」（教育部，2010）。此轉銜服務資料乃依據生涯轉銜計畫會議決議而來，也因此特殊教育通報網的轉銜服務資料應等同於生涯轉銜計畫內容，未來期待兩者的內容應能同一，直接將「個別化教育計畫」內容第 5 款或「個別化支持計畫」內容第 3 款和「轉銜服務資料」連結，以避免教育人員需要對相同的任務，操作兩次內容不一樣的作業，以節省行政業務工作。

▶ 肆、美國轉銜服務的實務運作與轉銜計畫

無論是美國的全國性資料還是各州的資料，很明顯的呈現在高中期間接受特殊教育的學生，很難在繼續高等教育或就業方面取得正向的成果。教育工作者（教師、行政人員和服務提供者）應該善用全國和各州高中畢業後身心障礙學生流向調查資料，以改善學生在學校就讀時的各種經驗，從而提高學生在高中畢業後可以成功轉銜的可能性；教育人員應該根據學生流向調查結果確認哪些群體的畢業學生表現良好，哪些群體的畢業學生

處於掙扎困難狀況，教育工作者應而調整他們所提供的教育內容，以滿足學生的個人需求。

Kohler（1996）提出了「轉銜觀點的教育模式」（transition perspective of education model），她認為能促成身心障礙者成功的轉銜服務有五個向度，此完整的全方位介入模式乃是目前美國實施轉銜教育與服務的主要參考架構（Flexer, Baer, Luft, & Simmons, 2013; Morgan & Riesen, 2016）。Kohler、Gothberg、Fowler 與 Coyle（ 2016）又提出更周延的「轉銜方案向度 2.0 版」（Taxonomy for Transition Programming 2.0）（如圖 1-3 所示），以作為轉銜服務實施的參考。

此新版轉銜方案包含五個關鍵向度，分述如下：(1)以學生為主的規劃（含個別化教育計畫、執行計畫的策略、學生的參與）；(2)考量學生的發

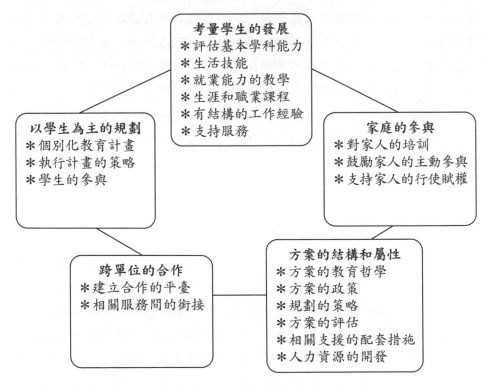

圖 1-3　轉銜方案五向度

展（含評估基本學科能力、生活社交和情緒處理能力、職業技能和就業能力、學生所需的支持、教學上的需求）；(3)整合相關單位的合作（含合作的機制、相關服務的銜接）；(4)家庭的參與（含家人的主動參與、家庭的賦權、家庭的準備度）；(5)學校有系統的規劃相關活動（含計畫的內容、計畫的評估、計畫的策略、實施辦法和程序、相關支援的配套措施、學校的氛圍）。

美國勞工部之身心障礙者就業政策處（Office of Disability Employment Policy, ODEP）曾建議教育工作者可以參考「成功指南」（Guideposts for Success），以作為身心障礙者轉銜教育的教學內容。所謂「成功指南」是由身心障礙者就業政策處（ODEP）與其所轄屬的「全國青年工作力與身心障礙協同合作中心」（National Collaborative on Workforce and Disability for Youth, NCWD/Youth）所共同研發，這份指南廣泛回顧三十多年以來在青年發展、教育和工作力發展方面的相關研究和最佳實務報告，而提出對一般人和身心障礙者皆適用的教育和生涯發展之正向成效的五項關鍵要素：(1)學校本位的預備經驗；(2)生涯發展本位的預備以及職業基礎的學習經驗；(3)青年的發展與領導才能；(4)連結的活動；(5)家庭的參與和支持。此五項關鍵要素非常適合作為身心障礙學生轉銜的教育教學指標，也因此在設計學生的個別化轉銜計畫時，學生現況亦將需包含上述五個向度的能力，亦即是「引導學生高中畢業後朝向成功的五項指標」（National Collaborative on Workforce and Disability for Youth, 2016），此關鍵要素可以作為轉銜計畫教學目標之參考，五項指標內容分述如下。

一、學校本位的預備經驗

為了讓身心障礙學生在不同教育環境中達到最佳的學習水準，學校應該提供身心障礙學生適性且有合理期待標準的學習方案，這些方案對身心障礙學生有明確的期望和具有意義，同時規劃符合他們狀況的不同畢業標準要求，此些方案的課程目標乃為教導學生及其未來成為成人相關的知識和技能，此學校本位的預備經驗可以包括：

1.能夠達到或超過所屬年級水準的學科表現水準。

2.高中畢業時,能夠以相當於大學預備標準的能力水準完成學業;亦即是進入學院或大學時無需再進行補救教學。

3.對學科的學習目標有動機和毅力。

4.了解自己的未來教育和職業的選擇,有能力選擇適合自己的學科課程以及高中畢業後的規劃,以實現個人的學術、職業和人生目標。

5.能夠處理妨礙自己學習的學科性和非學科性的困難,這些挑戰包含社交與情緒的自我管理、自我決策和自我倡權等能力。

6.社交和情緒自我管理技能,包括自我覺知、自我管理、社交覺知、人際關係技能、解決問題能力、解決衝突能力和負責任的決策。

7.能有效將輔助科技運用於各種目的所需的技能和知識上,包括應試、學習線上課程、組織、時間管理,或者是個人學習領域或職業上所需要的工作。

8.中學階段和高中畢業後,能夠在規劃的歷程和學習環境中,為自己的特殊教育需求和目標主動發聲及爭取資源。

9.了解自己在教育環境中需要哪些學習調整和支援,包括輔助科技等,以及該如何使用它們。

10.在教育環境中,能夠為自己的學習調整和支援主動提出說明和爭取資源。

二、生涯發展本位的預備以及職業基礎的學習經驗

職業準備和基於工作所需的學習經驗對於青年而言非常重要,因為這些學習經驗能夠讓他們得到啟發,以做出明智的職業選擇。這些經驗可以在學校內發生,或是透過放學後的課外活動進行,例如:

1.了解就業在經濟上可以達到自給自足的功能,以及提升技能養成、職業探索和尋找工作以養活自己的動機。

2.培養自我探索的技能以讓青年找到自己的興趣、能力和價值觀。

3.培養職業探索技能,能讓青年識別不同種職業選擇,以及如何配合自己的興趣、能力和工作偏好。

4.訓練學生能夠辨明興趣、課程、職業證照的相關性，然後做出明智的抉擇：找到長期的職業興趣後，可以找到相對應的中學和高等教育的相關課程，以及達成這些職業興趣所必需的職業認可證照。

5.具備特定職業的工作技能和知識，以及就業能力或「軟」技能，「軟」技能包含溝通、領導、決策和衝突處理能力。

6.培養職業規劃和管理技能，包括學科學習規劃、高中畢業後路徑發展相關的決策、職業準備技能、求職技能和財務知識等。

7.了解工作場所和訓練場所中自己需要哪些調整和支援，包括輔助科技等，以及該如何使用它們。

8.訓練在工作場所和訓練場所中，能夠為自己的特殊需求之調整和支援，主動提出說明和爭取資源。

三、青年的發展與領導才能

青年發展歷程可使青年對迎接青春期和成年挑戰做好準備，青年領導力是這些技能的其中一部分，青年發展技能引導青年做出明智的決定，以為自己的未來生活定位，青年發展所應建立的能力包括：

1.自我效能或相信自己的信念。

2.自我決策的知識和技能，以及相信一個人能夠做到目標導向、自我約束和自主行動的信念。

3.相信在人生道路上，人有做選擇和主動出擊的能量和選擇。

4.人際交往能力。

5.批判性思考能力。

6.自我倡權的技能，包括自我覺知、公民權的知識、溝通和領導能力。

7.領導技能和主動性。

8.了解是否、何時，以及如何自我倡權，包括了解身心障礙的發展歷史、文化，以及身心障礙的公共政策及其權利和義務。

9.了解自己的身心障礙以及對身心障礙的認同，包括了解自己的長處，也會依據自己的障礙，爭取所處環境中可以提供給自己的調整和支援，使

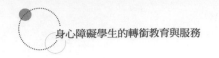

自己在各種情況下能夠參與群體和達成目標。

10.能夠在各種環境中，包括教育、工作、社會、娛樂、社區和其他發展環境裡，有效地對自己所需的調整和支援提出說明和爭取資源。

四、連結的活動

連結活動的目的是希望青年能與外界作有意義的聯繫與建立關係，內容包括如下：

1.如何透過醫療系統獲得醫療、精神、行為和懷孕生產服務的能力。

2.自我照護、健康維護決策和自我倡權的技能。

3.能夠選擇和參與促進個人健康與幸福的娛樂及休閒活動的能力。

4.尋找、確保和維護一個安全、穩定及無障礙住家的知識與技能。

5.確保可以使用公共或個人的可靠、無障礙的交通工具或方式的能力。

6.在自己的居住社區中可以獨立行動所需要的技能和自信心。

7.能夠獲得充足的營養食物，並且了解到選擇健康食品的好處之能力。

8.確保可以達到高品質的幼兒保育的知識和技能。

9.能成為負責任的父母。

10.知道如何獲得避孕和性健康資訊的能力。

11.能獨立生活和具備生活的技能。

12.能夠有效地管理自己的財務來源。

13.能夠為自己的繼續教育和訓練做出決定和擬定計畫，包括高中畢業後的教育和職業證照考試。

14.了解一個人的權利和能力，以便找到和運用適合個人需要及符合年齡的法律支援與服務，如針對英語是第二語言學習者、外來移民青年、退伍軍人、涉及法庭判決的青年、寄養家庭青年，以及有心理健康問題的人所提供的服務等。

15.能夠查詢和利用與身心障礙相關的服務，如輔助技術、社會福利諮詢和個人援助服務。

16.能夠為自己發聲和處理與身心障礙相關的社會性服務。

五、家庭的參與和支持

　　父母、家庭成員和其他長輩之參與和支援，都可以促進身心障礙青年的成長，並使他們在高中畢業之後有較佳的後續發展。家庭參與和支持的例子，包括：美國《復健法》504 條款（Section 504 of the 1973 Rehabilitation Act）的權利與美國《身心障礙者教育法》的規定，有何不同？

　　目前學校轉銜教育的實際運作中，轉銜計畫（Transition Plan）乃屬於個別化教育計畫的一部分，都是從學生的學科表現和實用能力的「現況」開始。設計個別化計畫時不宜僅關注身心障礙學生的缺陷短處，而是要強化學生的優勢、偏好和興趣。至於如何評估學生的優勢、弱勢、偏好和興趣，則應該要運用有證據資料的多元管道加以評估，包括學生的醫療診斷資料、正式或非正式性評量、個人興趣量表、檢核表、直接觀察、直接訪談學生，以及訪問非常熟悉學生的相關人員等。而現況的評估可以利用「無偏見和歧視評量」（non-discriminatory assessment）和「多元評量的結果」（multi-disciplinary assessment）進行分析，這些評量都必須經由受過訓練的合格專業人員執行，因為身心障礙學生的所有評量，都有可能受到學生本身的「障礙」而影響測驗結果，受過訓練的人員方能謹慎且有效地詮釋測驗的資料。設計個別化教育計畫時，應以學生學習現況（present levels of performance）作為後續設計轉銜目標和教學介入的起點。 所評量的學生學習現況，包括學科能力、日常生活技能、社交能力、行為表現、感官功能、溝通能力和行動能力等，以作為後續設計轉銜目標和教學介入的起點。

▶ 伍、轉銜服務的績效評鑑

　　美國《身心障礙者教育 2004 年修正法》非常重視評估身心障礙學生的高中畢業後成效，即是注重成果為導向的轉銜成效，同時也可以作為美國政府評鑑各州政府執行特殊教育法的績效。《身心障礙者教育法》B 篇主要規 範 3 至 21 歲身心障礙學生接受特殊教育及相關專業服務的內容，此法公

告之後，美國教育部特殊教育司（Office of Special Education Programs, OSEP）依據《身心障礙者教育法》B 篇的內容，制定了一套對各州政府實施特殊教育 B 篇的績效評估，類似於我國教育部對縣市教育局的特殊教育績效評鑑。剛開始共有 20 項績效指標，現今已經修正為 17 項指標，各州的教育部門必須依據這 17 項特殊教育績效指標制定各州的「州政府成效計畫」（State Performance Plan, SPP）和「年度績效報告」（Annual Performance Report, APR）。各州政府每六年要制定一次「州政府成效計畫」，並且透過每年的「年度績效報告」（Annual Performance Report, APR）向教育部特殊教育司（Office of Special Education Programs, OSEP）呈報各項指標的實施進展情況。此 17 項各州的特殊教育績效指標（IDEA, 2004, 20 U.S.C. 1416(a)(3)(A)）包括：

指標 1：提升身心障礙學生的畢業率。

指標 2：降低身心障礙學生的中輟率。

指標 3：提升身心障礙學生參與全州學力測驗的人數與成果表現。

指標 4：降低身心障礙學生的休學和退學。

指標 5：最少限制的環境中提供學齡階段身心障礙學生各項服務。

指標 6：在學校中提供學前身心障礙兒童與正常同儕一起學習的各項服務。

指標 7：改善學齡前兒童的學習成果。

指標 8：提升學校協助家長參與其子女的特殊教育計畫。

指標 9：減少種族和族裔群體在特殊教育中的不當比例現象。

指標 10：減少某些特定身心障礙類別內出現種族和族裔群體有不當比例的現象。

指標 11：提供及時的評估，以確保學生可以通過鑑定以接受特殊教育服務。

指標 12：確保在孩子 3 歲生日以前可以從嬰幼兒方案有效轉銜到學齡前方案。

指標 13：為 16 歲及以上的身心障礙學生提供有效的轉銜服務。

指標 14：提升學生從高中到高中畢業後的成果，包括繼續高等教育或

就業。

指標 15：提高有效運用協調會議以解決不符合正當程式的申訴事件。

指標 16：提升有效利用協調服務解決家庭和學校之間的意見歧異。

指標 17：呈報各州系統性改善計畫（State Systemic Improvement Plan, SSIP）。

上述 17 項特殊教育績效指標中，其中有 4 項指標直接涉及中等教育的轉銜成效，即是指標 1：身心障礙學生的畢業率、指標 2：身心障礙學生的中輟率、指標 13：個別化教育計畫內的轉銜目標、指標 14：學生高中畢業後的成果。這四個指標可以看作是一個簡單的邏輯模型， 其中輸入是個別化教育計畫內的轉銜目標， 近程結果是學生畢業率的增加和輟學率的下降， 遠程結果則是學生積極邁向四個高中畢業後的可能進路之一：(1)就讀高等教育；(2)競爭型就業；(3)其他高中畢業後的教育或職業訓練；(4)其他形態的就業（Unruh, 2009）。此四個與轉銜相關的指標評估標準乃分述如下：

指標 1：身心障礙學生的畢業率：具有特殊教育證明文件之高中生獲得普通畢業證書者占應屆畢業生的比率。

指標 2：身心障礙學生的中輟率：具有特殊教育證明文件之高中生中輟離校的比率。

指標 13：個別化教育計畫內有設計且落實執行的轉銜目標比例。16 歲及其以上具有特殊教育證明文件之高中生的有效「個別化教育計畫」比例，此個別化教育計畫必須載明具有整合性和可測量的轉銜年度目標與轉銜服務，而此些轉銜設計將可以呼應此一學生高中畢業後的下一階段目標。

指標 14：學生高中畢業後的成果。第 14 項指標要求各州政府提出比例數據，來說明具有《特殊教育法》資格之身心障礙學生：(1)高中畢業離校一年之內進入高等教育就讀的比例；(2)高中畢業離校一年之內進入高等教育或競爭型職場就業的比例；(3)高中畢業離校一年之內進入高等教育、其他高中畢業後教育場所或職業訓練方案，或是競爭型職場或其他類型職場就業的比例。

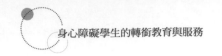
「全國轉銜技術協助中心」（National Technical Assistance Center on Transition, NTACT）是美國聯邦政府為了幫助各州或學區教育局，對於提報特殊教育績效指標的資料之技術協助所設立的機構，這個中心乃是「國立高中畢業後成果中心」（National Post School Outcomes Center, NPSO）的前身，「全國轉銜技術協助中心」彙整上述轉銜的四個重要指標之有益資料資源和結果分析，呈現了四項轉銜相關指標之間的關聯，此四項轉銜相關指標中，第13項指標（個別化教育計畫內的轉銜目標）和第14項指標（學生高中畢業後成效）又被視為可以造成學生實質性和可持續性改變的轉捩點，值得所有相關人員的重視。

▌陸、轉銜的重要盟友：職業復健服務

身心障礙學生在決定高中畢業後的繼續教育和訓練方案（包括獨立生活和與就業有關的目標）時，身心障礙學生及其家長必須了解社區現有的相關服務範圍，以及如何在學區裡獲得這些服務。學區應該鼓勵家長和學生充分參與關於其他服務的需求和可用性的討論會，包括說明職業復建服務的申請條件和申請方式，並確保學生高中畢業之後與這些支援機構建立了正式的連結。

根據美國2017年出版的《身心障礙青年學生中學後教育和就業轉銜指南》（*A Transition Guide to Postsecondary Education and Employment for Students and Youth with Disabilities*）（U.S. Department of Education, Office of Special Education and Rehabilitative Services, 2017），職業復建機構的主要作用之一是賦予身心障礙者（學生）權力，協助他們能對其生涯做出通盤了解後的決定，例如：了解有哪些連續和後續服務，可以協助他們達成有競爭力的綜合就業或支持性就業。此外，職業復建服務也可以協助身心障礙學生「就業前的轉銜服務」，不管學生是否已經申請了職業復建的服務，「就業前的轉銜服務」乃是提供給符合資格的學生職業試探的啟蒙活動，以幫助他們確定自己的職業興趣，就業前的轉銜服務內容包含：

1.職業探索諮詢。

2.協助校內或放學後的工作經驗，包括實習的選擇。

3.提供諮詢如何在高等教育機構，或是在中學畢業後的教育方案註冊入學。

4.協助職業場所預備訓練，以發展社交技能和獨立生活技能。

5.教導自我倡權和以個人為主體的生涯規劃

《身心障礙青年學生中學後教育和就業轉銜指南》中也提出轉銜成功的八項關鍵因素（U.S. Department of Education, Office of Special Education and Rehabilitative Services, 2017, p. 21）：

1.主動參與：家長應是學生個別化教育計畫團隊的正式成員之一，其主動參與可確保轉銜服務在 16 歲或更早之前在個別化教育計畫中落實。（註：轉銜服務年齡的啟動依各州的規定，不得晚於 16 歲）

2.熟悉流程：家長和學生應熟悉轉銜計畫實施的步驟，包括所使用的評估工具、個別化教育計畫擬定的教育目標應該和轉銜目標相配合、確定轉銜服務並且諮詢和聯繫過其他機構，特別是職業復健機構。

3.學校責任：學校應實施轉銜服務，包括在個別化轉銜計畫加入職業復健服務所提供的「就業前的轉銜服務」。

4.轉介服務：學校應將身心障礙學生轉介至職業復健機構和／或是其他成人機構。

5.職訓申請：提醒學生要在招生面試和職業復健的申請過程中提出他們的職業興趣。

6.就業規劃：個別化教育計畫／個別化轉銜計畫應該為學生就業擬定量身定制規劃。

7.善用資源：學校在進行轉銜服務時可善用《工作力的創新和機會法》（WIOA）所提供的共通職業復健服務，包括：轉銜服務、職業諮詢、職業培訓、高中畢業後的教育、支持性就業服務、職業發展和就業安置等。

8.轉銜終點：當轉銜歷程結束時，身心障礙學生或青年將可以實現就業的目標，職業復健的服務也可圓滿落幕。但如果身心障礙學生或青年決定不再尋求就業，他們也將喪失接受職業復健服務的資格。

轉銜的最終目標乃是協助達成符合學生高中畢業後期望的目標，也因

此相關單位應該對哪些是可行服務，以及接受這些服務後的對應活動有所共識。明智決策、合理責任分配是轉銜成功要件；了解個別化轉銜計畫團隊的每個成員的貢獻均等也是非常重要。轉銜計畫中應考慮身心障礙學生／青年及其父母所關切的議題，轉銜規劃的歷程應重視溝通，彼此尊重，努力化解分歧和相互信任，以包容的心盡量結合所有的資源，讓身心障礙學生和青年能夠以正向積極的態度面對前景，無接縫地過渡到成年期。

▍柒、結論

在每一個人生命的過程中，充滿著許多變化、考驗，也就是相伴而來的不同轉銜議題。我們為什麼要重視轉銜？美國和臺灣的《特殊教育法》揭舉了相同的特殊教育的精神與目標，即是期待所有的身心障礙學生都可以得到適性教育的引導，成人之後仍然可以服務社會，成為社會的一分子，而此亦正是轉銜教育與服務的核心目標。

每位學生的養成教育都需要父母、師長、家人、社會資源的人力挹注，持續關懷，身心障礙學生也不例外。從學前早療、學齡階段的教育，以至最後的轉銜至成人角色，這些歷程都需要我們在跨角色、跨專業和跨機構的攜手合作。本書主題所討論的轉銜是特殊教育長程馬拉松接力賽的最後一棒，不管在美國或在臺灣，對所有身心障礙者及其家庭來說，這是一段漫長、艱辛但值得傾力投入的旅程，身心障礙學生能夠走到成功的終點，必須藉由所有重要相關人的長期縝密周延的規劃，一棒接一棒的交棒傳承；家人、教育工作者、勞政和社政單位的服務提供者，都是最佳的陪跑者，但身心障礙學生最後是否能跑到成功目標的終點，仍然端視身心障礙學生自己是否願意親自坐在自己生命的駕駛座上，掌握自己的未來，為自己的前途而奮力勇敢向前跑。

談及教育創新時，教育工作者 Berman 與 McLaughlin（1976）曾說：「『執行』可將教育理想轉化為對學生的實質影響，可惜創新的理想很少能按原本的創意去執行。」轉銜教育也可算是教育史上的創新之舉，但是如果沒有一個有毅力、有遠見的領導，和一群有共識的團隊，願意克服困

難，一步一腳印地深耕，轉銜教育有可能淪為立意良善的理想空談。

　　臺灣的轉銜教育發展比美國晚起步約十九年，雖然實務上大家都一直在執行身心障礙學生的轉銜教育與服務，但是不管在定義、實施程序、運作模式到績效評估等方面，我們都需要加緊腳步向前行。社會文化與制度、教育制度和家庭文化都是影響學生轉銜成效的關鍵因素，我們必須從臺灣的社會制度與人文的獨特性，創造出我們對身心障礙者生涯輔導與轉銜教育的方向和目標。然而，不管在哪一個國家或文化，轉銜服務的設計和實施都必須依靠許多人員和跨單位共同合作的實踐。我們需要搭建出一座轉銜橋梁，完成我們對身心障礙學生和家長的「有教無類」及「因材施教」之承諾。所有人員的努力皆會對學生產生深遠的影響，誠願臺灣的身心障礙學生在良好的特殊教育轉銜教育與服務之後，最後都可以跨越自身的限制，跟所有人一樣自由翱翔於成人的世界。

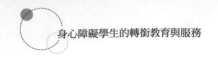

參考文獻

中文部分

林素貞（1995）。社區本位之生涯教育轉銜模式：生活技能網路系統。特
　　教園丁季刊，**11**（2），1-13。

教育部（2009）。**特殊教育法**。臺北市：作者。

教育部（2010）。**各教育階段身心障礙學生轉銜輔導及服務辦法**。臺北
　　市：作者。

教育部（2013）。**特殊教育法**。臺北市：作者。

教育部（2019a）。**特殊教育法**。臺北市：作者。

教育部（2019b）。**108 年度特殊教育統計年報**。臺北市：作者。

英文部分

Berman, P., & McLaughlin, M. W. (1976). Implementation of educational innova-
　　tion. *The Educational Forum, 40*(3), 345-370. doi:10.1080/00131727609336469

Blackorby, J., & Wagner, M. (1996). Longitudinal post-school outcomes of youth
　　with disabilities: Findings from the National Longitudinal Transition Study.
　　Exceptional Children, 62(5), 399-413.

Cameto, R. (2007). *4-years out: Postschool outcomes, and experiences of youth with
　　disabilities*. Presentation at the Division on Career Development and Transi-
　　tion Conference, Orlando, FL.

Career Education Implementation Incentive Act of 1977, Pub. Law 95-207.

Carnevale, A. P., Smith, N., & Strohl, J. (2013). *Recovery: Job growth and education
　　requirements through 2020*. Center on Education and the Workforce: Georget-
　　own University. Retrieved from https://reurl.cc/RdglO6

deJung, J. E., & Reed, D. M. (1978). *Measurement of community adjustment of mil-*

dly retarded young adults: Final Report. Eugene, OR: University of Oregon.

Edgar, E. (1985). How do special education students fare after they leave school? A response to Hasazi, Gordon, and Roe. *Exceptional Children, 51*, 470-473.

Edgar, E. (1987). Secondary programs in special education: Are many of them justifiable? *Exceptional Children, 53*, 555-561.

Edgar, E. (1988). Employment as an outcome for mildly handicapped students: Current status and future directions. *Focus on Exceptional Children, 21*, 1-8.

Flexer, R. W., Baer, R. M., Luft, P., & Simmons, T. J. (2013). *Transition planning for secondary students with disabilities* (4th ed.). Upper Saddle River, NJ: Pearson.

Flexer, R. W., Simmons, T. J., Luft, P., & Baer, R. M. (2001). *Transition planning for secondary students with disabilities.* Upper Saddle River, NJ: Merrill Prentice-Hall.

Haber, M., Mazzotti, V. L., Mustian, A. L., Rowe, D. A., Bartholomew, A. L., Test, D. W., & Fowler, C. H. (2016). What works, when, for whom, and with whom: A meta-analytic review of predictors of postsecondary success for students with disabilities. *Review of Educational Research, 86*(1), 123-162. doi: 10.3102/0034654315583135

Halpern, A. S. (1985). Transition: A look at the foundations. *Exceptional Children, 51*(6), 479-486.

Halpern, A. S. (1992). Transition: Old wine in new bottles. *Exceptional Children, 58*(3), 202-211.

Hasazi, S. B., Gordon, L. R., & Roe, C. A. (1985). Factors associated with the employment status of handicapped youth exiting high school from 1979 to 1983. *Exceptional Children, 51*, 455-469.

Hoyt, K. B. (1982). Career education: Beginning of the end? Or a new beginning? *Career Development for Exceptional Individuals, 5*, 3-12.

Individuals with Disabilities Education Act (IDEA) Pub. L. 101-476 (1990).

Individuals with Disabilities Education Act (IDEA) Pub. L. 105-17 (1997).

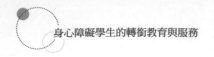

Individuals with Disabilities Education Act (IDEA) Pub. L. 108-446. (2004).

Individuals with Disabilities Education Act (IDEA), 20 U.S.C. 1416(a)(3)(B) (2004).

Individuals with Disabilities Education Act (IDEA), 34 CFR §300.1(a) (2004).

Kohler, P. (1996). *A taxonomy for transition programming: Linking research and practice.* Champaign, IL: University of Illinois, Transition Research Institute.

Kohler, P. D., Gothberg, J. E., Fowler, C., & Coyle, J. (2016). Taxonomy for transition programming 2.0: A model for planning, organizing, and evaluating transition education, services, and programs. Retrieved from https://reurl.cc/xDv0jZ

Kohler, P., Gothberg, J., & Coyle, J. (2017). Using the taxonomy for transition programming 2.0 to guide transition education. In A. L. Ellis (Ed.), *Transitioning children with disabilities: From early childhood through adulthood* (pp. 169-182). Rotterdam, The Netherlands: Sense Publishers.

Kranstover, L. L., Thurlow, M. L., & Bruininks, R. H. (1989). Special education graduates versus nor-graduates: A longitudinal study of outcomes. *Career Development for Exceptional Individuals, 12*, 153-166. https://doi.org/10.1177/088572888901200211

Liebert, D. E., & Weissman, C. S., (1982). *Support and advocacy for vocational training of handicapped postsecondary adults: Final report.* Westbury, NY: Nassau County Board of Cooperative Educational Services.

Lipscomb, S., Haimson, J., Liu, A. Y., Burghardt, J., Johnson, D. R., & Thurlow, M. L. (2017). *Preparing for life after high school: The characteristics and experiences of youth in special education. Findings from the National Longitudinal Transition Study 2012. Volume 1: Comparisons with other youth: Full report* (NCEE 2017-4016). Washington, DC: U.S. Department of Education, Institute of Education Sciences, National Center for Education Evaluation and Regional Assistance.

Liu, A. Y., Lacoe, J., Lipscomb, S., Haimson, J., Johnson, D. R., & Thurlow, M. L.

(2018). *Preparing for life after high school: The characteristics and experiences of youth in special education. Findings from the National Longitudinal Transition Study 2012. Volume 3: Comparisons over time (Full report)* (NCEE 2018-4007). Washington, DC: U.S. Department of Education, Institute of Education Sciences, National Center for Education Evaluation and Regional Assistance.

Mithaug, D. E., Horiuchi, C. N., & Fanning, P. N. (1984). A report on the Colorado statewide follow-up survey of special education students. *Exceptional Children, 51*(5), 339-404.

Morgan, R. L., & Riesen, T. (2016). *Promoting successful transition to adulthood for students with disabilities*. New York, NY: The Guilford Press.

National Center for Education Statistics. (2006). *Profile of undergraduates in U.S. postsecondary education institutions: 2003-2004*. Retrieved from https://reurl.cc/pD2jZa

National Center for Education Statistics. (2019). *Digest of education statistics, 2017* (2018-070). Retrieved from https://reurl.cc/5gQy8V

National Collaborative on Workforce and Disability for Youth. (2016). *Guideposts for success* (2nd ed.). Retrieved from https://reurl.cc/RdqK9D

Newman, L., Wagner, M., Cameto, R., & Knokey, A. M. (2009). *The post-high school outcomes of youth with disabilities up to 4 years after high school. A report of findings from the National Longitudinal Transition Study-2 (NLTS2)* (NCSER 2009-3017). Menlo Park, CA: SRI International.

Newman, L., Wagner, M., Cameto, R., Knokey, A. M., & Shaver, D. (2010). *Comparisons across time of the outcomes of youth with disabilities up to 4 years after high school. A report of findings from the National Longitudinal Transition Study (NLTS) and the National Longitudinal Transition Study-2 (NLTS2)* (NCSER 2010-3008). Menlo Park, CA: SRI International.

Newman, L., Wagner, M., Knokey, A.-M., Marder, C., Nagle, K., Shaver, D., Wei, X., Cameto, R., Contreras, E., Ferguson, K., Greene, S., & Schwarting, M.

(2011). *The post-high school outcomes of young adults with disabilities up to 8 years after high school. A report from the National Longitudinal Transition Study-2 (NLTS2)* (NCSER 2011-3005). Menlo Park, CA: SRI International.

Part B State Performance Plan/Annual Performance Report [SPP/APR] 2019 Indicator Analyses (2019). Available from https://reurl.cc/L1gzXK

Poppen, M., & Alverson, C. Y. (2018). Policies and practice: A review of legislation affecting transition services for individuals with disabilities. *New Directions for Adult & Continuing Education, 160*, 63-76.

Schalock, R. L., Wolzen, B., Ross, I., Elliott, B., Werbel, G., & Peterson, K. (1986). Post-secondary community placement of handicapped students: A five-year follow-up. *Learning Disability Quarterly, 9*, 295-303

Test, D. W., & Fowler, C. H. (2018). A look at the past, present, and future of rural secondary transition. *Rural Special Education Quarterly, 37*(2), 68-78. doi: 10.1177/8756870517751607

Test, D. W., Aspel, N. P., & Everson, J. M. (2006). *Transition methods for youth with disabilities*. Upper Saddle River, NJ: Pearson.

U.S. Department of Education, Office of Special Education and Rehabilitative Services. (2017). *A transition guide to postsecondary education and employment for students and youth with disabilities*. Retrieved from https://reurl.cc/31X8bL

Unruh, D. K. (2009). *Data use toolkit*. National Post-School Outcomes Center. Eugene, OR: University of Oregon.

Wagner, M., Blackorby, J., Cameto, R., & Newman, L. (1993). *What makes a difference? Influences on postschool outcomes of youth with disabilities. The third comprehensive report from the National Longitudinal Transition Study of special education students* (ED 365085). Menlo Park, CA: SRI International.

Wagner, M., Newman, L., Cameto, R., & Levine, P. (2005). *Changes over time in the early post-school outcomes of youth with disabilities. A report of findings from the National Longitudinal Transition Study (NLTS) and the National*

Longitudinal Transition Study-2 (NLTS2). Menlo Park, CA: SRI International.

Will, M. (1983). *OSERS programming for the transition of youth with disabilities: Bridges from school to working life* (EC 172533). Washington, DC: Office of Special Education and Rehabilitative Services.

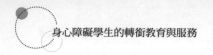

第二章　身心障礙學生高中畢業後能成功轉銜的有效教學與預測指標
Effective Practices and Predictors of Post-School Success for Students with Special Education Needs

Charlotte Y. Alverson

中文摘錄：林素貞

中文重點摘錄

　　特殊教育的目的乃為協助身心障礙學生高中畢業之後，能繼續在接受教育、就業和獨立生活上獲得積極的成效，因此他們的學校學習經驗需要透過嚴謹的證據，以證明學生確實接受了有效的特殊教育服務，才能夠有理想的教育成果；但是這樣的證據是什麼？又要如何呈現這樣的證據？1996 年，Sackett、Rosenberg、Gray、Haynes 與 Richardson（1996）將「實證醫學」（evidence-based medicine, EMB）定義為：謹慎地、精確地、小心地採用目前的最佳證據，以作為照顧病人之臨床治療決策參考，「實證醫學」意指醫療人員執行專業時，必須結合個人的專業知識與外部系統性研究所得到的臨床證據，以做出正確的決策。1999 年，Davies（1999）也闡述「實證教育」（evidence-based education）為：將個人教學專業知識與外部系統性研究所提供的最佳證據相結合；他強調：(1)採用現有來自全世界的研究和文獻綜合分析的證據；(2)建立可靠證據的重要性，確立最好的教學實務……，實證教育不僅是做簡單的談話、批判性建議和執行研究的結果，它還涉及如何將知識、專業判斷與經驗結合運用。亦即是教育工作者需要參考教育研究的結果，以作為他們教學決策與實施的依據。

　　美國推動「實證教育」的催化劑是 2001 年修正的《小學和中學教育

法》（Elementary and Secondary Education Act），此法案的標題為「帶起每一位學生」（No Child Left Behind, NCLB），此法案強調教師的教學法必須有正向的研究結果支持，亦即是學生必須能接受到教師採用有效且科學的教學策略，以及教導他們具有挑戰性的學科內容。2001 年至今，美國要求教師使用有科學證據支持的教學法／策略，乃標榜著「實證本位教學」（evidence-based practices, EBP）時代的來臨。隨著其他運動的推波助瀾，「實證本位特殊教育」（evidence-based special education）儼然也成為中等階段特殊教育和轉銜領域的首要優先議題。美國政府在建構與發展「實證本位教學」的相關配套措施包括：(1)建立「哪些是有效教學法」（What Works Clearinghouse, WWC）的資訊平臺；(2)在特殊教育研究中制訂品質標準指標；(3)資助建構技術援助中心，以識別哪些教學法或策略屬於「實證本位教學」，並且支援各州的教育實施能採用這些有效的教學法。

What Works Clearinghouse（WWC）成立於 2002 年，這是一個政府資助的資訊開放平臺，它的目的是促進高教學研究的品質，檢驗不同水準的教學研究成果，以提供教師、教育行政人員和教育政策制訂者，在需要根據研究的證據做出不同決策時所需的資訊。WWC 的教育研究結之果評估標準分為三種等級：(1)完全符合 WWC 的研究設計標準；(2)符合 WWC 的研究設計標準，但有所保留；(3)不符合 WWC 的研究設計標準。

美國的教師除了要遵守《小學和中學教育法》來實施「實證本位教學」外，《身心障礙者教育法》也要求提供給身心障礙學生的特殊教育和相關專業服務以及輔助支援，都必須依據有專業審查通過的研究結果。「實證本位教學」是一種教學決策，它必須使用由數個高品質的研究所提出的結論，這些研究的設計可以推斷因果關係，以證明此教學方法可以對學生產生正向且有意義的學習成果。從 2001 至 2004 年這短短數年間，美國普通教育和特殊教育的聯邦法律都要求教師、教育行政人員和教育政策制訂者，在學校的教學和學生畢業後的進路輔導，都需要運用研究證據以做出適當的教育決策。

為了增進特殊教育實施「實證本位教學」，美國教育部特殊教育司（OSEP）在全國成立了幾個技術援助和傳播中心，包括：奧瑞崗大學

（University of Oregon）的「國立學生高中畢業後成果研究中心」
（NPSO），以及北卡羅來納大學夏洛特分校（University of North Carolina
Charlotte）的「國立中學轉銜技術支援中心」（National Secondary Transition
Technical Assistance Center, NSTTAC）等。2015 年，美國教育部特殊教育司
和復健服務管理局（Rehabilitation Services Administration, RSA）共同將這些
中心與「國立身心障礙學生輟學預防中心」（National Dropout Prevention
Center for Students with Disabilities）整合，成立了「國立轉銜技術協助中
心」（NTACT），此中心的研究人員不斷進行研究文獻的綜合分析，以確
認哪些是對中學轉銜有效的教學策略，並宣導中學轉銜方案的發展，這些
努力都對身心障礙學生高中畢業後的發展有正向的貢獻。

壹、何謂中學階段轉銜的有效教學策略和預測指標？

　　實務（practices）是指教育的教學策略，預測指標（predictors）是指學
生的校內經驗因素，NTACT（2018a）的教學研究評定結果有三種層次：(1)
實證水準；(2)研究水準；(3)可能會有效的水準，表 2-1 呈現 NTACT 委員會
對上述三種層次的定義（詳見英文原文）。被評定為實證水準的教學策略
／法，其必須有足夠的高品質實驗研究以證明它的有效性，這些研究皆以
科學化設計呈現教師和服務提供者使用某種策略，以教導身心障礙學生成
功學會某些特定技能。表 2-2 是 2009 年 NSTTAC 所認證的 32 項「實證本位
教學」的清單（詳見英文原文），這些認證過程一直持續進行中，所以認
證名單也會有變化，有興趣者可上以下網站瀏覽：http://www.transitionta.org
；此 32 項「實證本位教學」的內容為：讓學生參與自己的個別化教育計畫
會議、使用電腦輔助教學教導生活技能、自我倡權策略、運用自我管理教
導生活技能、自主自己的個別化教育計畫、教導特定工作的職業技能、教
學生活技能、運用電腦輔助教學教導特定職業技能、教導購物技能、運用
「one more then」策略教導購物技能、教導使用銀行技能、教導餐廳的採買
技能、教導完成工作申請技能、教導安全技能、教導烹飪技能、教導自我
倡權技能、運用社區本位教學教導就業技能、教導自我決策技能、教導食

物準備技能、教導自我管理的就業技能、教導實用性數學能力、教導社會技能、教導實用性閱讀技能、教導與工作相關的社交溝通技巧、教導大賣場（超市）購物技巧、教導家長和家庭關於轉銜的議題、教導家庭的維護技能、教導社區運用、教導休閒技能、結構性課程教導運用高中畢業以後的資源、運用社區教導生活技能、為身心障礙學生實施「Check & Connect 計畫」。

▎貳、身心障礙學生高中畢業後可以成功發展的 實證本位預測指標

2009 年，NSTTAC 為了確認學生的高中學校經驗和畢業後結果之間的聯結關係，進行了第二次的文獻綜合分析，結果找出 16 個有實證水準的學生高中畢業後能成功發展的預測因素；然而，與「實證本位教學」不同，「實證本位預測指標」來自高品質的相關研究，並不是實驗研究，因此學生的校內經歷和畢業後結果之間無法具有因果關係，而僅有相關性。表 2-3 列出了高中生畢業後能成功的 20 項預測指標清單（詳見英文原文），這些指標是指學校所提供的相關課程或活動因素，內容如下：生涯覺知課程、社區經驗、通過高中畢業考試和要求／取得高中畢業資格、設定目標、在普通學校接受融合教育、跨機構合作、個別化職涯探索課程、有給薪的工作經驗、家長期待子女高中畢業後能繼續升學大學或就業、家長／家庭參與、基本學科或實用性學科課程、自我倡權／自我決策、自我照顧／獨立生活技能、能與他人溝通和合作的態度和行為之社交技能課程、學生的支持網絡（家庭、朋友、教師和社福人員）、中學階段為畢業後成人生活預做準備的轉銜計畫、使用交通工具到不同地方的能力、特定技能的職業教育、發展工作態度和基本工作能力課程、青年自主／自己做決定；基於NSTTAC 的研究工作仍然持續進行中，所以此清單也會更新變化。

參、為何學生高中畢業後能成功的「實證本位教學」和「實證本位預測指標」很重要？

　　首先，因為這些「實證本位教學」和「實證本位預測指標」的運用，中學階段特殊教育和轉銜議題發展出至今最佳的科學性和同儕審查之研究標準，因應這些研究標準的要求，相關研究的品質也相對提升了。第二，運用實證本位教學和預測指標，教師可以有效教導身心障礙學生，引導學生為中學後的繼續教育、就業和獨立生活目標做好準備。第三，實施有效的實證本位教學和預測指標，可以提高學生獲得新知識與技能的有效性和效率。

肆、如何有效運用「實證本位教學」和「實證本位預測指標」？

　　從圖 2-1 中可知「實證本位教學」和「實證本位預測指標」存在於教育系統的三個層級：學生（即微觀／中量）、學校（即 中量／巨觀），以及學區和政府（即巨觀）（詳見英文原文）。微觀層面是針對學生實施「實證本位教學」，指教師用來教導學生特定技能的教學策略；也包含個別化教育計畫團隊會根據每個學生的獨特需求、優勢和特點，為每個學生擬定適當的學習目標或轉銜目標。中量和巨觀層面是指學校、學區和州政府運用「實證本位預測指標」，這些預測指標將促使行政單位可以更廣泛地關注學校對學生的各種學習經驗的提供，以及政策和行政結構等會影響到個別學生的大範圍因素。表 2-4 呈現了如何將「實證本位教學」和「實證本位預測指標」有效地融入一位 17 歲學生之個別化教育計畫的範例（詳見英文原文）。

　　「實證本位教學」和「實證本位預測指標」的運作可以參考下列的步驟：(1)確認學生為了要達成他們高中畢業後的目標，現階段他們必須學

習、改善或展現的技能、行為或經驗；(2)找到與學生需要學習、改善或展現的技能、行為或經驗相關的實證本位教學和指標，而且兩者皆選用最高等級的實證水準內容；(3)有目標地忠實執行所選用的「實證本位教學」和「實證本位預測指標」；(4)定期監測學生的學習狀況，以了解所採用的「實證本位教學」和「實證本位預測指標」是否有效。

　　總結而言，「實證本位教學」和「實證本位預測指標」是兩項系統性和實證性的教育方法，它們並非是能解決所有特殊教育問題的仙丹妙藥，但是它們仍然是值得努力發展的教師專業素養。研究上為了要區辨出有效的實證本位教學和預測指標，我們需要訓練有素的教師，他們知道何時和如何實施差異化教學；也因此在特殊教育教師的職前訓練上，未來的教師需要具備和準備好特殊教育教學之必要基礎知能，如精確教學法、直接教學法、個別化教學等，而專業教師也需要在特殊教育基礎知能和新研發的有效教學法上，持續地研習進修精進專業能力之發展。

Effective Practices and Predictors of Post-School Success for Students with Special Education Needs

Charlotte Y. Alverson

In order for children with disabilities to achieve positive post-school outcomes in further education, employment, and independent living, their school experience needs to be grounded in interventions that have strong evidence showing their effectiveness, but what is evidence? According to the Merriam-Webster (n.d.) Online Dictionary evidence is "something that furnishes proof". In 1996, medical researchers defined evidence-based medicine as the "conscientious, explicit and judicious use of current best evidence in making decisions about the care of individual patients. The practice of evidence-based medicine means integrating individual clinical expertise with the best available external clinical evidence from systematic research" (Sackett, Rosenberg, Gray, Haynes, & Richardson, 1996, p. 71). A few years later, Davies (1999) described evidence-based education as "integrating individual teaching and learning expertise with the best available external evidence from systematic research" (p. 117). Davies emphasized the importance of (a) using the existing "evidence from worldwide research and literature" (p. 109), and (b) establishing sound evidence, stating, "establishing best practice ... is more than a matter of simply accessing, critically appraising, and implementing research findings. It also involves integrating such knowledge with professional judgement and experience" (p. 116). Furthermore, Davies recognized, that for evidence to be used, educational research literature would need "... to be better registered, indexed, classified, appraised, and made accessible to researchers and teachers alike" (p. 117). In other words, educators need access to research findings to inform their practice (Alverson & Yamamoto, 2016; Carnine, 1997). Thus, accessibility - "the ease and quickness with which practitioners can obtain research findings and extract the necessary information related to a certain goal" - and usability - "the likelihood that the research will be used by those who have the responsibility for making decisions" (Carnine, 1997, p. 363) are hallmarks of data-based decision-making frameworks and paramount to an evidence-based education.

In 2001, a catalyst for evidence-based education in the United States was the reauthorization of the Elementary and Secondary Education Act, titled No Child Left Behind (NCLB), with an emphasis on evidence supporting educational practices. Along with flexibility, accountability, and parent choice, research proven effectiveness was a pillar of NCLB (Poppen & Alverson, 2018). The Act required that children have access "... to effective, scientifically based instructional strategies and challenging academic content" (20 USC 6301 §1001(9)) and defined scientifically-based research as "(A) ... research that involves the application of rigorous, systematic, and objective procedures to obtain reliable and valid knowledge relevant to education activities and programs; and (B) includes research that— (i) employs systematic, empirical methods that draw on observation or experiment; (ii) involves rigorous data analyses that are adequate to test the stated hypotheses and justify the general conclusions drawn; (iii) relies on measurements or observational methods that provide reliable and valid data across evaluators and observers, across multiple measurements and observations, and across studies by the same or different investigators; (iv) is evaluated using experimental or quasi-experimental designs in which individuals, entities, programs, or activities are assigned to different conditions and with appropriate controls to evaluate the effects of the condition of interest, with a preference for random-assignment experiments, or other designs to the extent that those designs contain within-condition or across-condition controls; (v) ensures that experimental studies are presented in sufficient detail and clarity to allow for replication or, at a minimum, offer the opportunity to build systematically on their findings; and (vi) has been accepted by a peer-reviewed journal or approved by a panel of independent experts through a comparably rigorous, objective, and scientific review." (20 USC 7801 §9101(37).

Mandating the use of scientifically-based instructional strategies marks the genesis of the evidence-based practices era, 2001 through present day (Test & Fowler, 2018). Combined with several seminal events that helped inaugurate the movement, evidence-based special education is now a priority in the field of secondary special education and transition. Key among these events were (a) establishing the What Works Clearinghouse, (b) developing quality indicators in special education research, and (c) funding technical assistance centers to identify evidence-based practices and support states' use of them.

To facilitate the identification of high-quality research and make it accessible to educators, the United States (US) Department of Education Institute of Education Sciences (IES) established the What Works Clearinghouse (WWC) in 2002. The purpose of the WWC is to provide educators, administrators, and policymakers with the information needed to make decisions based on evidence. WWC staff regularly conducts a comprehensive search of the literature and review of research studies to determine the highest quality research on an educational policy, program, or practice. Studies meeting the WWC standards are rated as (a) Meets WWC Design Standards Without Reservations, (b) Meets WWC Design Standards with Reservations, or (c) Does Not Meet WWC Design Standards. Findings from the review of studies are combined and made available to the public through intervention reports and practice guides (see http://www.whatworks.ed.gov).

Reauthorization of the Individuals with Disabilities Education Improvement Act (known as IDEA) in 2004 further strengthened the need for evidence on effective instructional practices. Congressional findings for IDEA indicated "... the implementation of this title has been impeded by low expectations, and an insufficient focus on applying replicable research on proven methods of teaching and learning for children with disabilities" (P. L. 108-446) (IDEA 2004). Furthermore, the Act's Findings indicated "... providing effective transition services to promote successful post-school employment or education is an important measure of accountability for children with disabilities" (P. L. 108-446) (IDEA 2004). In addition to incorporating the definition of scientifically-based research as defined in NCLB, IDEA requires "... special education and related services and supplemental aids and services, based on peer-reviewed research to the extent practicable, to be provided to the child ..." (34 CFR §300.320(a)(4)) (IDEA, 2004). Thus, in a short period of time, two federal laws governing education in the US established expectations that educators, administrators, and policymakers would use evidence when making educational decisions. Each Act also included accountability mechanisms focused on both in-school and post-school outcomes.

In a special issue of *Exceptional Children*, researchers with expertise in four research methodologies - qualitative, correlation, single-subject, and group and quasi-experimental - put forth a set of quality indicators "... for research in special education and guidelines for evidence of effective practices" (Graham, 2005, p. 135). The indicators and guidelines represented rigorous methodological application in group and quasi-experimental research (Gersten, Fuchs, Compton, Coyne, Greenwood, & Innocenti, 2005), single-subject research (Horner, Carr, Halle, McGee, Odom, & Wolery, 2005), correlational research (Thompson, Diamond, McWilliam, Snyder, & Snyder, 2005), and qualitative research (Brantlinger, Jiménez, Klingner, Pugach, & Richardson, 2005). Collectively, the authors' intent was to improve the quality of special education research. Improving the quality of special education research has enabled researchers to develop, identify, judge, and establish interventions based on their effectiveness. Interventions that meet prescribed criteria related to four defining elements: "research design, quality of research, quantity of research, and magnitude of effect of supporting studies" (Cook & Cook, 2011, p. 73) are deemed evidence-based. Evidence-based practices are instructional techniques "··· that are supported by multiple, high-quality studies that utilize research designs from which causality can be inferred and that demonstrate meaningful effects on student outcomes" (Cook & Cook, 2011, p. 73).

Recognizing the significant changes mandated by NCLB and IDEA, as well as the need to measure outcomes and identify effective interventions educators could implement in schools and classrooms, the US Department of Education Office of Special Education Programs funded several technical assistance and dissemination centers, including the National Post-School Outcomes Center (NPSO) at the University of Oregon, and the National Secondary Transition Technical Assistance Center (NSTTAC) at the University of North Carolina Charlotte. NPSO was charged with helping states develop a rigorous, yet practical data collection system to measure the outcomes of former students with disabilities as part of a results driven accountability system. The post-school outcomes of former students who had an IEP in effect when they left high school was one measure of how well states were meeting the purposes of IDEA (Alverson & Yamamoto, 2014), particularly preparing children with disabilities for further education, employment, and independent living. NSTTAC was charged with helping state and local education agencies implement sound transition programming that would lead to better in-school and post-school outcomes for students experiencing a disability. In 2015, these centers, along with the National Dropout Prevention Center for Students with Disabilities, collaborated to form the National Technical Assistance Center on Transition (NTACT). Funded by the US Department of Education Office of Special Education Programs (OSEP) and the Rehabilitation Services Administration (RSA), the purpose of NTACT is "... to assist State Education Agencies, Local Education Agencies, State VR agencies, and VR service providers in implementing evidence-based and promising practices ensuring students with disabilities, including those with significant disabilities, graduate prepared for success in postsecondary education and employment" (http://www.transitionta.org). Through NTACT, researchers have continued to conduct literature syntheses to identify effective practices in secondary transition and advocate for secondary transition program development that contributes to positive post-school outcomes for students with disabilities.

This chapter describes evidence-based practices and predictors of post-school success in secondary transition, why they are important, and how they can be used to inform educational decision making.

What are Effective Practices and Predictors in Secondary Transition?

Collectively, instructional strategies (i.e., practices) and in-school experiences (i.e., predictors) that contribute to students attaining skills and achieving positive post-school outcomes are referred to as effective practices and predictors. Effective practices and predictors "... have been evaluated regarding the amount, type, and quality of the research conducted, and are labeled as either (a) evidence-based, (b) research-based, or (c) promising" (NTACT, 2018a). Table 2-1 shows NTACT's Broad Definitions (NTACT, 2018a) of the levels of evidence used to categorize practices and predictors in secondary transition.

Table 2-1. NTACT's Broad Definitions

Evidence-Based Practices	Research-Based Practices	Promising Practices
• Are based on group experimental, single-case, and/or quasi-experimental correlational research designs; • Requires 2 to 5* studies demonstrating effectiveness; • Contributing studies: must utilize methodologically sound research designs; and adhere to quality indicators for evaluation; and • Include 60 participants in group experimental studies and 20 participants in single-case design studies.	• Are based on group experimental, single-case, and or a priori correlational research designs; • Requires 1 to 4* studies demonstrating effectiveness; and • Contributing studies: must utilize methodologically sound research designs and adhere to quality indicators for evaluation.	• Are based on group experimental, single-case, and or a priori or exploratory correlational, or qualitative research designs; • Requires 1 to 2* studies demonstrating effectiveness; and • Contributing studies may or may not utilize methodologically sound designs, and may or may not adhere to quality indicators for evaluation.

Note: * number of studies required to determine level of effectiveness is based on the research design. See NTACT's (June 2018) Introduction to NTACT Criteria for Levels of Evidence.

Evidence-Based Practices. Evidence-based practices are instructional strategies, shown to be effective based on high quality experimental research, used by educators and services providers to teach specific skills to students with disabilities. In 2009, NSTTAC conducted a literature synthesis to identify evidence-based practices in secondary transition (Test, Fowler et al., 2009). Table 2-2 shows the initial list of 32 practices.

Table 2-2. Evidence-Based Practices

Involving students in Individualized Education Program (IEP) meetings	Teaching life skills using computer-assisted instruction
Self-Advocacy Strategy	Teaching life skills using self-management
Self-Directed IEP	Teaching job-specific employment skills
Teaching life skills	Teaching job-specific employment skills using computer-assisted instruction
Teaching purchasing skills	Teaching purchasing using the "one more than" strategy
Teaching banking skills	Teaching restaurant purchasing skills
Teaching completing a job application	Teaching safety skills
Teaching cooking skills	Teaching self-advocacy skills
Teaching employment skills using community- based instruction	Teaching self-determination skills
Teaching food preparation skills	Teaching self-management for employment skills
Teaching functional math skills	Social skills training
Teaching functional reading skills	Teaching job-related social communication skills
Teaching grocery shopping skills	Teaching parents and families about transition
Teaching home maintenance skills	Provide community-based instruction
Teaching leisure skills	Structure program to extend services beyond secondary school
Teaching life skills using community-based instruction	Implement Check & Connect program for students with disabilities

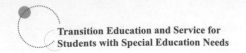
Researchers at NTACT continue synthesize the current literature to identify new predictors and practices that have been shown to be effective. For the most recent list of effective practices and predictors in secondary transition, as identified by NTACT, visit www.transitionta.org.

Evidence-Based Predictors of Post-School Success

Absent from the initial literature synthesis conducted by NSTTAC was a link between in-school experiences and students' outcomes after exiting high school. To identify a link between experiences and outcomes, NSTTAC conducted a second literature synthesis. The result of which was the identification of 16 evidence-based predictors of post-school success (Test, Mazzotti, Mustian, Fowler, Kortering, & Kohler, 2009). The predictors, unlike the evidence-based practices, were based on high quality correlational studies, not experimental research, therefore no causation could be drawn between a student's in-school experience and their post-school outcome. At this time, a correlation provides the best available evidence between in-school experiences and post-school outcomes. On-going syntheses resulted in the addition of four predictors - goal setting, travel training, youth autonomy, and parent expectations (Mazzotti, Rowe, Sinclair, Poppen, Woods, & Shearer, 2016). Table 2-3 shows the list of predictors of post-school success. In 2014, Rowe et al. conducted a Delphi study with experts in the field to operationally define the 16 original predictors and identify essential program characteristics of each predictor. The resulting operational definitions and essential program characteristics provide consistency for developing, implementing, and evaluating secondary transition programming.

Table 2-3. In-School Predictors of Post-School Success

Career Awareness	Program of Study
Community Experiences	Self-Advocacy /Self-Determination
Exit Exam Requirements / High School Diploma Status	Self-Care /Independent Living
Inclusion in General Education	Social Skills
Interagency Collaboration	Student Support
Occupational Courses	Transition Program
Paid Employment /Work Experience	Vocational Education
Parental Involvement	Work Study
Goal Setting	Travel Training
Youth Autonomy	Parent Expectations

Why are Evidence-Based Practices and Predictors of Post-School Success Important?

The importance of effective practices and predictors are grounded in three factors. First, used together, these evidence-based practices and predictors provide the best available peer-reviewed research to date that meets the criteria of scientifically-based and peer-reviewed research in secondary special education and transition. Educators and educational leaders can use the practices and predictors as a framework for developing, expanding, and implementing effective secondary transition programming. Second, using effective practices and predictors help educators better prepare students with disabilities for success in their postsecondary education, employment, and independent living goals. Third, and most important, implementation of effective practices and predictors increases the effectiveness and efficiency with which students gain new knowledge and skills. Children who experience disabilities "do not have time to waste while their teachers try methods that might work. These students need teachers to use the methods that are the most likely to work" (Lloyd & Lloyd, 2015, p. 78). Therefore, utilizing instructional strategies that produce the intended result in the least amount of time is preferred.

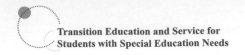
How Can Evidence-Based Practices and Predictors of
Post-School Success be Used?

Identifying effective practices and predictors is just the starting point for an evidence-based education. Formulating a list of effective practices and predictors contributes to the accessibility of evidence, but for students to benefit from the evidence, the reliance on and use of practices and predictors must become ubiquitous across multiple organizational levels. As shown in Figure 2-1, practices and predictors occur at different levels of the educational system - student (i.e., micro/mezzo), school (i.e., mezzo/macro), and state or nation (i.e., macro). At the micro-level, practices are the instructional strategies used to teach specific skills to individual students. At the mezzo- and macro-levels, predictors are more broadly focused on in-school experiences of formal groups, and the large-scale endeavors such as policy and administrative structures (Mattocks, 2018).

At the micro level, the IEP team is responsible for identifying appropriate instructional strategies and experiences for each individual student based on his or her unique needs, strengths, and characteristics. Instructional strategies and experiences should be considered when a student's IEP team identifies the students'

a) preference, interests, needs and strengths,

b) annual goals,

c) supplemental aids and services,

d) modifications and or accommodations needed to ensure the student can access the general curriculum and benefit from instruction, and for students who are transition age

e) transition services, that is the instructional, related services, community experiences, vocational evaluation, daily living skills, employment and adult objectives need to achieve his or her postsecondary goals.

Each juncture of the process affords an opportunity to ask the questions: what instructional strategies have been (or have not been) effective for this student and what experiences does the student need to have? Relevant evidence-based practices and predictors should be identified through formal and informal assessment and evaluation procedures, past-performance data, input from families, and/or observations of astute educators, and services providers.

Predictors of post-school success are in-school experiences that transpire at the mezzo- and/or macro-organizational levels of schools, districts, or states. At the mezzo level, evidence-based practices and predictors should be incorporated into lesson plans and other program or group structures (e.g., jobs club, transition program) to address the similar needs of a small group of students. At the macro-level, educational administrators and leaders, such as school principals, school district administrators, and national leaders should set policy and infrastructures that support the wide-scale development, implementation, and evaluation of evidence-based practices and predictors.

To understand how implementation of predictors and practices occur at different organizational levels, consider the following illustration. The IEP team determines that a student would benefit from being in the general education setting for a portion of her school day. *Inclusion in general education* is a predictor of positive post-school outcomes. Furthermore, the IEP team identifies two instructional strategies - *mnemonics* and *graphic organizers* - have been effective based on her unique learning characteristics and the skills she needs to learn. The classroom teacher, whether a general or special educator, can implement the instructional strategies. However, ensuring the student's success in general education classes requires more than a decree from the IEP team. Organizational structures must be in place if implementation of the predictor is going to be successful for the student. These structures include the general and special educators working together through consultation, collaboration, and or co-teaching models to meet the student's unique needs. School- and district-level administrators supporting inclusive practices by providing professional development opportunities, being flexible, and focusing on solving problems (Boscardin, Mainzer, & Kealy, 2011). State-level policies and procedures aligning special education services within the context of general education (Pugach, & Peck, 2016), and students and families understanding the benefit of general education (Rojewski, Lee, & Gregg, 2015). Thus, successful implementation of a predictor involves multiple people working at multiple organizational levels toward a shared outcome.

Table 2-4 shows examples of how effective practices and predictors can be incorporated into an IEP. The column on the left contains the student's present level of academic achievement and functional performance. The column on the right contains examples of practices and/or predictors incorporated into different areas of the IEP - annual goal, a supplemental aids/service, or a modification or accommodation. In the first example, multiple sources report Kuan-lin struggles with comprehension and recall. A mnemonic is an instructional strategy that has been shown to be effective in improving comprehension, based on high quality experimental research. The

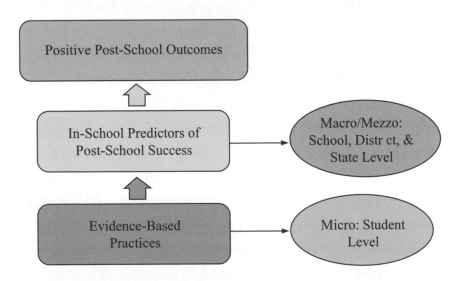

Figure 2-1. Organization of Practices and Predictors

Resource: Alverson, Unruh, Post, & Rowe (2014).

use of a mnemonic could be specified in the annual goal or as a supplemental aid in the IEP. Since Kuan-lin is now 17 years old, in the second example, the IEP team is considering his postsecondary goals and determining the transition services he needs in order to achieve his goals.

Table 2-4. Examples of effective practices and predictors incorporated into an IEP

Child's Present Level of Academic Achievement and Functional Performance	Use of Effective Practices in···
Kuan-lin's scores for verbal comprehension, working memory, and processing speed on the Wechsler Adult Intelligence Scale 4th edition are all within the low range.	**Annual goal:** Using a mnemonic either developed by the teacher or himself, Kuan-lin will answer 6 of 8 comprehension questions correctly 9 of 10 times.
During an observation of Kuan-lin in the summer school reading program, the school psychologist observed Kuan-lin responded with "I don't know" 12 times when asked reading comprehension questions after reading several passages. Kuan-lin's teachers report he frequently replies "I don't know" when asked questions during class and leaves questions blank on tests. Based on his testing scores, observations, and teacher reports, Kuan-lin needs strategies to help his recall memory and comprehension.	**Supplemental aids and services:** Use a mnemonic device to recall lists of characteristics, steps, stages, parts, phases, or other important information for tests or assignments. *The effective practice is mnemonic.*
Kuan-lin plans to work after completing high school. Currently, his vocational interests are in manufacturing and retail. Based on results from his age-appropriate transition assessment, he prefers to work alone or with a small number of people. Kuan-lin has had no paid or unpaid work experiences.	**Transition services:** To learn about manufacturing and retail occupations, Kuan-lin will participate in three, 4-week unpaid work experiences in his community during the first semester to increase his employability skills. *The effective predictor is unpaid work experiences.*

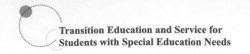

To use evidence-based practices and predictors, consider this process:

1. Identify the skill, behavior, or experiences the student needs to learn, improve, or demonstrate in order to achieve his or her post-school goals. This information will come from a variety of sources, including:

- age-appropriate transition assessments used to identify the student's preferences, interests, needs, and strengths and determine his or her post-school goals for further education, employment, and independent living;
- input from the student and family;
- eligibility assessment data from psychoeducational evaluations including academic and adaptive behavior skills;
- observations, case notes or progress monitoring from teachers and/or service providers;
- grades and results from academic achievement testing;
- industry-based skills and behaviors the student will need in order to obtain and maintain his or her desired post-school employment goal;
- functional skills and behaviors the student will need to enroll and persist in his or her desired further education or training goal; and
- daily living skills and behaviors needed to achieve adult outcomes.

2. Identify the evidence-based practice/s or predictor/s, with the highest level of evidence, associated with the skill, behavior, or experience the student needs to acquire. That is, choose research-based practices over promising practices; evidence-based practices over research-based practices, and promising practices when there is no other evidence. When the targeted skill, behavior, or experience is not associated with a practice or predictor, professionals should use the best available evidence paired with their professional judgement to decide which practice or predictor is most appropriate. To the extent possible, select evidence-based practice/s or predictor/s that have been used with the student's population.

3. Implement the practice or predictor with fidelity. Implementation with fidelity requires intentionality. If possible, replicate the procedures for implementation

outlined by the original study/studies used to establish the practice or predictor. Pay attention to the materials used, the dosage (how long and how often), and procedures used to establish the practice or predictor. When this level of detail is not available in peer-reviewed publications, consider contacting the authors of a study and requesting guidance. When implementing the practice or predictor, do so with consistency; use the same materials, presented in the same way, for the same amount of time.

4. Monitor the student's progress regularly to determine its effectiveness. Take copious notes and collect data on both procedures and results. Collect data regularly and consistently about the process used and the outcomes attained to inform decision making. First, collect data as a measure of the implementation process. At this level, the underling question is whether the intervention was implemented with fidelity. Record how often the intervention occurred, the dosage, materials, and situational context. Second, student-level data must be collected to measure outcomes- that is, did implementation of the practice or predictor result in the student learning the intended information or performing the desired behavior? Only through progress monitoring can determine effectiveness of a practice or outcome for a particular student.

Conclusion

"The evolution away from methods driven by premature hypotheses and poorly founded theories toward those firmly grounded in empirical research is one of the most important developments in special education ..." (Lloyd & Lloyd, 2015, p. 78). However, evidence-based practices and predictors are not panaceas; they are but two components of a systemic, evidence-based approach to education. Although, federal policies, like those in the US, may emphasize utilization of strategies and experiences with proof of effectiveness, establishing and embracing such an approach requires more. It requires public and private investments in research. High-quality, experimental research on a scale that provides the empirical evidence to differentiate

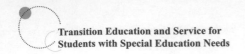

instructional strategies and experiences by multiple categories (e.g., disability, race/ethnicity, gender, and geographic location) (Haber et al., 2016; Lloyd & Lloyd, 2015) in order to determine for whom which practices and predictors are effective. It requires well trained educators who know when and how to differentiate instruction. It requires teacher preparation in the essential foundations of special education (e.g., precision teaching, direct instruction, individualization) (Lloyd & Lloyd, 2015), as well as on-going professional development and technical assistance in both the foundations of special education and emerging effective practices (Test & Fowler, 2018).

References

Alverson, C. Y., & Yamamoto, S. H. (2014). Talking with teachers, administrators, and parents: Preferences for visual displays of education data. *Journal of Education and Training, 2:2*. doi:10.11114/jets.v2i2.253.

Alverson, C. Y., & Yamamoto, S. H. (2016). Educational decision making with visual data and graphical interpretation: Assessing the effects of user preference and accuracy. *Sage Open, October-December*, 1-13. doi:10.1177/21582440 16678290

Alverson, C. Y., Unruh, D. K., Post, C., & Rowe, D. (2014). *State Toolkit for Examining Post-School Success- Professional Development* (STEPSS-PD). Available from http://www.transitionta.org

Boscardin, M. L., Mainzer, R., & Kealy, M. V., (2011). Commentary: A response to "preparing special education administrators for inclusion in diverse, standards-based contexts," by Deborah L. Voltz and Loucrecia Collins. *Teacher Education and Special Education, 24*(1), 71-78.

Brantlinger, E., Jiménez, R., Klingner, J., Pugach, M., & Richardson, V. (2005). Qualitative studies in special education. *Exceptional Children, 71*(2), 195-207.

Carnine, D. W. (Ed.). (1997). *Bridging the research-to-practice gap*. Mahwah, NJ: Lawrence Erlbaum Associates.

Cook, B. G., & Cook, S. C. (2011). Unraveling evidence-based practices in special education. *The Journal of Special Education, 47*(2), 71-82. doi:10.1177/00224 66911420877

Davies, P. (1999). What is evidenced-based education? *British Journal of Educational Studies, 47*(2), 108-121.

Gersten, R., Fuchs, L. S., Compton, D., Coyne, M., Greenwood, C., & Innocenti, M. S. (2005). QIs for group experimental and quasi-experimental research in special education. *Exceptional Children, 71*(2), 149-164.

Graham, S. (2005). Preview. *Exceptional Children, 71*(2), 135.

Haber, M., Mazzotti, V. L., Mustian, A. L., Rowe, D. A., Bartholomew, A. L., Test, D. W., & Fowler, C. H. (2016). What works, when, for whom, and with whom: A meta-analytic review of predictors of postsecondary success for students with disabilities. *Review of Educational Research, 86*(1), 123-162. doi: 10.3102/0034654315583135

Horner, R. H., Carr, E. G., Halle, J., McGee, G., Odom, S., & Wolery, M. (2005). The use of single-subject research to identify evidence-based practice in special education. *Exceptional Children, 71*(2), 165-179.

Individuals with Disabilities Education Act (IDEA) Pub. L. 108-446. (2004).

Individuals with Disabilities Education Act (IDEA), 34 CFR §300.320(a)(4)(2004).

Lloyd, J. W., & Lloyd, P. A. (2015). Reinforcing success: What special education could learn from its earlier accomplishments. *Remedial and Special Education, 36*, 77-82. doi:10.1177/0741932514560025

Mattocks, N. O. (2018). Social action among social work practitioners: Examining the micro-macro divide. *Social Work, 63*, 7-16.

Mazzotti, V. L., Rowe, D. A., Sinclair, J., Poppen, M., Woods, W. E., & Shearer, M. L. (2016). Predictors of post-school success: A systematic review of NLTS2 secondary analyses. *Career Development and Transition for Exceptional Individuals, 39*(4), 196-215.

Merriam-Webster (n.d.). *Evidence.* Retrieved January 2, 2019, from https://www.merriam-webster.com/dictionary/evidence

National Technical Assistance Center on Transition. [NTACT] (2018a). *Broad definitions.* Retrieved from https://transitionta.org/system/files/effectivepractices/LOE_Definitions_Simplified_Final_Spring2018.pdf?file=1&type=node&id=1474&force=

Poppen, M., & Alverson, C. Y. (2018). Policies and practice: A review of legislation affecting transition services for individuals with disabilities. *New Directions for Adult and Continuing Education, 160*, 63-75.

Pugach, M. C., & Peck, C. (2016). Dividing practices preservice teacher quality assessment and the (re)production of relations between general and special education. *Teacher Education Quarterly, 43*, 3-23.

Rojewski, J. W., Lee, I. H., & Gregg, N. (2015). Causal effects of inclusion on post-secondary education outcomes of individuals with high-incidence disabilities. *Journal of Disability Policy Studies, 25*(4), 210-219.

Sackett, D. L., Rosenberg, W. C., Gray, J. A. M., Haynes, R. B., & Richardson, W. S. (1996). Evidence based medicine: What it is and what it isn't. *BMJ, 312*, 71-72.

Test, D. W., & Fowler, C. H. (2018). A look at the past, present, and future of rural secondary transition. *Rural Special Education Quarterly, 37*(2), 68-78. doi: 10.1177/8756870517751607

Test, D. W., Fowler, C. H., Richter, S. M., White, J., Mazzotti, V., Walker, A. R., Kohler, P., & Kortering, L. J. (2009). Evidence-based practices in secondary transition. *Career Development for Exceptional Individuals, 32*, 115-128. doi: 0.1177/0885728809336859

Test, D. W., Mazzotti, V. L., Mustian, A. L., Fowler, C. H., Kortering, L. J., & Kohler, P. H. (2009). Evidence-based secondary transition predictors for improving post-school outcomes for students with disabilities. *Career Development for Exceptional Individuals, 32*, 160-181.

Thompson, B., Diamond, K. E., McWilliam, R., Snyder, P., & Snyder, S. W. (2005). Evaluating the quality of evidence from correlational research for evidence-based practice. *Exceptional Children, 71*(2), 181-194.

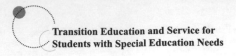

第三章　學校與家庭如何促進身心障礙學生的自我決策

Promoting Self-Determination at School and at Home

Michael L. Wehmeyer、趙本強（Pen-Chiang Chao）

中文摘錄：趙本強

中文重點摘錄

▶ 壹、緒論

　　促進轉銜階段身心障礙青少年之自我決策對其學校表現及社區生活皆有正面助益，而當教師在思考實施自我決策介入教學時，教學場域的文化背景是必須考量的重要因素之一。「自我學習導向教學模式」（Self-Determined Learning Model of Instruction, SDLMI）即是強調此概念的介入教學，其教學成效及實用性在包含亞洲在內的許多國家均已獲得實證研究的支持。有鑑於自我決策對於身心障礙青少年的生涯轉銜極為重要，故當致力於提升這群學子的轉銜成效時，務必提供他們在自我決策能力成長與發展所需的支持及教學。本章討論的內容包括概述自我決策概念、探究其發展沿革，以及闡述文化背景因素在促進學生自我決策過程中扮演的重要性。此外，亦介紹適於在學校及家庭中應用的自我決策介入教學策略。就臺灣自我決策介入教學的實施而言，則以「從做中學自我決策課程」（Learning by Doing Self-Determination Curriculum, LDSDC）為例，並概述其內涵。

　　促進身心障礙青少年自我決策已廣泛被世界各國視為是轉銜服務中的重要一環。誠如本章後半段所述，身心障礙青少年有能力成為一位自我決策者，而當此成真時，即意謂他們在學校學習及轉銜成果會有更好的表

現。在本章中，首先介紹自我決策的概念及其定義，並簡述此概念的發展沿革，另亦以文獻佐證資料闡明提升自我決策能力發展的重要性。之後，則進一步探討一個能協助個體成為自我決策者之終身學習方法，包括當其處於自我決策發展初期階段時，家庭該扮演何種角色，而隨其成長至青少年時期及進入求學階段後，教師與家長又該有何作為，方能提升個體自我決策能力之發展。本章最後將論述在亞洲及其他國家地區經實證研究證明為有效的介入教學策略——「自我學習導向教學模式」（SDLMI）。

貳、了解自我決策概念

在特殊教育領域中，致力於促進學生自我決策的首要任務之一，乃是對此概念做明確定義。自我決策此概念最早係用於 17 世紀的歐洲哲學界，以探討個體的自由意志與自主性，及至 20 世紀初方被心理學界引用，以討論與人類自主行為相關之議題（Wehmeyer, Shogren, Little, & Lopez, 2017）。自 1990 年代初期的 25 年間，為了致力促進身心障礙學生自我決策，Wehmeyer 等學者已明確界定此名詞的意涵。Shogren、Wehmeyer、Palmer、Forber-Pratt、Little 與 Lopez（2015）近年則進一步以「自我掌控理論」（causal agency theory）說明個體如何成為一位自我決策者。此理論將自我決策定義為：「……能在生活中展現掌控自己行為的一種先天特質。自我決策者（即自我行為代理人）能按己意選定目標而行。自我決策行為具有促使個體成為自己生活代理人的功能」（p. 258）。

藉由將自我決策定位為一種先天特質，Shogren 等學者實乃暗示著：自我決策者具有持續在其生活中扮演自我行為代理人的特質。自我行為代理人可以在生活中主動讓事情發生。此外，自我決策者在生活中亦能達成具體目標或做必要調整。簡言之，此理論最核心的論述是：自我決策行為係指個體在生活中主動促使事情發生，而非假他人之手。自我決策行為係一種目標導向且以個人喜好與興趣作為驅力的行為，此行為最終將有助於個體提升其生活品質（Shogren, Wehmeyer, Palmer, Forber-Pratt et al., 2015）。

Wehmeyer 等人（2017）曾闡述個體在其成長過程中自我決策的發展歷

程。雖然完整地陳述此歷程並非本章重點，但基本而言，該理論主張自我決策係個體在其所處環境中由需求與機會兩者交互作用後產生的結果，個體藉此自我決策行為來滿足其在自主、勝任及歸屬等心理層面的需求（Shogren, Little, & Wehmeyer, 2017）。更具體而言，個體在具有自主性、勝任心及歸屬感等三項需求上的交互作用激盪出一連串掌控行為的連續交錯，此行為掌控即個體的意志行為（在生活中促使某事發生）及引導行為（持續去完成目標的行為）。此意志行為及引導行為間的循環互動，即由個體自認其能成為一位自我掌控者的信念居間協調（Mumbardó-Adam, Guàrdia-Olmos, & Giné, 2018; Shogren et al., 2017）。更簡單來說，由 Wehmeyer 等人（2017）提出的發展模式主張，人類自兒童期早期開始即具按個人自由意志展現行為的動機（如自主動機或內在動機）且能駕馭相關的自我掌控行為，此行為即是由自認能成為自我掌控者之信念所協調管理的意志行為及引導行為。個體反覆地經歷與體驗自我掌控行為，將漸次促使其自我決策能力之提升。

▌參、自我決策對身心障礙青少年的重要性

有愈來愈多的研究顯示，能自我決策對身心障礙青少年的生活非常重要。首先，在文獻中有明顯的佐證資料證明，各不同障礙類別的身心障礙學生多未具備應有的自我決策能力（Wehmeyer & Shogren, 2017）。一份近期在美國調查的大規模研究，其評估學生的障礙身分別（即身心障礙或非身心障礙）、性別及種族背景對學生自我決策的影響情形，其結果顯示：非身心障礙學生（一般普通生）普遍較其各不同障別之身心障礙同儕有更高的自我決策程度。另外，學生的自我決策程度亦深受其家庭社經地位及種族背景等因素之影響，例如：那些在學校具有午餐費全額或部分減免資格的身心障礙青少年（即來自低社經地位家庭者），在自我決策評估量表的得分較其非來自低社經地位家庭身障生同儕的分數更低（Shogren, Shaw, Raley, & Wehmeyer, 2018）。因此，當檢視學生的自我決策程度時，其障礙身分別及家庭社經地位等因素均是必須考量的因素之一。

　　另一份近期在臺灣進行的大規模調查研究也再度證明上述論述。Chao、Chou 與 Cheng（2019）以臺灣「特殊教育長期追蹤資料庫」的資料，分析 630 名智能障礙、學習障礙、情緒行為障礙及自閉症等四類青少年的自我決策程度。此外，當其與一般普通生同儕相較時，感官障礙或身體病弱青少年的自我決策程度亦顯著較低；此突顯相同型態的差異結果亦可見於南韓（Lee, Hong, Yeom, & Lee, 2018）。

　　有許多研究顯示，當提供學生自我決策介入教學時，他們有潛力可以成為更具自我決策能力的個體（Wehmeyer, Palmer, Shogren, Williams-Diehm, & Soukup, 2012; Wehmeyer, Shogren, Palmer, Williams-Diehm, Little, & Boulton, 2012），在本章後半段會將有關於這些研究之內容做更詳細的說明。但近期一份針對自我決策介入教學進行的後設分析結果，再次印證先前之後設分析早已得到的結論，即當提供有助提升身心障礙學生自我決策之介入教學時，對於不同年級、障礙類別及安置班級型態的學生而言，皆具教學成效（Burke et al., 2018）。

　　很明顯地，如此的研究結果並非僅限於美國，在世界其他國家亦有相似的發現，例如：Lee、Wehmeyer 與 Shogren（2015）在南韓國家研究基金會（National Research Foundation of Korea）的補助下進行一項後設分析研究，此研究應用單一論文探討設計法針對 15 篇以「自我學習導向教學模式」（SDLMI）作為介入教學的實證研究論文（6 篇來自南韓、9 篇來自美國）進行分析。其研究結果發現，「自我學習導向教學模式」（SDLMI）介入教學的實施不但有助身心障礙青少年在普通班接受教學，且亦有助於其在轉銜相關成果上有更佳的表現。接受此教學模式教導的學生可以展現的具體成果目標，包括：有進步的問題解決能力、更佳的自我調整能力、更有能力參與生涯與職業規劃及做選擇、有更成熟的工作表現等。

　　最後，很明顯地，具備更好的自我決策能力對身心障礙學生在學期間或畢業後均有助益。有非常明確的證據顯示，更高的自我決策程度有助於各不同障礙類別學生在學習相關的成果上有更好的表現，包括：至普通班接受教育的機會、學業成就與轉銜目標的達成、轉銜知識與技能的習得等（Shogren, Palmer, Wehmeyer, Williams-Diehm, & Little, 2012; Wehmeyer, Pal-

mer, Lee, Williams-Diehm, & Shogren, 2011）。另外，對那些已經離校且自我
決策程度相對較好的學子而言，他們在就業及社區生活上則會有更好的表
現（Shogren, Wehmeyer, Palmer, Rifenbark, & Little, 2015）。

肆、促進自我決策

一、情境脈絡因素在促進自我決策中的重要性

　　Lee（2009）指出，當致力於促進自我決策時，將文化及跨文化因素納
入考量非常重要。Wehmeyer、Abery 等人（2011）亦曾探討在提升自我決策
能力過程中以文化作為中介變項的重要性。筆者在此釐清促進自我決策與
文化因素間的關聯性，乃是由於一般大眾太常將某些特定的做決定或問題
解決行為視為是自我決策。但如前所述，自我決策係指個人在其生活中促
使某事發生，而非指其能展現某特定的行為特質，例如：Frankland、Tur-
nbull、Wehmeyer 與 Blackmountain（2004）在探討將自我決策概念應用於美
國原住民納瓦荷印第安人〔Diné（Navajo）〕時提到：「……表達自我決策
的方式與歐裔美國白人不同。當納瓦荷人評斷自我決策與自主性時，他們
更強調互助依賴與團體凝聚力，而非僅是獨立性與自主性」（p. 195）。
　　有許多自我決策介入教學，或許特別是在美國，其發展及成效評估乃
是奠基於強調個人獨特性與自主性的立論基礎。但必須了解的是，促進自
我決策的真諦並非關乎個體該如何行動方能成為一位自我掌控者，而是指
個體能實際按其自由意志而行。Wehmeyer、Abery 等人（2011）引用一個有
關因個人主義／集體主義文化之差異而表現出的不同自我決策特質。Ewalt
與 Mokuau（1995）兩位學者則從太平洋島國民族的角度來討論自我決策，
指出：「自我決策對太平洋地區人民的文化而言，乃是被定義為集體隸屬
關係而非個人主義」（p. 170），並提供以下例子做說明：「Debra 是位住
在夏威夷的女性，她近期甫完成醫學教育取得醫生資格，並想繼續待在學
校附近的地區當醫生。她如願在一間名聲頗佳的家醫科診所擔任醫師且薪
資優渥。對 Debra 來說，繼續待在學校附近的社區確實很吸引人，因為她不

但能住得舒適且朋友圈也都在此。然而她的家人，特別是她的父母卻希望 Debra 能回到自小成長的家鄉當醫生。但若是這麼做的話，她就必須從都市搬回家鄉社區。雖然 Debra 一開始有些遲疑，但她仍很快地改變自己的想法以順應父母的期待。她認為回到家鄉社區不但能與家人團聚，且亦能為家人及社區中其他有嚴重健康問題的鄉親提供醫療照護」（p. 171）。

二、如何在家庭中促進自我決策

家庭中的成員往往是兒童人生中的第一位教師。當他們年幼時，父母與手足便開始扮演其在發展過程中最初且最重要的導師，自我決策的發展歷程即是如此。隨著兒童逐漸成長且變得更成熟，家庭對其自我決策發展的重要性並不會因此消失，而僅是在影響的形式上有所改變（Palmer, 2010）。自我決策的發展主要係在青少年時期，雖然兒童年幼時必須倚賴他人「照料滿足他們在物質、社會及心理層面的需求，養育並提供其在發展與教育上的支持，以及確保他們的生活安全與保障」（Palmer, Wehmeyer, & Shogren, 2017, p. 72），但他們在日後發展自我掌控與自我決策所需的基本技能卻均始於兒童時期（Wehmeyer & Palmer, 2000）。

Palmer 等人（2013）指出，有助於日後發展自我決策所需的基本技能，係指「讓身心障礙兒童習得：(1)做選擇與問題解決；(2)自我調整；(3)參與技能」（p. 38）。詳述這些基本技能發展的重要歷程雖非本章討論的重點，但簡言之，上述所謂做選擇與問題解決主要係指，鼓勵並支持兒童表達個人喜好、做決定、參與問題解決，此為其日後具備獨立自主（auto-nomy）、自我倡權及自主行動能力的基石。必須注意的是，此所謂的獨立自主並非指個體能單獨地去行動，而是指其能按個人自由意志去行動。上述理論模式中的第二個要素——自我調整，則係指教導兒童能根據環境變化調整自己的行為，並能在行為表現及學習上具備自我引導的能力。同樣地，自我調整技能並非強調兒童能獨自去解決問題或調整行為，而是指在兒童行使這些行為過程中提供其必要的鷹架（scaffolding）支持。兒童早期的行為發展模式多是如此。最後，所謂促進學生參與，係指教導他們自我

引導、堅持不懈及實踐目標所需的相關基本技能。

　　為了提出一套能用於提升那些有助於日後發展自我決策所需之基本技能的架構，Palmer 與 Wehmeyer（2003）兩位學者探究應用「自我學習導向教學模式」（SDLMI）此架構的成效。「自我學習導向教學模式」（SDLMI）提供兒童和青少年一個可以幫助他們有效解決問題的方法，並進而具備設定及達成目標的能力。Palmer 與 Wehmeyer 的研究結果顯示：當給予身心障礙學生需要的支持時，他們可以受惠於此教學模式的教導，提升其在問題解決及自我調整等層面的能力。此外，Palmer 與 Wehmeyer（2002）兩位學者同樣亦將「自我學習導向教學模式」（SDLMI）應用於家長，使其可以建構能有效提升子女自我決策的親子間互動之能力。

三、如何在學校中促進自我決策

　　「自我學習導向教學模式」（SDLMI）是一種讓教師教導學生如何自我教導的教學模式。所謂的教學模式乃係指「可在教室或其他情境中用於發展長期性課程、設計教材、引導教學的一種計畫或型態」（Joyce & Weil, 1980, p. 1）。 教學模式係起源於與人類行為或學習相關之理論，教學者在其平時教學過程中，則根據學習者的特質與學習方式（型態）而使用不同的教學模式，例如：角色扮演教學模式（role-playing model）可用於教導社會技巧及歸納思考；探究訓練教學模式（inquiry training model）可用於教導推理及學業學習技能；另源自於操作心理學的權宜／情境管理教學模式（contingency management model）則時常應用於特殊教育領域。

　　「自我學習導向教學模式」（SDLMI）乃係根據自我決策及自我引導學習理論所發展，並用於教導學生自主學習的教學模式（Mithaug, Wehmeyer, Agran, Martin, & Palmer, 1998; Wehmeyer, Palmer, Agran, Mithaug, & Martin, 2000）。雖然此模式最初係針對身心障礙學生發展而來，但其亦同時適用於普通生（Shogren, Wehmeyer, & Lane, 2016）。另如前所述，此模式亦可用於不同年齡層的學生，其中包括幼童。最後，「自我學習導向教學模式」（SDLMI）已被應用於多個亞洲國家中的不同教學情境（Lee et al.,

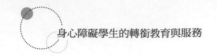

2015; Ohtake & Wehmeyer, 2004）。

　　「自我學習導向教學模式」（SDLMI）的實施是一個含括三階段教學的歷程（如圖 3-1、圖 3-2 及圖 3-3，詳見英文原文）。整體而言，在每個教學階段中皆有一道讓學生解決的問題，而每階段中又各有四個「學生問題」，學生藉由回答這些問題去認識自己的學習特質與教育需求，學習如何在個人或環境上做調整，並能實際去達到自己設定的目標。另在教學過程中，每個「學生問題」皆可連結至數個「教師目標」，而每個「教師目標」又可連結至有助於教導及引導學生回答問題的「教育支持」，藉由此有系統的教學，學生最終被期待能自行解決問題、設定目標及達成目標。

　　在每個教學階段中，學生皆是行為的自我掌控者，包括：做選擇、做決定及設定目標。在「自我學習導向教學模式」（SDLMI）中的「學生問題」，係藉由一系列的問題解決步驟引導學生，而每個階段的解答又可導出（成為）下個階段的問題，整個問題解決步驟可以循環進行。在各階段中，學生要解決的問題分別為：階段一「我的目標是什麼？」；階段二「我的計畫是什麼？」；階段三「我學會了什麼？」。而各教學階段中的四個「學生問題」則用不同的文字敘述來表達，以使學生能針對每個獨特的問題做出回答。但各階段中的四個「學生問題」皆為相同的解決問題步驟，包括：(1)提出問題；(2)找出可能的解決方法；(3)評估解決問題時會遇到的阻礙；(4)評估問題解決的結果。「自我學習導向教學模式」（SDLMI）是一種教學模式，故其是針對教師教學而設計，因此「學生問題」係以具體文字陳述，以利教師清楚了解題意。在教師首次針對某個別學生使用此教學模式時，可以和學生一起唸讀每個「學生問題」，或必要時僅由教師唸給學生聽。另外，教師亦可為學生解釋問題的意思，若學生有需求，教師亦可用不同的文字敘述來取代原有的字詞，以利學生了解題意。當教師和學生共同完整練習整個過程後，學生即可自行練習去提出問題與解決問題。

　　如前所述，「自我學習導向教學模式」（SDLMI）中的「教師目標」提供教師在支持學生回答問題時所需的具體資訊。基本而言，「教師目標」提供教師一套能引導學生習得解決「學生問題」中所陳述問題之準

則，例如：就第一個「學生問題」而言（我想要學什麼？），「教師目標」是讓學生找出自己的優勢能力及學科學習上的需求，確認並傳達自己在學科學習上的偏好、興趣、看法及價值觀，以上這些因素與其成人成果（即未來進入社會的生活表現）的關聯性，以及在學習過程中將其個人的教育需求視為是優先的考量。

每個「教師目標」可以連結到至少一個以上的「教育支持」，這些支持作法的理念多數來自於自我管理與自我引導領域的參考文獻。既然「自我學習導向教學模式」（SDLMI）的目的是讓教師教導學生自我引導與自我決策式的學習，故教師教導其以自我引導的學習方式習得自我管理與自我調整策略自當屬合理，但並非所有的教學策略皆是學生自我導向式的策略。一個教學模式的主要目的是促進學生學習，但有時達成某特定教育成果最有效的方法或策略反而是教師引導式的策略。而在「自我學習導向教學模式」（SDLMI）的教學歷程中，不論是自我導向或教師引導式學習，學生皆是按自己的想法確認其教育計畫。

有明顯證據強烈支持「自我學習導向教學模式」（SDLMI）的實施成效。許多在美國進行的實證研究於實驗過程中，皆設有以隨機方式選取與形成的對照組樣本做為比較對象，這些研究的結果均確認了「自我學習導向教學模式」（SDLMI）的實施與學生在自我決策、學校與成人成果良好表現間的因果關係，這些多已於前述提及。Wehmeyer、Palmer 等人（2012）在一個有控制組設計之實驗研究中，評估「自我學習導向教學模式」（SDLMI）用於提升高中身心障礙學生自我決策之成效，其結果顯示：接受介入教學之實驗組學生的自我決策有明顯進步。當 Shogren、Wehmeyer、Palmer 與 Rifenbark 等人（2015）追蹤參與此研究之學生其後續表現時，亦進一步確認自我決策程度愈高的學生更具備融入社區生活的能力且其職業表現亦更佳。另外，Wehmeyer、Shogren 等人（2012）則針對國中與高中階段學生進行「自我學習導向教學模式」（SDLMI）教學之實驗研究，此研究同樣亦是有控制組設計之實驗研究，其結果亦顯示：有接受介入教學的學生更能展現自我決策。Shogren 等人（2012）的研究則發現，參與此研究的實驗組學生同樣亦在目標達成及在普通班接受融合教育的表

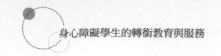

現上有更好的成效。另外，亦有證據顯示，「自我學習導向教學模式」（SDLMI）具跨國間的教學成效，包括亞洲國家在內。

　　提升身心障礙學生之自我決策能力，近年亦受到臺灣特殊教育學界的重視。本章另舉「從做中學自我決策課程」（LDSDC）為例並概述其內涵（詳細內容請見英文原文）。Chao（2011）發展的「從做中學自我決策課程」（LDSDC），其目的係協助臺灣高中輕度智能障礙學生提升其自我決策的知識與能力。「從做中學自我決策課程」（LDSDC）的主要特色是強調 John Dewey 所提出的從做中學（learning by doing）概念，並教導學生如何藉由在日常生活中練習做選擇與決定、問題解決及自主行動等，習得自我認識、自我倡權、自我調整及獨立自主等自我決策能力。除了融入強調教育生活性及實踐性的從做中學理論外，「從做中學自我決策課程」（LDSDC）也融入了發現學習（discovery learning）和鷹架作用（scaffolding）兩種學習理論的概念。前者強調學生能主動學習並從錯誤中學習，後者則強調教師的支持與引導對學生在學習過程中的重要性。簡言之，Chao 將「從做中學自我決策課程」（LDSDC）定義為：「一種強調實踐性、主動性及支持性的課程，學生藉由實際做選擇與決定、解決問題及自主行動的過程中，學習主動去思考自己的理想、興趣、優弱勢、問題解決策略及行為目的等，而教師則隨時給予必要的協助與教導」（p. 99）。有關此課程的完整內容及其應用，請參閱〈提升高職特教班學生自我決策能力成效之研究：從做中學之教學模式〉（Chao, 2011）此篇論文之內容。

Promoting Self-Determination at School and at Home

Michael L. Wehmeyer & Pen-Chiang Chao

Promoting self-determination has been shown to have positive impacts on school and community outcomes for transition-age youth with disabilities. It is important, when considering the implementation of interventions to promote self-determination that the cultural context in which the intervention is being implemented be considered. One intervention that has strong evidence of its efficacy and utility across the world, including in Asia, is the *Self-Determined Learning Model of Instruction* (SDLMI). Given the importance of enhanced self-determination for youth with disabilities, it is important to ensure that efforts to support the development of self-determination and to provide interventions to promote self-determination be included in efforts to improve transition outcomes. This chapter overviews the self-determination construct, examines its development, and describes the importance of cultural contexts to its promotion. Interventions to promote self-determination are introduced that can be used to promote self-determination at home and at school. Furthermore, the *Learning by Doing Self-Determination Curriculum* (LDSDC) aimed at promoting the self-determination knowledge and skills of Taiwanese high school students with mild intellectual disabilities is also described in this chapter.

Promoting the self-determination of youth with disabilities has been identified, worldwide, as a critical element of transition services. As described in more detail later in this chapter, we know that young people with disabilities can become more self-determined and if they do so, that they achieve more positive school and transition outcomes. This chapter introduces and defines self-determination and briefly examines its development. Data with regard to the importance of promoting self-de-

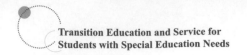

termination is presented. The chapter then discusses a lifelong approach to promoting self-determination, beginning with the role of families in the early development of self-determination and, then, examining efforts to promote self-determination in schools and during adolescence. Evidence-based practices that have been implemented in Asia and elsewhere are examined, in particular the *Self-Determined Learning Model of Instruction* (SDLMI).

Understanding the Self-Determination Construct

A focus on the importance of promoting self-determination began, in the United States, in the early 1990s in response to growing evidence that students with disabilities were not achieving positive postschool outcomes (Wehmeyer, 1996). One potential reason identified for this lack of positive outcomes was that, by and large, students with disabilities were not involved in their transition planning, goal setting, and goal attainment. If students were not involved in and engaged with their transition activities, it was argued, then they would be less likely to invest time and effort toward transition-related goals and activities. Thus, a focus on promoting the self-determination of youth with disabilities became a focal point for transition services.

Among the important early tasks in implementing efforts to promote self-determination in the special education context was to define the construct. Self-determination is a construct that was first used in late 17th century in philosophical discourses in Europe pertaining to free will and volition and, then, later in the early 20th century in psychological discussions regarding human agentic behavior (Wehmeyer, Shogren, Little, & Lopez, 2017). Beginning in the early 1990s and over a 25-year period, Wehmeyer and colleagues defined self-determination so as to support efforts to promote the self-determination of students with disabilities. Most recently, Shogren, Wehmeyer, Palmer, Forber-Pratt Little & Lopez (2015) introduced Causal Agency Theory to explain *how* people become self-determined. Causal agency theory defined self-determination as:

...a dispositional characteristic manifested as acting as the causal agent in one's life. Self-determined people (i.e., causal agents) act
in service to freely chosen goals. Self-determined actions function to
enable a person to be the causal agent in his or her life. (p. 258)

By positioning self-determination as a dispositional characteristic, Shogren
and colleagues implied that people who are self-determined can be characterized as
having an enduring tendency to act as causal agents in their lives. Being a causal agent means that a person makes or causes things to happen in his or her life. Moreover,
self-determined people act to accomplish specific ends or to cause or create change
in their lives. At its heart, then, acting in a self-determined manner implies that a person makes or causes things to happen in their own lives, rather than someone or
something else making them act in other ways. Self-determined action is goal oriented, driven by preferences and interests, and ultimately serves to enable people to enhance the quality of their lives (Shogren, Wehmeyer, Palmer, Forber-Pratt et al.,
2015).

Wehmeyer and colleagues (Wehmeyer et al., 2017) described the life-course
development of self-determination. A full description of this development is beyond
the scope of this chapter, but fundamentally, self-determination develops as a function of the interaction between the demands and opportunities in one's environment
and attempts by the person to meet basic psychological needs of autonomy, compet-
ence, and relatedness (Shogren, Little, & Wehmeyer, 2017). These interactions between the person's need to be autonomous, competent, and maintain meaningful
relationships energizes a causal action sequence that involves volitional action (initiating action to make or cause things to happen in one's life) and agentic action
(sustaining action toward a goal). These volitional and agentic action cycles are
mediated by action-control beliefs about one's ability to act as a causal agent (Mumbardó-Adam, Guàrdia-Olmos, & Giné, 2018; Shogren et al., 2017). Put more simply,
the developmental model proposed by Wehmeyer and colleagues (Wehmeyer et al.,

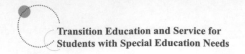

2017) proposed that from early in childhood forward, humans are motivated to act volitionally (e.g., based upon autonomous or intrinsic motivation) and employ a causal action sequence involving volitional and agentic action mediated by action-control beliefs that enable them to act as a causal agent in their lives (e.g., make things happen). Repeated experiences of causal agency, in turn, result in enhanced self-determination.

Describing a developmental course for the development of self-determination is important if we are to understand how to promote self-determination across the life course at home and at school. Before exploring interventions to promote self-determination, however, it is relevant to consider the importance of being self-determined in the lives of transition-age youth.

Importance of Self-Determination to Youth with Disabilities

There is an expanding body of research showing that being self-determined is important in the lives of young people with disability. First, there is clear evidence in the literature that students across disability categories are less self-determined than necessary (Wehmeyer & Shogren, 2017). A recent analysis examining the impact of disability status, gender, and race ethnicity on self-determination scores from a large database in the U.S. indicated that, in general, youth without disability were more self-determined than their peers across disability categories, but self-determination status was impacted by such factors as socio-economic status and race. For example, youth who were eligible for free and reduced lunches at school (determined by socio-economic criteria) had lower self-determination scores across disability categories than their peers with disabilities who did not experience poverty (Shogren, Shaw, Raley, & Wehmeyer, 2018). So, when considering relative self-determination status, disability status is one of a number of variables that must be considered.

A recent large scale study confirmed that this is the case in Taiwan as well. Chao, Chou, and Cheng (2019) analyzed data from the Special Needs Education Longitudinal Study to examine the self-determination status of 630 youth with intellectual disability, learning disabilities, emotional disturbance, and autism. Compared with youth with sensory or health impairments (but otherwise with typical functioning), these youth had significantly lower levels of self-determination. The same patterns have been identified in Korea (Lee, Hong, Yeom, & Lee, 2018).

It seems clear, then, that disability status impacts self-determination. It is also clear that this has nothing to do with whether or not students with disabilities can become self-determined, but instead about opportunities available to them to acquire and practice skills that enable them to be causal agents in their lives. Numerous studies show that when students are provided instruction to promote self-determination, they become more self-determined (Wehmeyer, Palmer, Shogren, Williams-Diehm, & Soukup, 2012; Wehmeyer, Shogren, Palmer, Williams-Diehm, Little, & Boulton, 2012). Specifics about these studies will be provided in the intervention section later in the chapter. But, a recent meta-analysis of interventions to promote self-determination confirmed again what prior meta-analytic studies had established; that when students with disabilities are provided interventions to promote self-determination, such efforts are effective across grade levels, student disability categories, and settings (Burke et al., 2018).

Again, this is clearly the case across the world and not just in the U.S. Working from a grant supported by the National Research Foundation of Korea, Lee, Wehmeyer, and Shogren (2015) conducted a meta-analysis of single-case design research studies ($n = 6$ from South Korea, $n = 9$ from the U.S.) of the Self-Determined Learning Model of Instruction (SDLMI, described subsequently). This analysis found that implementation of the SDLMI resulted in greater access to the general education curriculum and more positive transition-related outcomes for youth with disabilities. Examples of goals attained by students taught using the model included improved problem-solving skills, enhanced self-regulation, enhanced involvement

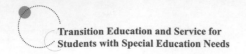

in career and vocational planning and decision making, and improved work perform-ance.

Finally, it is equally clear that being more self-determined has benefit to stu-dents with disabilities during and after school. There is strong evidence that beco-ming more self-determined results in more positive school related outcomes for stu-dents across disability categories, including access to the general education, educa-tional and transition goal attainment, and transition knowledge and skills (Shogren, Palmer, Wehmeyer, Williams-Diehm, & Little, 2012; Wehmeyer, Palmer, Lee, Wil-liams-Diehm, & Shogren, 2011) and that students who leave school as more self-de-termined young people achieve more positive employment and community out-comes (Shogren, Wehmeyer, Palmer, Rifenbark, & Little, 2015).

Again, this is true not only in the U.S., but in Asia as well. In their large study, Chao et al. (2019) found that the transition outcomes of three-quarters of the youth with intellectual, learning, and developmental disabilities could be correctly predic-ted based on their degree of self-determination. Lee and colleagues (Lee et al., 2018) reviewed 121 studies published related to the self-determination of students with di-sabilities in Korea, finding that self-determination status predicted more positive school-related outcomes.

Given that students with disabilities are not as self-determined as desired and that interventions to promote self-determination have been shown to result in enh-anced self-determination and more positive school and adult outcomes, it is import-ant to consider how to promote self-determination across the lifespan.

Promoting Self-Determination

Importance of Contextual Variables in Promoting Self-Determi-nation

As noted by Lee (2009), it is important to consider cultural and cross-cultural factors when considering the implementation of efforts to promote self-determination. Wehmeyer and colleagues (Wehmeyer, Abery et al., 2011) discussed the importance of culture as a mediating variable in efforts to promote self-determination. The issue in ensuring that efforts to promote self-determination are culturally relevant is that too often people conflate particular ways of making decisions or solving problems with being self-determination. But, as has been discussed, being self-determined means making or causing things to happen in one's life, and not actually acting in a specific manner. For example, Frankland and colleagues (Frankland, Turnbull, Wehmeyer, & Blackmountain, 2004) examined the applicability of the self-determination construct to members of the Diné (Navajo) indigenous people in the U.S., noting that:

> ...the ways in which [self-determination is] expressed differs from an Anglo perspective. While the Diné people value self-regulation and autonomy, they are operationalized more in an emphasis on the importance of interdependence and group cohesion above independence and autonomy. (p. 195)

Many interventions designed to promote self-determination, perhaps particularly in the U.S., have been developed and evaluated within contexts that emphasize individualism and autonomy. But, it is important to understand that promoting self-determination is not about how a person acts to be a causal agent, but in fact that one acts volitionally. Wehmeyer and colleagues (Wehmeyer, Abery et al., 2011) cited an example of self-determination as being relevant to cultural contexts that vary on the individualistic/collectivist continuum. Ewalt and Mokuau (1995) discussed self-determination from the Pacific Islander perspective, noting that "self-determination for the cultures of the Pacific region is defined by values of collective affiliation rather than by individualism" (p. 170) and providing the following example:

> Debra, a Hawaiian woman, was interested in practicing medi-

cine in the community in which she had recently completed her medical education. Here she was offered a physician's position with a reputable family clinic and a good salary. Combined with her comfortable living quarters and her network of friends, remaining in this community was an attractive option for Debra. However, her family, and in particular her parents, wished for Debra to establish her practice in the community in which she was raised. To do so would require her to move from the city back to her native community. Although there were a few moments of hesitation, Debra quickly adjusted and aligned her values with those of her family. She reasoned that by returning to her native community she would be reunited with her family and be available to provide medical care to members of her family and a community with severe health problems. (p. 171)

To people from more individualistic-oriented cultures, Debra's chosen option might appear to "limit" her self-determination by going from a context in which she had a lot of personal freedom to one where she would have less personal control over decisions. But, of course, such an interpretation misses the point of self-determined behavior; acting in a self-determined manner means that one endorses decisions made about one's own life, not that one makes all of one's decisions independently.

This is true in an Asian context, certainly. Ohtake and Wehmeyer (2004) addressed this in a Japanese context by noting that "introducing theories and practices from the USA often produces conflict with theories and practices developed in educational settings in Japan ... partly due to the disparity of the cultural values deeply rooted in the practices in both countries, specifically, individuals vs. collectivism values" (p. 170). It is clear from the abundance of research on promoting self-determination in Asian countries that the construct itself is deemed as relevant to the transition of young people. What is important, then, is that interventions to promote self-determination are culturally and contextually relevant. To that end, the following sections examine promoting self-determination in the home and in school.

Promoting Self-Determination in the Home

Family members are, in essence, a child's first teachers and as is the case with every developmentally important area, promoting self-determination begins when children are young and the child's parents and siblings the first (and most important) teachers. As the child grows and matures, the importance of the family in promoting self-determination does not end, but changes in nature (Palmer, 2010). The development of self-determination is associated mainly with adolescent development. Young children are, necessarily, dependent upon others to "care for their physical, social, and psychological needs, nurture and support their growth, development, and education; and ensure their safety and protection" (Palmer, Wehmeyer, & Shogren, 2017, p. 72). But, the foundational skills for the later expression of causal action and the development of self-determination emerge in early development (Wehmeyer & Palmer, 2000).

Palmer and colleagues (Palmer et al., 2013) described the foundational skills leading to later self-determination as enabling "young children with disabilities to gain skills in (a) choice-making and problem solving, (b) self-regulation, and (c) engagement" (p. 38). A full description of the developmental milestones associated with these foundational skills is beyond the scope of this chapter, but, briefly, supporting children to express preferences, make decisions, and engage in problem-solving activities serves as building blocks to later autonomy, self-advocacy, and volitional action. Importantly, autonomy here does not refer expressly to acting independently, but instead, to acting volitionally. Promoting self-regulation, the second element of the foundations model, involves enabling children to regulate their action in response to changes in the environment and to self-direct behavior and learning. In this area, and indeed across all of early development, the emphasis may not be on solving problems or self-regulating actions completely independently, but instead supporting the child to engage in such activities with the scaffolding and support

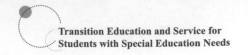

they need to be successful. Finally, promoting the engagement of children involves teaching the early skills leading to self-direction, persistence, and goal pursuits.

It is true in both the U.S. and in Asia that there has been too little focus on issues pertaining to promoting the foundational skills leading to later self-determination (Wehmeyer, 2014). That said, research has shown that U.S. parents report significantly higher levels of engagement in self-determination – fostering behaviors at both elementary and secondary levels and across all items than do parents in Taiwan, a finding attributed to cultural values in the two countries (Zhang, Wehmeyer, & Chen, 2005). Research in Korea has found that parents tend not to give their children with disabilities sufficient chances to learn and practice self-determination at home because they may have low expectations for their children and lack awareness of self-determination (Kim, 2014, 2015). Lee, Hong, Yeom, and Lee (2019) explained that this is likely due to numerous factors: including "hierarchical relationships (e.g., parent-children, teacher-student) based on Confucianism, paternalism toward people with disabilities, the 'hurry-up' culture that prevents students with disabilities from making their decisions in a timely fashion, and various conflicting situations or perceptions (e.g., individualism vs. collectivism, self-advocacy vs. talebearing)."

To provide a structure to promote foundational skills leading to later self-determination, Palmer and Wehmeyer (2003) examined the efficacy of the *Self-Determined Learning Model of Instruction* (SDLMI; discussed in detail in the next section). The SDLMI provides a means to enable children and youth to self-regulate problem solving leading to goal setting and attainment. Palmer and Wehmeyer found that young children with disabilities could, with supports, benefit from instruction through the SDLMI and improve skills related to problem solving and self-regulation. Further, Palmer and Wehmeyer (2002) used the SDLMI as a model to enable parents to, similarly, structure interactions to promote self-determination.

Promoting Self-Determination at School

There is clear evidence that focusing on promoting what Shogren and colleagues (Shogren, Wehmeyer, Palmer, Forber-Pratt et al., 2015) refer to as the component elements of self-determined action (choice-making, problem-solving, decision-making, goal-setting and attainment, planning, self-regulation, self-advocacy, self-awareness, and self-knowledge) can lead to more positive outcomes for youth (Burke et al., 2018). There have been very few school-based interventions, however, that have cross-cultural validation and given the prior discussion pertaining to the importance of the cultural context for promoting self-determination, this section will focus on the Self-Determined Learning Model of Instruction (SDLMI), which was mentioned previously and that does have efficacy data both in the U.S. and in Asia.

The SDLMI is a teaching model designed to enable teachers to teach students to teach themselves. A teaching model refers to "a plan or pattern that can be used to shape curriculums (long term courses of study), to design instructional materials, and to guide instruction in the classroom and other settings" (Joyce & Weil, 1980, p. 1). Teaching models are derived from theories about human behavior or learning and educators use multiple models of teaching through the day, depending on the characteristics of the learner and types of learning. For example, the role-playing model may be used to teach social behaviors, the inductive thinking and inquiry training models to teach reasoning and academic skills, or, as is frequently the case with special education, the contingency management model derived from operant psychology.

The SDLMI was developed using theories from self-determination and self-directed learning to provide a teaching model to support student self-determined learning (Mithaug, Wehmeyer, Agran, Martin, & Palmer, 1998; Wehmeyer, Palmer, Agran, Mithaug, & Martin, 2000). Though developed initially with students with disabilities, the model is applicable for use with students with and without disabilities (Shogren, Wehmeyer, & Lane, 2016), and, as discussed previously, has been used to support instruction across age ranges, including with younger children. Finally, the SDLMI has been applied to multiple contexts in Asian countries (Lee et al., 2015; Ohtake & Wehmeyer, 2004).

Implementation of the SDLMI consists of a three-phase instructional process that is illustrated in Figures 3-1, 3-2, and 3-3. [A full description of the SDLMI process is available in *The Self-Determined Learning Model of Instruction Teacher's Guide* (Shogren, Raley, Burke, & Wehmeyer, 2019), available at http://www.self-determination.org. The following description is a shortened version from this source.] Each phase presents a problem to be solved by the student. The student solves each problem by answering a series of four *Student Questions* in each phase that they learn, modify to make their own, and apply to reach self-set goals. Each student question is linked to a set of *Teacher Objectives* and each teacher objective is linked to *Educational Supports* that can use to teach or support students to answer the question and, thus, self-regulate problem-solving to set and attain goals.

In each phase, the student is the causal agent for actions, including choice and decision making and goal setting. The student questions in the SDLMI direct students through a problem-solving sequence, the solution to which in each phase leads to the problem in the next phase, and the problem-solving sequence is repeated. The problems to be solved are: Phase 1-What is my Goal? Phase 2-What is my Plan? and Phase 3-What have I Learned? The four questions in each phase are worded differently to enable the student to solve the unique problem posed in each phase, but in each phase, the four questions represent identical steps in a problem-solving sequence: (1) identify the problem, (2) identify potential solutions to the problem, (3) identify barriers to solving the problem, and (4) identify consequences of each solution. The SDLMI is an instructional model, and so it is designed for teachers to implement and, as such, the student questions are worded so that teachers understand the intent of the question. The first time a teacher uses the model with a student, the teacher can read each question with or (if necessary) to the student, talk about what the question means with the student, and, if it is the student's preference, to reword the question so that student can understand the intent. By the time a teacher and student go through the model once, students will have a set of questions that are their own.

Phase 1: Set a Goal

Educational Supports Defined

Self-assessment of interests, abilities, and instructional needs
Assisting students to determine what he or she enjoys, does well, and what he or she needs to learn.

Communication skills training
Communication skills involve non-verbal components (e.g., looking a person in the eye) of conversations and responding to a conversational partner's question or statement with a relevant statement or answer, initiating conversations at appropriate times, appropriate turn taking, and showing continued interest in a conversation by employing brief speech acknowledgements.

Decision-making instruction
Decision-making is a process of identifying various options and weighing the adequacy of various options. Decision-making is broader than choice-making as it involves weighing different outcomes and picking the best one.

Problem-solving instruction
The teaching of strategies to assist a student with problems they encounter. In problem solving, a solution is not previously known and must be identified. Problems may be simple to complex, depending on the instance. Social problem solving involving interpersonal communication is one of the most difficult problems to attempt to solve.

Awareness training
To be self-aware, a student learns to identify basic physical and psychological needs, interests, and abilities. He or she knows which of these interests are common and which are unique. A student also knows how their behavior affects others. To become self-aware, the student develops a broader sense of themselves, learning to apply that knowledge to building a positive self-image and gaining self-confidence.

Self-advocacy instruction
Self-advocacy instruction involves a variety of skills to promote leadership, and teamwork including assertive behavior, communication, decision-making skills, goal setting and attainment, leadership skills, legal and citizenship rights and responsibilities, problem-resolution skills, public speaking skills, transition planning, and use of community resources.

Choice-making instruction
Teaching a student to choose from two or more alternatives, based on individual preference. Choice making can be as simple as indicating preferences, as being a part of the decision-making process, and ultimately as an expression of autonomy and dignity.

Goal-setting instruction
Goal setting instruction involves teaching the skills to create plan for what one wants to accomplish or achieve (Sands & Doll, 2000).

Phase 1: Set a Goal

Student Problem to Solve: What is my goal?

Student Questions

Teacher Objectives And Primary Educational Supports*

Enable student to identify specific strengths and instructional needs
- Student self-assessment of interests, abilities, and instructional needs

Enable student to communicate preferences, interests, beliefs and values
- Communication skills training

Enable student to prioritize needs
- Decision-making, problem-solving instruction

1. What do I want to learn?

Enable student to identify current status in relation to the instructional need
- Problem-solving instruction, decision-making instruction

Enable student to gather information about opportunities and barriers in their environments
- Awareness training, self-advocacy instruction

2. What do I know about it now?

Enable student to decide if actions will be focused on capacity building, modifying the environment or both
- Decision-making instruction, problem-solving instruction

Enable student to choose a need to address from the prioritized list
- Choice-making instruction

3. What must change for me to learn what I don't know?

Enable student to state a goal and identifies criteria for achieving goal
- Goal-setting instruction

4. What can I do to make this happen?

Go to Phase 2

* In addition to the primary educational supports, other supports may be used as needed. See the Teacher's Guide for more information.

Figure 3-1   SDLMI Phase 1

Phase 2: Take Action

Student Problem to Solve: What is my plan?

Phase 2: Take Action

Educational Supports Defined

Goal attainment strategies
Instruction in methods to attain particular goals or outcomes that the student self-identifies. Goal attainment is another way to state the concept of goal-setting instruction.

Self-management strategies
Self-management incorporates self-monitoring, self-instruction, self-evaluation, self-scheduling, and antecedent cue regulation. Self-management is a set of behaviors a student utilizes to complete tasks through awareness and modification of their behavior.

Communication skills training
Communication skills involve non-verbal components (e.g., looking a person in the eye) of conversations and responding to a conversational partner's question or statement with a relevant statement or answer, initiating conversations at appropriate times, appropriate turn taking, and showing continued interest in a conversation by employing brief speech acknowledgements.

Antecedent cue regulation
An action taken to alter conditions before a target behavior so as to influence the probability of its occurrence. This can be a picture, symbol, or word that reminds individuals to engage in a target behavior. A variety of prompts are used in this way by people in everyday life.

Self-instruction
A specific type of "self-talk" related to a task that a student verbalizes while completing the task.

Self-scheduling
The student learns to scheduling times with a teacher or mentor to discuss goal-setting activities using a system of written scheduling in a day planner or using technology. The strategy of scheduling will focus on a target (the goal), but be of general use in the life of the student to maintain assignments and class requirements.

Self-monitoring
Self-monitoring involves systematic observation and recoding of a target behavior. In other words, a student must acknowledge his or her own behavior and monitor it. The monitored behavior should be thoroughly understood by the student in terms of how it relates to the larger goal. In behavioral terms, self-monitoring affects change because it is thought to function as a discriminative stimulus to desired cure, responding prior to and during task performance.

Teacher Objectives
And Primary Educational Supports*

Enable student to self-evaluate current status and self-identified goal status
- Goal attainment strategies

Enable student to determine plan of action to bridge gap between self-evaluated current status and self-identified goal status
- Goal attainment strategies, self-management

Collaborate with student to identify most appropriate instructional strategies
Teach student needed student-directed learning strategies
Support student to implement student-directed learning strategies
- Communication skills training
- Antecedent cue regulation
- Self-instruction, self-scheduling
Provide mutually agreed upon teacher-directed instruction

Enable student to determine schedule for action plan
Enable student to implement action plan
Enable student to self-monitor progress
- Self-scheduling
- Self-instruction
- Self-monitoring

Student Questions

5. What can I do to learn what I don't already know?

6. What could keep me from taking action?

7. What can I do to remove these barriers?

8. When will I take action?

Go to Phase 3

* In addition to the primary educational supports, other supports may be used as needed. See the Teacher's Guide for more information.

Figure 3-2   SDLMI Phase 2

Copyright ©Shogren, Raley, Burke, & Wehmeyer, 2019, used with permission.

Phase 3: Adjust Goal or Plan

Educational Supports Defined

Self-evaluation

Self-evaluation involves the comparison of a behavior being self-monitored (observed and recorded) and the performance goal. Students can learn to provide themselves with immediate feedback using self-monitoring and evaluate to determine if the appropriate response was given.

Self-recording

Self-recording involves a student recording a target behavior, generally by marking whether the behavior is absent or present (Menzies, Lane, & Lee, 2009). Self-recording is one component of self-monitoring.

Self-monitoring

Self-monitoring involves systematic observation and recording of a target behavior. In other words, a student must acknowledge his or her own behavior and monitor it. The monitored behavior should be thoroughly understood by the student in terms of how it relates to the larger goal. In behavioral terms, self-monitoring affects change because it is thought to function as a discriminative stimulus to desired cure, responding prior to and during task performance.

Goal attainment strategies

Instruction in methods to attain particular goals or outcomes that the student self-identifies. Goal attainment is another way to state the concept of goal-setting instruction.

Decision-making instruction

Decision-making is a process of identifying various options and weighing the adequacy of various options. Decision-making is broader than choice-making as it involves weighing different outcomes and picking the best one.

Self-reinforcement

Self-reinforcement is a student's method of rewarding a target behavior identified with self-monitoring. Examples may include a small break from work or access to a preferred activity (Menzies, Lane, & Lee, 2009).

Phase 3: Adjust Goal or Plan

Student Problem to Solve: What have I learned?

| Student Questions | Teacher Objectives And Primary Educational Supports* |

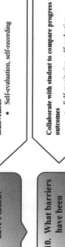

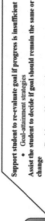

9. What actions have I taken?

Enable student to self-evaluate progress toward goal achievement
- Self-evaluation, self-recording

10. What barriers have been removed?

Collaborate with student to compare progress with desired outcomes
- Self-monitoring, self-evaluation

11. What has changed about what I don't know?

Support student to re-evaluate goal if progress is insufficient
- Goal-attainment strategies

Assist the student to decide if goal should remain the same or change
- Decision-making instruction

Collaborate with student to identify if action plan is adequate or inadequate given revised or retained goal
- Self-evaluation

Assist student to change action plan if necessary
- Decision-making instruction

12. Do I know what I want to know?

Enable student to decide if progress is adequate, inadequate or if goal has been achieved
- Self-evaluation, self-reinforcement

© 2007 – Kansas University Center on
Developmental Disabilities, Lawrence, KS US

Figure 3-3   SDLMI Phase 3

Copyright ©Shogren, Raley, Burke, & Wehmeyer, 2019, used with permission.

As mentioned, the teacher objectives in the SDLMI provide specific information to teachers on what they need to support students to do when answering a question. The teacher objectives provide, in essence, a road map for the teacher to enable students to solve the problem stated in the student question. For example, with the first student question (What do I want to learn?), the teacher objectives are to enable the student to identify his/her specific strengths and instructional needs related to the content area, identify and communicate his/her preferences, interests, beliefs and values about the content area and its link to adult outcomes, and prioritize his/her instructional needs.

Each teacher objective is linked to at least one educational support. The majority of these supports are identified from the self-management and self-directed learning literature. Since the purpose of the SDLMI is to enable teachers to teach students to self-directed and self-determine learning, it makes sense that teachers should enable students to use self-management and self-regulation strategies that enable them self-direct learning. But, not every instructional strategy is student directed. The purpose of a teaching model is to promote student learning. Sometimes the most effective method or strategy to achieve a particular educational outcome will be a teacher-directed strategy. Within the SDLMI context, students are active in determining these educational plans, whether self- or teacher-directed.

There is strong evidence to support the implementation of the SDLMI. Randomized trial studies conducted in the United States have established causal relationships between implementing the SDLMI and more positive student self-determination and school and adult outcomes, most of which has been mentioned previously. Wehmeyer and colleagues (Wehmeyer, Palmer et al., 2012) included the SDLMI as an intervention in a randomized trial control group study of the effect of interventions to promote self-determination, with high school youth with disabilities, and determined that youth with disabilities in the treatment group became more self-determination. Shogren and colleagues (Shogren, Wehmeyer, Palmer, Rifenbark et al., 2015) followed up with the students in this study, determining that students who were more self-determined achieve more positive community inclusion and employ-ment outcomes. Wehmeyer, Shogren et al. (2012) conducted a randomized study of the SDLMI with middle and high-school students, determining that students who re-ceived the intervention became more self-determined. Shogren et al. (2012) found that students in the treatment group in this study also had better goal attainment and engagement with the general education curriculum.

There is also evidence of the efficacy of the model internationally, including in Asia. In a study of interventions to promote the self-determination of elementary school students with and without disabilities in Korea, Cho and Seo (2019) found several studies that had implemented the SDLMI as the intervention, each showing benefit in academic domains in inclusive settings. Lee and colleagues (Lee et al., 2015) conducted a meta-analysis of single-case studies of the SDLMI, half of which were conducted in Korea, and determined that the intervention has strong effects. Seo, Wehmeyer and Palmer (2014) conducted a single-case study and determined that the SDLMI was an effective intervention to promote academic goal attainment for high school students in Korea. Finally, Ohtake and Wehmeyer (2004) showed that the SDLMI conformed well to a Japanese school context.

With respect to the efforts to support the development of self-determination In Taiwan, Chao (2011) developed the *Learning by Doing Self-Determination Curriculum* (LDSDC) aimed at promoting the self-determination knowledge and skills of Taiwanese high school students with mild intellectual disabilities. The LDSDC is characterized by its emphasis on the notion of *Learning by Doing* proposed by John Dewey, which teaches students skills pertaining to self-awareness, self-advocacy, self-regulation, and independence through decision-making, problem-solving, and exercising autonomous behaviors in daily life. In addition to incorporating *Learning by Doing* theory that emphasizes the everyday life and practical aspects of educa-tion, the LDSDC also incorporates the theoretical concepts of *Discovery Learning* and *Scaffolding*. *Discovery Learning* proposes that students can learn actively and learn from their mistakes, while *Scaffolding* emphasizes the importance of teacher

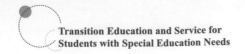
support and guidance of students during the learning process. In other words, the LDSDC is a curriculum that emphasizes practicality, initiative, and support. Students learn to actively think about their interests/strengths and weaknesses, apply problem-solving strategies, and set behavioral goals by actually making decisions/ choices, solving problems, and acting autonomously while teachers provide assistance and guidance when required.

The LDSDC consists of six teaching units: (1)*Choosing a Career*, (2)*Determining Future Lifestyle*, (3)*Resolving Daily Life Problems*, (4)*Resolving Academic Problems in Everyday Life*, (5)*Self-Care Ability*, and (6)*Autonomous Action*. The first two units consist of two classes each, while the last four units consist of six classes each. The entire curriculum lasts for sixteen weeks, with a total of thirty-two classes. The teaching objectives and content of each unit are described below.

The teaching objectives of units (1)*Choosing a Career* and (2)*Determining Future Lifestyle* are to train students to make appropriate decisions/choices about future careers and lifestyles. The teaching steps used by the teacher include arousing motivation, describing goals, demonstrating and explaining, practicing autonomously, providing feedback, and evaluating performance. Specifically, teachers first guide students to think about their ideals, interests, needs, strengths, and weaknesses. Students then make decisions based on this self-awareness. The most important consideration is not whether they can make the right decisions/choices, rather the curriculum emphasizes whether students are able to know themselves better after making decisions and are willing to have a positive and affirmative attitude about their own decisions/choices. The hypothesis of this curriculum is that if students are able to practice making career and lifestyle choices based on self-aware and self-advocacy attitude, this will improve their self-cognition and confidence, producing a virtuous circle.

Units (3)*Resolving Daily Life Problems* and (4)*Resolving Academic Problems in Everyday Life* mainly teach students the steps to resolve problems they encounter in their daily lives and academic studies. Teachers describe problem solving steps and methods in advance through explanation and demonstration. After the students understand the concepts at each step, they are offered the opportunity to practice independently. Specifically, problem solving strategies include six steps: (a)Identifying problems: the teacher guides students through identifying a problem to be solved in their life or studies based on their personal circumstances. For example, addiction to mobile games. After students identify problems, teachers assess the clarity and importance of the problem, and whether it can be effectively resolved. For students who do not identify problems clearly, suggestions are provided for revisions to ensure that the problems identified by students are clear and can be easily resolved. (b) Setting goals: teachers encourage students to set observable goals based on the problems identified. For example, for the problem of addiction to mobile games, the goal of "quitting mobile games" can be set. If students are unable to set reasonable and feasible goals after multiple attempts, teachers will provide the necessary assistance to students by making suggestions or providing examples, ensuring that the goals set by students are reasonable, feasible, and clear. (c)Making conjectures: teachers guide students to use "if...then..." statements to make conjectures. For example, "If I uninstall the game software, then I can give up my addiction to mobile games." For students who are unable to make conjectures teachers will provide guidance by making suggestions or providing examples, so that the conjectures made by each student are logical. (d)Thinking strategy: the teacher guides students to think more broadly about the "if..." part of the making conjectures step. For example, "If I asked my parents to remind me more often not to play games" or "If I became more active in outdoor activities." (e)Implementation strategy: students actually implement their problem solving strategies. Teachers evaluate whether students implement strategies correctly through observation and discussion. If the method is incorrect, the teachers will provide suggestions so that students are able to apply the strategy correctly. (f) Assessment of effectiveness: teachers and students discuss and evaluate whether problems are effectively resolved. If the problem is resolved, the teacher encourages the student to apply the model again to resolve another problem. If the problem per-

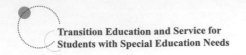
sists, the teacher encourages the student to think about other possible problem-solving strategies. In the two units on problem solving, the teacher repeatedly emphasizes students' training in self-regulation and independence.

Units (5)*Self-Care Ability* and (6)*Autonomous Action* provide students with the opportunity to practice autonomous behaviors. During training, students must care for themselves, carry out jobs at home, and complete teachers' assignments on their own initiative. Teachers mostly use 6W strategies to teach students relevant autonomous action skills. Take grocery shopping as an example, teachers first ask the students if they have experience shopping by themselves in the supermarket and if they had any pleasant/unpleasant or strange experiences. After students' learning motivation is aroused, the teacher tells the students why they need to have the ability to shop autonomously, and then explains the concept of 6W and its application. For example, for the purpose of purchasing fruit and vegetables, the teacher asks students to think about who they are purchasing for, what type of fruit/vegetables to choose, when to purchase, where to purchase, why they are purchasing, and how to purchase (for example, what transportation to take to the supermarket or how to pay). Through brainstorming, the students have a deeper understanding of the six concepts. After the oral practice is completed, teachers ask students to complete an actual shopping task after they go home and share it with their classmates during the next class. Chao (2011) conducted a randomized study of the LDSDC with senior high school students with intellectual disabilities, determining that students who received the intervention ($n = 41$) become more self-determined.

Conclusion

Promoting self-determination has been shown to have positive impacts on school and community outcomes for transition-age youth with disabilities. It is important, when considering the implementation of interventions to promote self-determination, that the cultural context in which the intervention is being implemented be considered. One intervention that has strong evidence of its efficacy and utility across the world, including in Asia, is the Self-Determined Learning Model of Instruction (SDLMI). Given the importance of enhanced self-determination for youth with disabilities, it is important to ensure that efforts to support the development of self-determination and to provide interventions to promote self-determination be included in efforts to improve transition outcomes. Furthermore, it is also clear that the Learning by Dong Self-Determination Curriculum (LDSDC) developed in Taiwan is effective in enhancing the self-determination of youth with disabilities.

References

Burke, K. M., Raley, S. K., Shogren, K. A., Hagiwara, M., Mumbardó-Adam, C., Uyanik, H., & Behrens, S. (2018). A meta-analysis of interventions to promote self-determination for students with disabilities. *Remedial and Special Education*. https://doi.org/10.1177%2F0741932518802274

Chao, P. C. (2011). A study of promoting self-determination skills of vocational high school students with disabilities: A learning by doing teaching model. *Journal of Special Education (Taiwan), 33*, 93-124.

Chao, P. C., Chou, Y. C., & Cheng, S. F. (2019). Self-determination and transition outcomes of youth with disabilities: Findings from the Special Needs Education Longitudinal Study. *Advances in Neurodevelopmental Disorders, 3*, 129-137.

Cho, E., & Seo, H. (2019). Self-determination studies for elementary students with and without disabilities in Korea. *Advances in Neurodevelopmental Disorders, 3*, 161-172.

Ewalt, P. L., & Mokuau, N. (1995). Self-determination from a Pacific perspective. *Social Work, 40*, 168-175.

Frankland, H. C., Turnbull, A. P., Wehmeyer, M. L., & Blackmountain, L. (2004). An exploration of the self-determination construct and disability as it relates to the Diné (Navajo) culture. *Education and Training in Developmental Disabilities, 39*, 191-205.

Joyce, B., & Weil, M. (1980). *Models of teaching* (2nd ed.). Englewood Cliffs, NJ: Prentice-Hall.

Kim, S. J. (2014). A study on perceptions of parents on self-determination of young children with disabilities. *Journal of Emotional & Behavioral Disorders, 30* (3), 151-176.

Kim, S. J. (2015). A study on the experience of self-determination of young children with disabilities at home. *Journal of Special Education & Rehabilitation Sci-*

ence, 54(2), 73-95.

Lee, S. H. (2009). A review on cross-cultural understanding and applications of self-determination. *Asia Journal of Education, 10*(1), 1-32.

Lee, S. H., Hong, J., Yeom, J. H., & Lee, J. (2018). Perceptions and experiences of self-determination of students and youth with intellectual disabilities in Korea. *The Korean Society of Special Education, 53*, 123-127.

Lee, S. H., Hong, J., Yeom, J. H., & Lee, J. (2019). Perceptions and experiences of self-determination of students and youth with intellectual disabilities in Korea. *Advances in Neurodevelopmental Disorders, 3*, 138-151.

Lee, S. H., Wehmeyer, M. L., & Shogren, K. A. (2015). The effect of instruction with the self-determined learning model of instruction on students with disabilities: A meta-analysis. *Education and Training in Autism and Developmental Disabilities, 50*(2) , 237-247.

Mithaug, D. E., Wehmeyer, M. L., Agran, M., Martin, J. E., & Palmer, S. B. (1998). The self-determined learning model of instruction: Engaging students to solve their learning problems. In M. L. Wehmeyer & D. J. Sands (Eds.), *Making it happen: Student involvement in education planning, decision making and instruction* (pp. 299-328). Baltimore, MD: Paul H. Brookes.

Mumbardó-Adam, C., Guàrdia-Olmos, J., & Giné, C. (2018). *An integrative model of self-determination latent trait and related contextual variables*. Manuscript submitted for publication.

Ohtake, Y., & Wehmeyer, M. L. (2004). Applying the self-determination theory to Japanese special education contexts: A four-step model. *Journal of Policy and Practice in Intellectual Disabilities, 1*, 169-178.

Palmer, S. B. (2010). Self-determination: A life-span perspective. *Focus on Exceptional Children, 42*(6), 1-16.

Palmer, S. B., & Wehmeyer, M. L. (2002). *A parent's guide to the self-determined learning model for early elementary students*. Lawrence, KS: Beach Center on Disability, University of Kansas.

Palmer, S. B., & Wehmeyer, M. L. (2003). Promoting self-determination in early elementary school: Teaching self-regulated problem-solving and goal setting skills. *Remedial and Special Education, 24*, 115-126.

Palmer, S. B., Summers, J. A., Brotherson, M. J., Erwin, E. J., Maude, S. P., Stroup-Rentier, V., Wu, H. Y., Peck, N. F., Zheng, Y., Weigel, C., Chu, S. Y., McGrath, G. S., & Haines, S. J. (2013). Foundations for self-determination in early childhood: An inclusive model for children with disabilities. *Topics in Early Childhood Special Education, 33*, 38-47.

Palmer, S. B., Wehmeyer, M. L., & Shogren, K. A. (2017). The development of self-determination during childhood. In M. L. Wehmeyer, K. A. Shogren, T. D. Little, & S. Lopez (Eds.), *Development of self-determination across the life course* (pp. 71-88). New York, NY: Springer.

Seo, H., Wehmeyer, M. L., & Palmer, S. B. (2014). The effects of the self-determined learning model of instruction on academic performance of students with high-incidence disabilities. *The Journal of Special Education: Theory and Practice, 15*(1), 305-330.

Shogren, K. A., Little, T. D., & Wehmeyer, M. L. (2017). Human agentic theories and the development of self-determination. In M. L. Wehmeyer, K. A. Shogren, T. D. Little, & S. Lopez (Eds.), *Development of self-determination across the life course* (pp. 17-26). New York, NY: Springer.

Shogren, K. A., Palmer, S. B., Wehmeyer, M. L., Williams-Diehm, K., & Little, T. D. (2012). Effect of intervention with the self-determined learning model of instruction on access and goal attainment. *Remedial and Special Education, 33*(5), 320-330.

Shogren, K. A., Raley, S. K., Burke, K. M., & Wehmeyer, M. L. (2019). *Teacher's guide to the self-determined learning model of instruction*. Lawrence, KS: Kansas University Center on Developmental Disabilities.

Shogren, K. A., Shaw, L. A., Raley, S. K., & Wehmeyer, M. L. (2018). Exploring the effect of disability, race-ethnicity, and socioeconomic status on scores on the self-determination inventory: Student report. *Exceptional Children, 85*(1), 10-27.

Shogren, K. A., Wehmeyer, M. L., & Lane, K. L. (2016). Embedding interventions to promote self-determination within multi-tiered systems of supports. *Exceptionality, 24*(4), 213-244.

Shogren, K. A., Wehmeyer, M. L., Palmer, S. B., Forber-Pratt, A., Little, T. D., & Lopez, S. (2015). Causal agency theory: Reconceptualizing a functional model of self-determination. *Education and Training in Autism and Developmental Disabilities, 50*(3), 251-263.

Shogren, K. A., Wehmeyer, M. L., Palmer, S. B., Rifenbark, G., & Little, T. D. (2015). Relationships between self-determination and postschool outcomes for youth with disabilities. *Journal of Special Education, 48*(4), 256-267.

Wehmeyer, M. L. (1996). Self-determination as an educational outcome: How does it relate to the educational needs of our children and youth? In D. J. Sands & M. L. Wehmeyer (Eds.), *Self-determination across the life span: Independence and choice for people with disabilities* (pp. 17-36). Baltimore, MD: Paul H. Brookes.

Wehmeyer, M. L. (2014). Self-determination: A family affair. *Family Relations, 63*, 178-184.

Wehmeyer, M. L., & Palmer, S. B. (2000). Promoting the acquisition and development of self-determination in young children with disabilities. *Early Education and Development, 11*(4), 465-481.

Wehmeyer, M. L., & Shogren, K. A. (2017). Applications of the self-determination construct to disability. In M. L. Wehmeyer, K. A. Shogren, T. D. Little, & S. Lopez (Eds.), *Development of self-determination through the life course* (pp. 111-123). New York, NY: Springer.

Wehmeyer, M. L., Abery, B., Zhang, D., Ward, K., Willis, D., Amin, W. H., ...Walker, H. (2011). Personal self-determination and moderating variables that impact efforts to promote self-determination. *Exceptionality, 19*, 19-30.

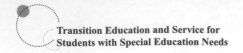
Wehmeyer, M. L., Palmer, S. B., Agran, M., Mithaug, D. E., & Martin, J. E. (2000). Promoting causal agency: The self-determined learning model of instruction. *Exceptional Children, 66*, 439-453.

Wehmeyer, M. L., Palmer, S. B., Lee, Y., Williams-Diehm, K., & Shogren, K. A. (2011). A randomized-trial evaluation of the effect of whose future is it anyway? on self-determination. *Career Development for Exceptional Individuals, 34*(1), 45-56.

Wehmeyer, M. L., Palmer, S., Shogren, K. A., Williams-Diehm, K., & Soukup, J. (2012). Establishing a causal relationship between interventions to promote self-determination and enhanced student self-determination. *Journal of Special Education, 46*(4), 195-210.

Wehmeyer, M. L., Shogren, K. A., Little, T. D., & Lopez, S. (2017). Introduction to the self-determination construct. In M. L. Wehmeyer, K. A. Shogren, T. D. Little, & S. Lopez (Eds.), *Development of self-determination through the life course* (pp. 3-16). New York, NY: Springer.

Wehmeyer, M. L., Shogren, K. A., Palmer, S. B., Williams-Diehm, K., Little, T. D., & Boulton, A. (2012). The impact of the self-determined learning model of instruction on student self-determination. *Exceptional Children, 78*(2), 135-153.

Zhang, D., Wehmeyer, M. L., & Chen, L. J. (2005). Parent and teacher engagement in fostering the self-determination of students with disabilities: A comparison between the U.S. and the Republic of China. *Remedial and Special Education, 26*, 55-64.

第四章　身心障礙學生的高等教育及就業轉銜歷程

Transition to Postsecondary Education and Preparation for Employment

張大倫（Dalun Zhang）、李依帆（Yi-Fan Li）、
Leena Jo Landmark、Kendra Williams-Diehm

中文摘錄：李依帆

中文重點摘錄

壹、21 世紀的轉銜教育

身心障礙學生進入高等教育為轉銜教育立下重要的里程碑（Newman, Wagner, Cameto, Knokey, & Shaver, 2010; Snyder & Dillow, 2010）。National Longitudinal Transition Study-2（NLTS2）的研究顯示，大約有 60% 的身心障礙學生高中職畢業後，進入高等教育（Newman et al., 2011）。以美國為例，不分種族、性別、社經地位、障礙類別的身心障礙學生，皆獲得充分的機會進入各種形式的高等教育，例如：四年制及二年制的大學、大學附設的技職中心，或是一些針對身心障礙人士附設的再教育方案。對於身心障礙學生的轉銜教育而言，從高中職畢業後，進入高等教育或職場就業為其中一個重要的轉銜目標。

其中一項促使身心障礙學生進入高等教育以及就業職場的重要因素，為相關法案的成立。以美國為例，《美國身心障礙法 2008 年修正案》（Americans with Disabilities Act Amendments Act of 2008）及《高等教育法》（Higher Education Opportunity Act of 2008）對於身心障礙者於高等教育

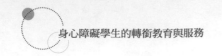

求學以及職場就業有直接的影響。這些法案使得身心障礙學生進入校園或職場能享有適當的權力。

然而，即使身心障礙學生進入高等教育的人數年年增加，身心障礙學生獲得高等教育學歷的比例仍然遠低於非身心障礙學生，進而影響這些身心障礙學生就業的可能性（Erickson, Lee, & von Schrader, 2016）。有鑑於此，幫助身心障礙學生進入高等教育學習，或進入其他教育方案接受持續性的訓練，將成為日後轉銜教育的重點工作之一（Zhang, Grenwelge, & Petcu, 2018）。轉銜教育的目標即是要幫助身心障礙學生發展就業技能，並且在經濟上自給自足，使得生活水準能夠提升。

▶ 貳、高中職畢業後進入高等教育或其他教育方案的轉銜現況

近年來，因轉銜教育品質的提升，使得身心障礙學生於高中職畢業後，有機會進入高等教育或其他教育方案持續學習。以美國為例，88%的公私立大學表示校內有身心障礙學生就讀。在這些身心障礙學生當中，以學習障礙（learning disabilities）及注意力缺陷過動症（attention deficit hyperactivity disorder, ADHD）為多數，各占31%及18%，其他障礙（如精神障礙及身體病弱）也不在少數（Raue & Lewis, 2011）。

高等教育或其他教育方案的形式可分為傳統型及非傳統型。以美國為例，高等教育分為四年制的大學、兩年制的社區大學、其他技職大學。以技職大學來說，身心障礙學生得以學習產業相關的技能，畢業後更加有機會找到業界的工作。值得一提的是，美國的 Landmark 學院（Landmark College）以招收身心障礙學生為主（Landmark College, 2019）。這些傳統型的高等教育形式，提供身心障礙高中職畢業生多重的選擇。

非傳統型的教育方案可以是高中職教育的延伸，學生自方案學習完成之後，或許能獲取結業證書，但不一定能取得高等教育的學歷。這些教育方案在美國如同雨後春筍般展開，並且基於這些方案成立的宗旨，提供不

同的課程內容及未來規劃。雖然教育方案的多元性提供身心障礙高中職畢業生不同的生涯規劃，身心障礙學生及其家長仍有必要對每一種教育方案提供的服務以及課程進行詳細的研究與了解（Grigal, Hart, & Weir, 2012）。

參、高等教育及其他教育方案轉銜面臨的挑戰

身心障礙學生的轉銜計畫應提早規劃，因為學生在高中職畢業後，將會遇到許多挑戰與阻礙（Francis, Stride, & Reed, 2018; Papay, Unger, Williams-Diehm, & Mitchell, 2015）。教師應對於以下的挑戰有充分的了解與探討。

一、來自家庭的低期待

家庭成員的期待對身心障礙學生轉銜往往是決定性的因素。研究顯示，若父母對轉銜計畫及目標期待不高，身心障礙學生容易持續依賴他人的協助與支持，因此在學習獨立生活方面也相對困難（Francis et al., 2018）。另一篇研究也表示，家庭的期待隨著身心障礙學生的障礙程度與障礙類型有所差異（Yamamoto, Stodden, & Folk, 2014），例如：智能障礙學生的家庭往往對其期待不高。家庭對身心障礙學生的轉銜目標期待不高可能來自於對轉銜的共識與知識的不足，因此教師可適時地提醒家庭未來身心障礙學生的轉銜目標，並且提供相關的資源。

二、缺乏自我決策的技能

自我決策意味著個體成為自己的主人，並且透過自己的意願與行動去維持並改善個人的生活品質（Wehmeyer, 2006）。研究顯示，身心障礙學生學習自我倡權以及人際溝通技巧，將有助於在高中職畢業之後，進入高等教育的適應與學習（Lyman, Beecher, Griner, Brooks, Call, & Jackson, 2016）。自我倡權及良好的溝通技巧有助於身心障礙學生表達自己需要的學習輔助（accommodation）。然而，身心障礙學生往往缺乏機會練習自我決策的相關技能，如自我管理及做決定。因此，教師需要於教學場合提供機會讓身

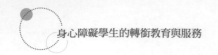

心障礙學生學習自我決策的技巧。

三、缺乏跨專業的合作與支持

　　跨專業合作與支持對於身心障礙學生的轉銜扮演重要的角色。一旦身心障礙學生自高中職畢業，他們需要從相關的職涯單位接受後續的服務。另一種合作的可能性是高中職端與高等教育學校的持續性合作。高中職端與高等教育的合作，可讓高中職教師更加了解如何協助身心障礙學生轉銜至大學。然而，缺乏跨專業或跨單位的合作，則難以將身心障礙學生所需要的服務整合，導致身心障礙學生接受到的服務不完整或是無法連續。因此，跨專業或跨單位的合作將有助於整合身心障礙學生所需要的服務與支持。

四、缺乏經濟上的協助

　　另一項阻擋身心障礙學生進入高等教育的因素，為缺乏經濟上的補助（Finnie, Wismer, & Mueller, 2015）。身心障礙學生的家庭可能面臨繳納大學學費的困境，因此經濟上的匱乏可能成為阻礙身心障礙學生上大學的原因之一。另外，依照各個大學的規定，學生可能需要具備相關條件才能符合資格接受獎學金的補助，這使得身心障礙學生獲取獎學金的機會更加受限。因此，教育工作者及學校單位應思考，如何提供適當的獎學金補助以協助身心障礙學生上大學。

▶ 肆、身心障礙學生於高等教育以及其他教育方案就學之適應策略

　　身心障礙學生從高中職畢業後，再次進入校園就讀，代表著人生進入新的扉頁，然而這也代表著，身心障礙學生要面臨的責任與挑戰。這些責任與挑戰除了來自課業的壓力，同時也考驗身心障礙學生的獨立生活能力與社交能力。以下提出針對身心障礙學生於高等教育以及其他教育方案就

學時的幾項適應策略。

一、充分了解高等教育及其他教育方案可提供的服務

　　身心障礙學生於高中職階段接受個別化的教育服務，以美國為例，在高中職就學階段，身心障礙學生可以享有免費且適性的公立教育（FAPE）。然而，進入高等教育以及其他教育方案之後，法律上雖可保護身心障礙學生免受歧視，但相對於高中職階段接受的個別化教育服務，學生在高等教育或其他教育方案接受的服務與保障相對減少很多。也因為缺乏個別化的教育服務，身心障礙學生需要學習自我決策以及自我倡權。在這過程中，父母或許仍可以給予支持與建議，但最後做決策者還是以身心障礙學生為主。

二、充分了解申請校內服務所需的文件與資格

　　不論是美國的身心障礙學生服務中心（disability services）或是臺灣的大學特教資源中心，在提供服務給身心障礙學生之前，需要審核資格與相關文件。身心障礙學生於高等教育階段或進入其他教育方案，需要自行揭露（disclose）自己的障礙因素，進而要求學習上的調整與服務（Newman & Madaus, 2015）。因此，申請校內的服務需仰賴身心障礙學生自行申請並提供相關的文件，待中心審核通過之後，身心障礙學生方可獲得合理且適當調整服務（reasonable accommodations）。以美國為例，身心障礙學生服務中心可提供的服務如：延長考試時間或是課堂筆記員（Office for Civil Rights, 2011）。

三、學習使用輔助科技

　　在高中職端進行轉銜規劃時，IEP 成員應將學生平時使用的輔助科技納入轉銜規劃之一。隨著科技的發達，科技著實改善了我們學習的方式，同時也意味著透過輔助科技，身心障礙學生在學習時能更加順利。其中一個融合輔助科技、建立無障礙學習環境的例子是全方位設計課程（universal

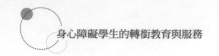

design for learning, UDL）。全方位設計課程的理念將輔助科技融入班級經營與課程設計，友善的學習環境及多元的課程呈現方式，將使每位學生充分學習（West, Novak, & Mueller, 2016）。

四、尋求同儕支持

同儕支持往往在學習上扮演重要的角色。研究顯示，同儕支持能給予身心障礙學生正向的影響，幫助他們適應校內及校外的生活。同儕扮演著不同的角色協助身心障礙學生，這些角色可能是課業上的協助者，也有可能是課後一同運動的好夥伴（Griffin, Wendel, Day, & McMillan, 2016）。適當的同儕支持也能給身心障礙學生融合的經驗，不論是同儕或身心障礙學生，兩方都獲得相等的益處。

除了以上的策略，身心障礙學生若具備良好的社交技巧及溝通能力將有助於經營人際關係。研究顯示，來自生活及課業的壓力將會是另一項挑戰（Jackson, Hart, Brown, & Volkmar, 2018），建議學生尋求情緒與社交支持團體。另外，身心障礙學生也應要考量健康照護的需要，若有請家人來協助照護或是聘請照護員，也須考量經濟層面及照護者能配合的時間。

伍、畢業與就業的歷程與策略

前述提及身心障礙學生進入高等教育或其他教育方案就學之適應策略，然而身心障礙學生仍然會面臨其他挑戰，影響持續就學直到畢業的可能性。研究顯示，身心障礙學生面臨最主要的挑戰為標籤化，這些標籤效應主要來自身旁的同學及老師對障礙因素而產生的觀感。標籤化的議題深深影響身心障礙學生是否要勇敢揭露自己的障礙，並且申請適當的學習調整（Dowrick, Anderson, Heyer, & Acosta, 2005）。另一項議題則是身心障礙學生沒有充分地了解校內可使用的資源，使得他們沒有申請適當的學習調整（Lindsay, Cagliostro, & Carafa,, 2018; Redpath, Kearney, Nicholl, Mulvenna, Wallace, & Martin, 2013）。以下提出針對協助身心障礙學生於高等教育或其

他教育方案持續學習的兩項策略。

一、運用自我決策能力

前述已提及適當地使用自我決策技巧，如自我倡權及溝通技巧，能協助身心障礙學生表達自己需要的學習調整。然而，為了讓身心障礙學生能順利地畢業，其他自我決策能力也相對重要。研究顯示，身心障礙學生在高等教育需學習擬訂合理的目標與計畫（Shepler & Woosley, 2012）。良好的目標與計畫包含課業學習及其他校園生活，例如：規劃要修習的課程、考量加入學校社團，以及為未來的職涯選擇做充分的準備。

於家庭支持方面，Francis 等人（2018）訪問身心障礙學生家長如何支持孩子於高等教育就讀，家長建議應適當地讓身心障礙學生自行做決定，允許犯錯的可能性，並且仍然維持適當程度的期待。這裡也值得一提的是，培養身心障礙學生獨立不代表不需要家庭或旁人的持續性支持；相反地，若身心障礙學生在遇到困難時，能適當地尋求協助也是一項必要的能力。

二、符合高中畢業資格

高等教育或其他教育方案對學生的畢業要求應有詳細的規定，比如最低學分修課要求，或是其他特殊課程要求（如語言課程、實作／實習）。課程的提供也可能有次序性，例如：要先完成基本的課程，才能選修進階的課程。對於身心障礙學生來說，一開始跟著班上同學一同修課，並且交換學習經驗，將有助於身心障礙學生對學分及畢業要求有進一步的了解。當必要的學分修習完成，身心障礙學生可以針對自己的興趣及未來規劃選擇其他選修課程。

每一間高等教育的修課及畢業規定相對差異不大，然而非傳統型的其他教育方案的修課規定及修業年限則較為不同。以美國的德州農工大學（Texas A&M University）提供的教育方案為例，此教育方案修業年限為一年，在這一年當中，學生學習職業相關的知識，並且到職場實習，身心障

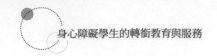

礙學生於此方案畢業後,將獲得一份證書。教育方案的規定較為多元,建議學生進入教育方案學習之後,要去了解畢業相關規定。

身心障礙學生離開校園並踏入職場,將是人生另一轉折點。不論是在高中職或是在高等教育就學,身心障礙學生需要在就學期間朝未來可能的職涯方向進行探索,並且培養必備的生涯和職業技能。教育工作者及研究者也漸漸地發展出許多策略,來協助解決身心障礙者就業上遇到的困難與挑戰。身心障礙者在尋找就業機會的過程中,首先面對的挑戰即是無法找到符合自己職業興趣的職業。因此,即使身心障礙者找到就業機會,但因為缺乏興趣,或是工作條件本身缺乏未來升遷的可能,身心障礙者往往會選擇離開。另一項挑戰即是在工作場所的標籤化議題,Toldrá 與 Santos (2013) 表示,工作場所的文化和氣氛影響身心障礙員工是否能被接納,並且影響員工之間關係的建立。

由於障礙的因素,工作場所可能要就身心障礙員工的需要進行合理的調整,比如物理空間的改善,協助身心障礙員工能在無障礙的環境工作,若工作環境對身心障礙員工不是很友善,這會是另一項身心障礙者就業的挑戰。最後一項挑戰是關於工作技能要求的提升,隨著產業的轉型,各個產業要求的人才條件不斷更新,過去幾十年所需要的技能於現今的就業市場來說恐怕已過時,這對於尋找就業機會的身心障礙者來說是一大困難 (Kocman, Fischer, & Weber, 2018)。為了協助身心障礙者順利進入職場,從事自己理想的工作,以下提出幾點建議。

一、培養職業技能

職業技能往往是影響個體是否能找到工作的原因之一。一般的職業技能都可以在學校的課程中學習,然而一項研究以雇主的觀點提出五項「軟技能」(soft skills)。若身心障礙者擁有這些軟技能,將有助於就業的歷程更加順利。

1.態度:保持正向且樂觀的態度,採行主動積極的態度。

2.可靠程度:良好且準時的出席率,能將交待的工作盡力完成,獲取他

人的信賴。

　　3.毅力／耐力：能接受工時長的工作。

　　4.溝通能力：學習表達自己的需要，工作上可能還需要使用溝通能力與客戶溝通。

　　5.彈性：適當地調整並且運用策略，完成多項工作任務。

　　除了這五項軟技能，其他如前述提及的自我決策能力也同樣重要。身心障礙者應特別留意軟技能的培養；技能的培養也有助於身心障礙員工獲得升遷的機會。職業的升遷是大部分人心中的渴望，就連身心障礙者也不例外。研究指出，一些基本的職業技能對於新進員工是相當重要的，如良好的職業道德、團隊合作、口語表達溝通能力、閱讀理解能力、遵行工作指導等（Casner-Lotto & Barrington, 2006; Ju, Zhang, & Pacha, 2012）。

二、尋求就業實習機會

　　於各種企業或產業實習將提供身心障礙者不同的經驗。相較於在課室學習，在社區中的產業實習能給予身心障礙學生實作的經驗（Lindstrom, Hirano, McCarthy, & Alverson, 2014）。身心障礙學生能藉由這些實習經驗，觀察並了解實際工作的樣貌，近而決定是否要在畢業後繼續往原本的職業興趣尋找就業機會。產業實習機會也能讓身心障礙學生了解必備的職業技能，並且思考自己是否已經具備該職業技能。

三、使用輔助科技

　　如同前述，輔助科技協助身心障礙學生的課業學習，輔助科技也同樣地能協助身心障礙員工完成工作任務（Edyburn, 2010）。但值得考量的是，於工作場所中，是否有提供輔助科技以協助身心障礙員工執行工作任務，或是提供的輔助科技是否符合身心障礙員工的需要。因此，在協助身心障礙者轉銜至工作場所時，教育工作者或其他專業人員應考量身心障礙者在使用輔助科技的偏好以及習慣，身心障礙者也應學習使用各樣的輔助科技，熟悉輔助科技的操作。

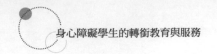

　　以上為針對身心障礙學生轉銜至職場的建議與策略。在轉銜至職場的期間，家庭對身心障礙者的期待也扮演關鍵的角色，適當良好的期待有助於身心障礙學生轉銜至職場以及未來獨立生活的可能性。

Transition to Postsecondary Education and Preparation for Employment

Dalun Zhang, Yi-Fan Li, Leena Jo Landmark & Kendra Williams-Diehm

Postsecondary Education in the 21st Century

More so than any time in history, individuals with disabilities are actively pursuing postsecondary education as an outcome following high school (Newman, Wagner, Cameto, Knokey, & Shaver, 2010; Snyder & Dillow, 2010). In fact, a report from the National Longitudinal Transition Study-2 determined that as many as 60% of high school graduates with disabilities continue into some form of postsecondary education (Newman et al., 2011). Within the United States, progress has been made for all groups (i.e., race, ethnicity, gender, socio-economic status, disability) on attendance into all forms of postsecondary education, including 4-year colleges, 2-year colleges, and vocational and career technical centers. Research clearly indicates the majority of students – including students with disabilities – desire to attend postsecondary education (Conner, 2012; Engle, 2007; Schneider, Broda, Judy, & Burkander, 2014). Many of these advancements are related to key legislation including the *Americans with Disabilities Act Amendments Act of 2008* (ADAAA) and the *Higher Education Opportunity Act of 2008*, which have had direct implications on postsecondary education. However, despite these improvements, individuals with disabilities are still not attending and graduating from postsecondary education programs at the same rate as their peers without disabilities (Katsiyannis, Zhang, Landmark, & Reber, 2009). The disparity between individuals with and without disabilities who hold a baccalaureate degree or higher is salient, reported as 14% for people with disabilities compared to 33% for people without disabilities (Erickson,

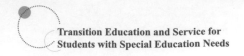
Lee, & von Schrader, 2016). Some have reported that individuals with disabilities represent the largest untapped pool of potential resource for tomorrow's workforce (Committee on Equal Opportunities in Science and Engineering, 2006).

The overall push and desire for postsecondary education changed dramatically over the second half of the 20th century. A high school diploma was considered highly valuable through the 1950s; even during the 1970s, a high school diploma typically resulted in many career opportunities (National Council on Disability, 2000) and a solid, stable income. However, times have changed and postsecondary education has become almost mandatory to achieve financial stability and job security. A survey by the U.S. Bureau of Labor Statistics (2014) determined that postsecondary education results in higher earning potential and lower unemployment rates. However, the need for postsecondary education is not only related to earnings and financial stability; it is also necessary for gaining entry-level employment in many fields. For example, 11 of the 15 fastest growing industries require postsecondary education for their entry-level positions (U.S. Bureau of Labor Statistics, 2015). Although the majority of these industries relate to STEM (science, technology, engineering, and math) fields advancement, others are more service oriented.

Because of the growing need for postsecondary education, helping students with disabilities access some form of postsecondary education and earn a degree or another credential has become necessary (Zhang, Grenwelge, & Petcu, 2018). Providing postsecondary education to students with disabilities increases their chance of economic self-sufficiency, reduces poverty rates, and enhances their quality of life (Zhang et al., 2018). Consequently, a great number of programs have become available for individuals with disabilities to access postsecondary education. The purpose of this chapter is to discuss the challenges and strategies for individuals with disabilities to attend, persist, and graduate from postsecondary education, as well as considerations for gaining employment after completing this level of education.

Current Status of Postsecondary Education Participation

The recent push for postsecondary education for many individuals with disabilities has resulted in higher rates of postsecondary education participation by this group than ever before (Newman et al., 2011; Raue & Lewis, 2011). In the United States, 88% of public and private 2-4 year postsecondary institutions report enrolling students with disabilities, with 11% of their undergraduate student population identified as a student with a disability (Raue & Lewis, 2011; Snyder, Brey, & Dillow, 2016). However, certain groups of undergraduate students report higher rates of disabilities. For example, 21% of undergraduates, who were also veterans, identified as a student with a disability; nontraditional-aged undergraduates also report higher rates of disability compared to traditional-aged undergraduates (Snyder et al., 2016). The most frequently reported types of disabilities by undergraduate students include specific learning disabilities (31%), attention deficit hyperactivity disorder/attention deficit disorder (ADHD) (18%), psychological/psychiatric conditions (15%), and health conditions (11%) (Raue & Lewis, 2011).

Traditional Postsecondary Education Programs

Postsecondary education options for individuals with disabilities include 2-4 year colleges and universities; community, junior, and technical colleges or schools; and special programs within institutions of higher education for students with specific disabilities such as learning disabilities, intellectual disability, or autism. Colleges and universities offer students opportunities to earn baccalaureate degrees in addition to professional and advanced degrees. Community, junior, and technical colleges allow students to earn a license, certificate, or associate degree. However, course credits may or may not transfer to a baccalaureate degree-granting college or university, so students need to be cautious when taking courses if their goal is to

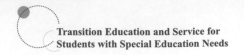
transfer to a baccalaureate degree-granting institution. This can be exceptionally rigid for technical and professional programs. Community, junior, and technical colleges often align their programmatic offerings to fast growing industries, so individuals can graduate from the program in one to two years and secure a job in a field with a high need for employees.

Some postsecondary educational institutions, such as Landmark College, only educate postsecondary students with disabilities (i.e., learning disabilities, attention deficit hyperactivity disorder, and autism spectrum disorders) (Landmark College, 2019). However, most individuals with disabilities attend postsecondary institutions that are not specifically designed for students with disabilities. Findings from the National Longitudinal Transition Study-2 (Newman et al., 2011) indicate former students who received special education services preferred to attend community colleges, followed by technical colleges, over other types of postsecondary institutions of higher education.

Specialized Postsecondary Education Programs for Individuals with Disabilities

Many postsecondary educational institutions house specialized postsecondary education programs for individuals with developmental disabilities such as intellectual disability or autism (Institute for Community Inclusion, 2019). Some of these programs are extensions of high school that occur on a postsecondary educational institution's campus as part of an 18-21 adult transition program facilitated by the high school. Other programs are for students with disabilities who have received a diploma or certificate of completion from their high school. Depending on how the program is set up, students may or may not receive course credit or a diploma from the postsecondary institution. Although there are many postsecondary programs for individuals with intellectual disability, Grigal, Hart, and Weir (2012) noted there is much variability among the programs in regard to program characteristics, admission criteria, course and campus activity access, accommodations, funding, residential services, and employment outcomes.

Additionally, some institutions of higher education have supplemental programs for students with autism or other developmental disabilities (e.g., the Connections for Academic Success and Employment at Texas Tech University) (Texas Tech University, 2019). In these programs, students must meet the admission requirements of the postsecondary school but believe more support for success is necessary than the disability services office provides. These supplemental programs are generally financed through vocational rehabilitation, private donations, or student fees. Finally, some institutions of higher education provide support groups, peer-mentoring, or counseling for their students with autism or intellectual disability (Hart, Grigal, & Weir, 2010).

Challenges Associated with the Transition to Postsecondary Education

Preparing students with disabilities to attend postsecondary education has been one of the primary foci of secondary schools because this is a common transition goal of many students. In order to help these students with disabilities, and really *all* students, prepare themselves for postsecondary education, transition planning should start early (Francis, Stride, & Reed, 2018; Papay, Unger, Williams-Diehm, & Mitchell, 2015) because there are challenges associated with transitioning to postsecondary education for students with disabilities (Yamamotoa, Stodden, & Folk, 2014). Having adequate awareness of these challenges helps educators understand some of the struggles students with disabilities may experience and adequately prepare students with disabilities to address these challenges.

Low Family Expectations

When a youth with a disability is considering postsecondary education, family expectation can be a determining factor. Francis et al. (2018) conducted interviews with parents of young adults with intellectual and developmental disabilities and found that parent expectation was one of the primary factors that contributed to the success of their transition to postsecondary education. When parents have low expectations, young adults with disabilities are less likely to be independent, and thus, continue to rely on parental support. Similarly, Yamamoto et al. (2014) determined that some family members tended to have low expectations for young adults with disabilities with regard to their educational achievement and career development. Family expectations may vary depending on the type and level of the disability. For example, young adults with an intellectual disability or have increased support needs may experience lower parental expectations. Yamamoto et al. believed that family members had low expectations for young adults with disabilities because family members did not have adequate information about postsecondary education opportunities for these individuals. Therefore, providing postsecondary education program information to parents will likely increase their awareness of opportunities and expectations for their sons and daughters.

Lack of Self-Determination Skills

"Self-determined behavior refers to volitional actions that enable one to act as the primary causal agent in one's life and to maintain or improve one's quality of life" (Wehmeyer, 2006, p. 117). This definition of self-determination recognizes that students themselves should be the causal agent in their lives and learn how to manage their career development. Lyman, Beecher, Griner, Brooks, Call, & Jackson, (2016) highlighted some successful cases about transitioning to postsecondary education. Some students with disabilities in these cases expressed that learning self-advocacy and communication skills was useful for them to adjust to life in postsecondary education. Students used these skills to communicate their needs for academic support and accommodations to staff in the office of disabilities services and to course instructors. These cases show how important self-determination skills are in the success of postsecondary education. However, many students with a disability are not given opportunities to make their own decisions and practice self-determination skills; thus, they do not possess important skills associated with self-determination, such as self-advocacy, self-management, and choice-making, to help them succeed in the transition to postsecondary education (Yamamoto et al., 2014).

Lack of Interagency Collaborations and System Support

Interagency collaborations play a pivotal role in the transition to postsecondary education. Yamamoto et al. (2014) proposed multiple collaborations among schools and different agencies. For example, the collaboration between secondary education and vocational rehabilitation services can support young adults with disabilities. Once these students graduate from secondary education, they may be eligible receive support and resources from vocational rehabilitation. Another collaboration is between actual secondary and postsecondary schools. When this collaboration occurs, secondary education teachers have a better understanding of how to prepare students with disabilities for postsecondary education. Noonan, Erickson, and Morningstar (2013) concluded that poor interagency collaborations resulted in low postsecondary education participation. Due to a lack of system support, young adults with disabilities wasted their time on navigating from one agency to another agency. The support they finally get may be insufficient and uncoordinated because many services require joint efforts from diverse stakeholders, such as vocational rehabilitation, schools, and other community agencies. Therefore, the importance of interagency collaborations deserves more emphasis when preparing students with disabilities for postsecondary education.

Lack of Funding Support

Another barrier that prevents students with disabilities from pursuing postsecondary education is the lack of funding support (Finnie, Wismer, & Mueller, 2015). Typically, in order to be eligible for financial aid, students need to meet a set of requirements associated with high levels of academic achievement. However, meet-

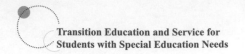
ing these requirements may be difficult or impossible for students with disabilities. For example, financial aid requires applicants to submit a standard high school diploma, but some students with disabilities may only have an alternative diploma such as a special education diploma, certificate of completion, occupational diploma, or others. This lack of a standard high school diploma prohibits these students from getting many forms of financial aid. In the Finnie et al. study, some participants expressed that their family could not afford the rising tuition of postsecondary education. However, after delving into the reasons why youth were not attending postsecondary education, it was found that some families simply assumed the investment in postsecondary education was not worthwhile. Based on this finding, Finnie and colleagues suggested efforts be focused on educating students and families about the benefits of postsecondary education as well as the financial aid system.

Preparing for Postsecondary Education

A number of strategies and suggestions are available to help secondary schools prepare students with disabilities for success in postsecondary education. Many of the strategies call for schools to equip students with both academic and non-academic skills that are essential for postsecondary education (McConnell et al., 2013). The following three strategies are especially helpful in planning the transition from school to postsecondary education for students with disabilities: (a) setting postsecondary education transition goals and ensuring compliance in transition planning, (b) ensuring access to general education and course alignment in transition planning, and (c) developing self-determination and advocacy skills.

Postsecondary Education Transition Goals and Compliance in Transition Planning

Appropriate transition planning is key to ensuring successful postsecondary outcomes and to ensure outcomes are aligned with student desires. In fact, proper transition planning should inform students about options following graduation and outline how the high school supports continue into postsecondary education (Test, Mazzotti, Mustian, Fowler, Kortering, & Kohler, 2009). This includes information about various types of postsecondary education (2-year, 4-year, vocational, technical, certificate) as well as helping students understand the education level needed to complete their individual career goals. This should also include educating students on the legal aspects and accommodations allowed at the postsecondary level (Rowe, Alverson, Unruh, Fowler, Kellems, & Test, 2014).

However, historically Individualized Education Programs (IEPs) and their transition components have retained more focus on compliance than quality when it comes to practice. This focus on compliance is further supported by findings of research that reviewed transition planning (Flannery, Lombardi, & Kato, 2015; Landmark & Zhang, 2013). Erickson, Noonan, Brussow, and Gilpin (2014) determined that compliant, well-written transition plans did result in more favorable postsecondary outcomes for students with disabilities. Therefore, schools are encouraged to not only ensure their transition plans are compliant, but also make sure appropriate planning and logical progression exist in these transition plans. This means transition plans must include the following four components: (a) measurable postsecondary goals to be updated annually, (b) postsecondary goals based on transition assessment (recommendation of two assessments in the areas of education, employment, and independent living) (Prince, Plotner, & Yell, 2014), (c) a course of study that reflects a student's postsecondary goals, and (d) annual IEP goals to reflect a student's transition needs (National Secondary Transition Technical Assistance Center, 2012).

Access to General Education and Course Alignment in Transition Planning

High school graduation continues to be a critical predictor of success in postsecondary education; but high school students with disabilities are less likely to en-roll in rigorous coursework at the high school level. However, students with disabili-ties can achieve the same graduation requirements as students without disabilities when awarded the opportunity for instruction and appropriate accommodations (Achieve, 2016). Therefore, it is imperative to hold students with disabilities to the same standards of achievement expected of all students. In fact, students who obtain more than 80% of their high school credits in general education classrooms are two times more likely to continue to postsecondary education when compared to stu-dents who received fewer credits in general education classrooms (Rojewski, Lee, & Gregg, 2015).

Ironically, the notions that good transition planning and maximizing access to the general curriculum have become conflicting concepts (Lee, Wehmeyer, Palmer, Soukup, & Little, 2008). This occurs because secondary education curriculum plac-es such an intense focus on academic outcomes that teachers feel they must decide between transition and academics (Kochhar-Bryant & Bassett, 2002). Therefore, educators must eradicate this notion and help foster the school's ability to incorpor-ate transition concepts into the general curriculum. In fact, research has shown this infusion to be effective in supporting student success in postsecondary education (Lee, Wehmeyer, Palmer, Williams-Diehm, Davies, & Stock, 2010; Lingo, Willi-ams-Diehm, Martin, & McConnell, 2018).

Self-Determination and Advocacy Skill Development

There has been almost fifty years of research demonstrating the strong link be-tween self-determined behavior and postschool outcomes (Agran, Sinclair, Alper, Cavin, Wehmeyer, & Hughes, 2005; Fowler, Konrad, Walker, Test, & Wood, 2007; Lee, Wehmeyer, Soukup, & Palmer, 2010). Although multiple definitions of self-de-termination exist, the overall consensus appears to focus on the individual being the primary decision maker within their life (Wehmeyer & Little, 2009). Several indi-vidual behaviors, often referred to as component elements of self-determination

(Wehmeyer, 1999), have been individually researched, including goal-setting and attainment, self-advocacy, and the decision-making process. School districts are encouraged to directly teach self-determination skills within their classrooms. Self-determination has been deemed an evidence-based practice due to the abundance of research demonstrating positive outcomes (Martin, Mithaug, Cox, Peterson, Van Dycke, & Cash, 2003; Wehmeyer, Palmer, Lee, Williams-Diehm, & Shogren, 2011).

High school students should practice self-determination related skills, such as self-advocacy skills and communication skills. Students can practice these skills during their IEP meetings. Wood, Karvonen, Test, Browder, and Algozzine (2004) demonstrated that students with disabilities can learn goal-setting, choice-making, and problem-solving skills by leading their own IEP meetings when they summarize what they have learned in class, communicate their course and career interests, and set goals for themselves. Students should have the necessary support to practice self-determination skills and learn to be independent. Shogren, Wehmeyer, and Lane (2016) recommended schools to build a system that promotes self-determination. In this way, students can practice self-determination on different occasions. Parents also expressed that allowing young adults with disabilities to make independent decisions is important (Francis et al., 2018).

Considerations for Access to Postsecondary Education

To help students with disabilities attain their postsecondary education goal and subsequent employment, teachers and parents need to help students equip themselves with knowledge about access to postsecondary education. In addition, schools need to implement some specific strategies to help students make a successful transition to postsecondary education. Researchers and educators proposed some evidence-based practices for transition to postsecondary education (Shaw, 2009; Shaw & Dukes III, 2013).

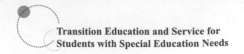
Develop Interagency Collaborations

Collaborations between secondary and postsecondary education systems can facilitate the continuities of accommodations from high school to postsecondary education. Because the different regulations governing secondary and postsecondary education cause disconnections of services, collaborations are necessary to help students with disabilities understand and obtain needed resources and accommodations. For example, staff from a postsecondary education institution's office of disability services can collaborate with high school counselors and special education teachers to teach students how to access college services and resources. Another example of collaborations is joint programs between high schools and colleges such as dual-credit programs. Shaw (2009) proposed joint programs that involve different stakeholders who can address different issues and concerns about the transition from secondary education to postsecondary education. One example is a joint disability documentation that was developed and agreed upon among stakeholders for the purpose of successful transition to postsecondary education.

Facilitate Skill Learning and Course Preparations

College courses prepare students for future careers, and students expect to learn and further their study in postsecondary education. However, college courses tend to not be as structured as high school courses, and heavy course loads might overwhelm students. Roberts (2010) suggested students must learn study and time-management skills that help individuals manage their time efficiently. Once students develop appropriate organizational and note-taking skills, they are able to apply these skills in college learning. Shaw and Dukes III (2013) indicated that students with attention deficit hyperactivity disorder (ADHD) can learn study skills through coaching and mentoring. Roberts further stressed the importance for students with disabilities to learn how to deal with schedule changes during high school. For those students who are anxious about unexpected schedule changes, instruction may be provided to teach them what to do if an unexpected schedule change occurs.

In addition to learning prerequisite skills for course preparations, Roberts (2010) suggested students consider their career paths and prepare for it during high school. The following are some guiding questions for this consideration which can also serve as guiding questions for students to prepare themselves for learning in postsecondary education.

- Is there a desired career path in a vocational or academic direction?
- What courses are available as college preparatory courses?
- Are there other online resources (e.g., online courses from open sources) available to support college learning?

Strategies for Adjusting to Academic Life in Postsecondary Education

Matriculating to a postsecondary educational institution marks the beginning of a new phase in a young adult's life. With the excitement of what is ahead also comes responsibilities. The expectation of graduating from postsecondary education requires sound planning that includes not only assurance of supports, resources, accommodations for coursework, but also adjustments to other on-campus and off-campus lives. Students with disabilities and their families need to understand the differences between high school and postsecondary education, the academic requirements of their chosen postsecondary program, where to get assistance when they need it, and the role of the disability services office. Any student entering postsecondary education needs to make various types of adjustments in order to lead to a successful life in college. New student orientation or similar programs provide some preparations for this adjustment. However, every student, particularly those with disabilities, needs to have additional strategies to cope with the change from being a high school student to being a college student, especially if the postsecondary institution requires the student to live away from home.

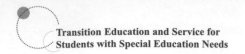

Understand the Differences between Secondary and Postsecondary Education

Students with disabilities, and sometimes their parents, do not always understand the difference between the laws that apply to education prior to college and those that apply during college. For example, in the United States, children who receive special education services are guaranteed a free appropriate public education (FAPE), but once the youth begins a postsecondary program, the individual is only guaranteed access to the education without being discriminated against due to their disability. Thus, students go from being entitled to an appropriate education based upon individual needs to having access to an education, if they otherwise meet the program's entrance requirements. Furthermore, in elementary and secondary school, students with disabilities may receive specially designed instruction, accommodations to access the curriculum, and modifications to the curriculum. In contrast, students with disabilities at the postsecondary education level will only receive accommodations to access learning. Specially designed instruction is not provided, nor are modifications (i.e., changes to the curriculum). Sometimes postsecondary programs will allow course substitutions such as not requiring a foreign language for a student who is deaf, but generally students with disabilities are required to meet the standards of the program.

Another difference between secondary and postsecondary education pertains to decision-making and the need for student self-advocacy. During elementary and secondary school, parents and educational professionals make the decisions about the child's educational programming. Ideally, by the time the youth completes their secondary education, they will have had a greater role in the educational decision-making as it pertains to their special education. Unfortunately, postsecondary students with disabilities are often not prepared for the entirety of the responsibility for their education. Yet, postsecondary students need to make decisions about courses to take, when to take the courses, how many credit hours to take a semester, and whether to disclose their disability and request accommodations. Certainly, parents can advise the postsecondary student, but the decision-making responsibility ultimately rests with the student. Indeed, the postsecondary institution of higher education does not communicate with the parents unless the student has given explicit, often written, permission for communicating with their parents.

Document Eligibility for Service at Postsecondary Education

As discussed earlier in this chapter, enrollment for disability services at a postsecondary educational institution is based on eligibility, not entitlement. Postsecondary education is required to, first, not discriminate on the basis of disability, and second, to provide appropriate academic adjustments or accommodations as necessary. Modifications, defined as changes in the curriculum or level of performance, are not found in postsecondary education settings. Instead, accommodations are available to ensure that students have equal access to all aspects of their educational experience (Newman & Madaus, 2015). Common academic adjustments and accommodations include arranging for priority registration; providing note takers; sign language interpreters; extended time for testing; and equipping computers with adaptive software or hardware (Office for Civil Rights, 2011). In order to obtain reasonable accommodations, the individual with a disability is responsible for disclosing their disability to the postsecondary institution. Although students are not required to disclose the presence of a disability, services will be not provided until all appropriate documentation is provided. Therefore, students in postsecondary education are advised to voluntarily disclose a disability early to help ensure academic success (Newman & Madaus, 2015). Most postsecondary institutions have a center on campus to provide services to students with disabilities. These centers have various names, such as the disability services office, student accessibility services, or services for students with disabilities. These centers help students navigate campus-specific guidelines to qualifying and receiving services as a student with a disability. Each institution has its legal obligation to require documentation for services. How-

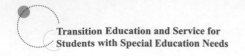

ever, the following are typical requirements:

- Documentation provided by professionals (e.g., medical doctor, psychologist, etc.)
- Diagnosis of a disability with any appropriate documentation
- Information on how the disability affects academic and/or life activity.

Although an IEP or Section 504 plan from high school may be helpful, these documents may not be sufficient for establishing qualification for services at the postsecondary level. Under certain circumstances, a student may need a new evaluation conducted to meet the requirements for services at the postsecondary level. Once determined to be eligible, postsecondary educational institutions will typically schedule a meeting with the student to determine appropriate accommodations and sign necessary paperwork. However, it is still imperative that individual students discuss needed academic adjustments with individual faculty, staff, and instructors across campus. Currently, there is a huge discrepancy between the percentage of students leaving the K-12 system and entering postsecondary education (67%) and the percentage of students who disclose their disabilities to receive disability services at the postsecondary level (28%) (Newman et al., 2011). The best way to alter this statistic is through education, training, and the transition process that occurs in secondary schools.

Learn to Use Assistive Technology

During each student's transition planning, the team should consider whether the student needs assistive technology. Traditional forms of assistive technology help students study independently; whereas modern technologies have changed the way we learn. For example, online courses and technology-based courses are commonly available. This new trend offers more opportunities and innovative ways for students to learn. Universal Design for Learning (UDL) offers another approach to teaching and learning that accommodates the different ability levels and learning preferences of learners. The principles of UDL have been applied in postsecondary education, facilitating full access to users without the needs for modifications or adaptations (West, Novak, & Mueller, 2016). By incorporating technology, UDL intends to create an environment that is accessible and inclusive to all people to the greatest extent. With these assistive technologies, instructors can deliver instruction in many different formats, and learners can use multiple ways to present what they have learned. Shaw and Dukes III (2013) suggested that teachers in secondary education apply UDL in their teaching because it creates an inclusive environment that benefits students of different backgrounds. The implementation of UDL in general education classrooms of secondary schools can facilitate student access to and adjustment in postsecondary education.

Get Help from Disability Services Office and Peer Supporters

Although there may be exceptions, if a postsecondary education program results in a degree or a professional license or certification, students with disabilities are held to the same standards as students without disabilities. This means students with disabilities must meet the same admission requirements and be able to complete the program with or without reasonable accommodations through the disability services office. Some of the assistance that students can receive include assistive or adaptive technology; direct instruction such as tutoring and remediation; strategy instruction in the areas of reading, writing, test-taking, and mastery of information; and comprehensive support programs for students with disabilities (Zeng, Ju, & Hord, 2018). However, students with disabilities need to know what resources are available on their campus and take the initiative to obtain these services.

Disability services office. The disability services office, also known as disability services, student accessibility services, or resource center for students with disabilities, is the office on the postsecondary education campus where students with disabilities use to get accommodations, academic adjustments, and auxiliary aids and services. Typically, when a student has been determined to be eligible for service, the disability service office will provide a letter for the student to present to course instructors. Some postsecondary education campuses send the letter to the faculty members instead of having the student present the letter to the faculty members. Regardless of the process, the disability services office will also advocate for the student if a faculty member does not want to provide reasonable accommodations. Some accommodations and related supports can be transferred from high school to college under Section 504 and the ADAAA. Roberts (2010) listed some reasonable accommodations that may be considered for transfer, including extended time for assignments or exams, accessible classrooms, and using assistive devises in class. Representatives of college disability services and educators in secondary education can have joint meetings to develop strategies for ensuring continuity of accommodations and the related supports (Shaw & Dukes III, 2013). Accommodations, adjustments, and auxiliary aids and services can be invaluable to students with disabilities at the postsecondary level. However, not all students who received special education services in secondary school register with the disability services office and request services. Squires, Burnell, McCarty, and Schnackenberg (2018) interviewed postsecondary students who self-identified as having a disability to learn their reasons for not seeking accommodations. Students indicated they did not disclose their disability and seek accommodations through the disability services office because they wanted to be independent, to challenge themselves to overcome their disability, and to avoid the stigma of having a disability. Postsecondary students who participated in a study by Lyman et al. (2016) noted they did not seek accommodations because they did not know about the disability services office, had negative experiences from their professors when asking for accommodations, or the services they received from the disability services office were inadequate.

Peer support. Some postsecondary education programs employ a peer-mentoring system to support students with disabilities. Research has shown peer support' s positive impact on students and their adjustments to postsecondary education. Griffin, Wendel, Day, and McMillan (2016) described a peer mentor model employed by a postsecondary education program. In this model, peer mentors played multiple roles in different areas, such as academics, daily planning, exercise, and lunch activities. Students with disabilities studied and participated in campus activities with these peer mentors and were able to get immediate help or support from peer mentors.

Peer support is also one of the major components in employment-oriented post-secondary education programs, in which peer-mentors provide considerable assistance to students with disabilities (Giust & Valle-Riestra, 2017; Hendrickson, Carson, Woods-Groves, Mendenhall, & Scheidecker, 2013; Zhang et al., 2018). Because typical college students from various disciplines and majors are invited into program-based courses with students with disabilities, the peer mentoring system also provides inclusion experiences to both students with and without disabilities. Both groups also learn from each other and increase their professional knowledge and skills.

Strategies for Adjusting to Campus Living during Postsecondary Education

For many students, attending a postsecondary educational institution requires them to live away from the home for the first time. Students with and without disabilities can struggle with this newfound freedom. For students with disabilities, this transition can be more complicated due to the impact of their disability on social relationships and health needs.

Social Relationships

Certain disabilities can have an impact on the individual's social relationships, and learning how to navigate the adult social environment is a part of the developmental growth process for these young adults. For example, autism, by its diagnosing criteria, includes deficits in social communication and interaction (American Psychiatric Association, 2013; World Health Organization, 2004). Jackson, Hart, Brown, and Volkmar (2018) surveyed college students with autism to learn about their academic, social, and mental health experiences. Although the college students reported high levels of comfort regarding their academics, they also reported loneliness, stress, anxiety, and depression. These stressors can lead to students dropping out or engaging in suicidal behavior (Jackson et al., 2018). Postsecondary students with disabilities, and in particular, those with autism, need social supports during this time. Undergraduate college students with autism in a case study (LeGary, 2017) indicated they received emotional, instructional (e.g., academic accommodations), and informational (e.g., information about library hours) support from parents, friends, and professors. University students with autism who participated in Cullen's (2015) study also noted they needed social support and that they were able to get the support from family, classmates, and social media.

Health Needs

Health conditions and healthcare needs of students with disabilities can impact their persistence and graduation from postsecondary education (Rosenbaum, 2018). Students with health conditions may need to take a reduced course load, and students with limited mobility due to physical disability or obesity require a campus and classrooms that are accessible (Stumbo, Hedrick, Weisman, & Martin, 2010/2011). Students who take medication may be solely responsible for taking the medications for the first time in their life, and it is not uncommon for young adults to stop taking medications, such as for ADHD or depression, after entering postsecondary education because they feel they no longer require the medication.

Additionally, there is a transition from child health care to adult health care, and families of children with disabilities who have health needs may not be aware of this transition and its ramifications. For example, an adolescent who has epilepsy may use a pediatric neurologist to manage their condition. However, once the adolescent turns 18 years old, the pediatric physician no longer will treat them, although some pediatric physicians may continue to see patients through age 21. Moreover, once the adolescent turns 18 years old, parents no longer have the right to be involved in the health care of the young adult unless there is written permission for the parent to be involved. If these changes have not been planned for and the adolescent has not started to incrementally be involved in their health care, there could be gaps in services.

Attendant Care

For postsecondary students who use wheelchairs and need assistance with daily life activities, going to college is likely the first time the individual is responsible for finding and managing personal care attendants. Until attending a postsecondary program, most individuals who need attendant care rely on their parents and teachers for that care and for managing outside personal care attendants (Burwell, Wessel, & Mulvihill, 2015). Another consideration is how the attendant care will be financed. Families need to plan for either paying the costs out of their pocket, using Medicaid or private insurance, using Medicaid waiver money, or using money from vocational rehabilitation.

Postsecondary students who use wheelchairs and have attendant care have to learn to schedule and manage their time around their attendant care and train the attendants (Burwell et al., 2015). Even with thorough scheduling, sometimes unforeseen circumstances occur, such as an attendant quitting and not showing up in the morning to get a student out of bed. In these situations, the student needs to have a back-up plan such as having a suitemate check to make sure the student is up or having access to a phone, if the student has the mobility to use a phone. Sometimes the student and the attendant are not compatible, and in those situations, the student needs to be able to fire and hire attendants as needed.

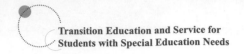

Completing Postsecondary Education and Gaining Employment

Challenges Associated with Persisting through Postsecondary Education

Since postsecondary education opened its door to students with disabilities, their retention and graduation rates have been a main concern. Although the retention and graduation rates of students with disabilities may be similar to students without disabilities in the first two years of college, students with disabilities seem to drop out more during fourth and fifth years (Wessel, Jones, Markle, & Westfall, 2009). However, failure to obtain postsecondary education credentials leads to frustrations in finding employment opportunities (Johnson, Stodden, Emanuel, Luecking, & Mack, 2002). To assist students with disabilities completing postsecondary education and obtaining subsequent employment, it is necessary to explore the challenges they face and develop strategies to support them.

Challenges in overcoming stigma issues. The most common challenges students with disabilities encounter are stigma and discrimination issues. Lindsay, Cagliostro, and Carafa (2018) stated that disability-related discriminations and negative effects of disclosing a disability prevented students from disclosing their disability and applying for accommodations at their postsecondary institutions. Many students worried that peers and course instructors would focus on their disabilities rather than seeing them as a whole person. Other negative feelings they may experience include discomfort or isolation. Similarly, Dowrick, Anderson, Heyer, and Acosta (2005) found that stigma issues were the primary reason why students decided to discontinue using accommodations. The fear of negative social reactions put students with disabilities at a disadvantage. The stigma issues get even worse for students with hidden disabilities, such as a learning disability, because people tend to think accommodation are not necessary (Moriña, 2017).

Challenges in identifying appropriate services and accommodations. In addition to stigma and discrimination issues, difficulties in identifying appropriate services or a lack of knowledge of supports is a common challenge experienced by students with disabilities at the postsecondary education level (Lindsay et al., 2018; Redpath, Kearney, Nicholl, Mulvenna, Wallace, & Martin, 2013). Some students with disabilities may not realize their need for accommodations. Even if they know their need for accommodations or other supports, they may not be aware of the eligibility and documentation requirements to access these accommodations. For example, an individual with mental health issues expressed she needed information about getting on-campus services, but ultimately found herself left alone with limited access to assistance (Redpath et al., 2013). Other students may choose to not disclose their disability for accommodations, but use their own coping styles to deal with learning-related challenges. Consequently, they may not be able to pass classes and make adequate progress toward graduation. The lack of provision and continuity of student services could be a challenge that negatively influences the inclusive experience of students with disabilities. If students cannot find appropriate services, such as student counseling services, to support their academic struggles and campus lives, they might easily give up on higher education.

Challenges related to other people's level of disability awareness and attitudes toward individuals with disability. Other people's levels of disability awareness and attitudes toward individuals with disabilities influence whether students with disabilities can persist through postsecondary education. In postsecondary education, faculty members play an important role in the academic learning of students with disabilities (Baker, Boland, & Nowik, 2012). If faculty do not have positive or favorable attitudes toward disabilities, it creates an additional challenge for students with disabilities to discuss academic accommodations with them. Unfortunately, most faculty lack some basic knowledge about policies and procedures to accommodate students' learning needs (Sniatecki, Perry, & Snell, 2015). Many factors influence faculty's levels of disability awareness and attitudes toward to disabilities. Bruder and Mogro-Wilson (2010) discovered that adequate and interactive experiences with individuals with disabilities increased faculty's levels of awareness and attitudes. Faculty who attended disability-related training have more positive attitudes towards disability-related issues (Dallas, Sprong, & Kluesner, 2016; Lombardi, Murray, & Gerdes, 2011). Therefore, providing disability-related training is a quick and effective way to increase faculty awareness and attitudes towards disability.

Strategies for Succeeding In Postsecondary Education

The ambition to succeed in postsecondary education is rooted in every student. Students with disabilities might encounter more challenges on the way to graduation and obtaining future employment compared to students without disabilities. By taking advantage of multiple strategies, students with disabilities can not only persist through postsecondary education, but can also experience the satisfaction of academic integration.

Self-determination. Strategies stemming from self-determination are helpful for college students to deal with the hardships in postsecondary education. Self-determination predicts enrollment and completion of postsecondary education for students with disabilities (Petcu, Van Horn, & Shogren, 2017). Getzel and Thoma (2008) identified self-awareness, problem-solving, and self-advocacy as self-determination strategies students can use to handle the challenges in postsecondary education settings. Students are encouraged to develop self-awareness of themselves regarding their disabilities, strengths, weaknesses, and learning preferences. The better they know themselves, the easier they can advocate for what they need in academic learning. Problem-solving skills help students understand their limitations and identify strategies to solve the problems in a systematic way.

Similarly, Shepler and Woosley (2012) recommended setting realistic goals and planning as a way to assist students with disabilities to succeed in postsecondary education. Because postsecondary education settings are less structured, students themselves usually take a lead role in managing their studies. Under this circumstance, goal setting and planning are critically important. As soon as, or even before, students enter a postsecondary education program, they need to set realistic goals for themselves. They can do so by developing short- and long-term goals with high expectations for themselves. These goals can address the aspects of involvement in campus life and academic integrations. For example, students can decide what student organizations they expect to join or determine the way they communicate their support needs to instructors. Educators and family members can work with students to develop realistic goals by identifying their potential strengths and needs. After setting a goal, students with disabilities need to develop actions they will take in order to achieve the goal and succeed in postsecondary education. High school educators or other professionals can guide students to identify effective strategies during high school and carry over to postsecondary education. Examples of these skills include specific study skills (e.g., note taking and learning with printed materials) and academic services (e.g., learning tutors).

Students should also plan their courses and programs based on adequate knowledge of credits required for graduation. They need to formulate a plan of courses based on their interests and career development. Other campus issues, such as transportation or housing, are also things to consider in a plan. The plan should include a budget section for independent living arrangements. A solid plan needs sound suggestions and advice from others. However, students with disabilities are owners of their own plans. If students lead the planning process, they become more confident to overcome the challenges associated with succeeding in postsecondary education (Shepler & Woosley, 2012).

Self-sufficiency. Lyman et al. (2016) conducted semi-structured interviews to investigate why disability services were not being fully used by students with disabilities. In addition to considering the stigma issues, participants expressed how they deal with academic struggles without using accommodations. These participants had the desire for self-sufficiency, which motivated them to learn the importance of being independent and self-accommodating their disabilities. Self-sufficiency is a unique aspect of the broader concept of self-determination. In this way, students with disabilities may use other resources to support their academic learning. For example, they can complete a class assignment by using on-campus tutoring services. They may also use assistive technology to help themselves read and write. Advanced technology has actually changed the way we learn (Edyburn, 2010). Thus, students with disabilities begin to use different tools to facilitate their own learning.

In addition, high levels of independence and self-sufficiency result in a lower level of homesickness-related distress (Shepler & Woosley, 2012). Students reduce the reliance on family support and try to deal with challenges by themselves. However, being independent does not mean that students with disabilities do not need any support or reasonable accommodations. Instead, students themselves make a choice and evaluate whether they really need any support. If they decide they need support from family, actively asking for help and support is part of learning to be independent. Similarly, if students with disabilities decide they need an academic accommodation from an instructor or disability services office, they are responsible for disclosing their disability and seeking accommodations. In this way, applying for a reasonable accommodation from disability services is just a backup. Being independent and self-sufficient has been the primary way to deal with hardships in postsecondary education.

Forming positive relationships with instructors and peers. Getzel and Thoma (2008) suggested that forming positive relationships with instructors and peers is a useful strategy for postsecondary education students with disabilities. Meeting instructors on a regular basis is a way to communicate accommodation needs. In this way, instructors can understand issues the student faces in class and serve as a natural support for the student. Peers are another source of natural support in postsecondary education settings. Students can form study groups with peers to study and work together to deal with challenges and difficulties. For example, sharing lecture notes provides a strong collaboration, learning how to collaborate and work together as a team (Rose, Harbour, Johnston, Daley, & Abarbanell, 2006).

Other strategies for succeeding in postsecondary education. Family members have recommended some other strategies for student success in postsecondary education. Francis et al. (2018) interviewed parents of individuals with intellectual and developmental disabilities who graduated from a postsecondary education program. Parents in this study suggested some strategies parents can use to help their young adult children with disabilities succeed in postsecondary education. The three most recommended strategies were maintaining high expectations, allowing for choices, and permitting risk-taking. Overall, parents expect young adults with disabilities to be independent from home and more engaged in college activities. Allowing these young adults to make a choice independently might take a risk, but this is a necessary process to help them grow and learn from mistakes. However, just because young adults with disabilities should be independent does not mean they do not need ongoing support from family; instead, asking for advice and help is a strategy every student should learn if they want to succeed in postsecondary education.

Meeting Graduation Requirements of Postsecondary Education Programs

The primary goal of attending postsecondary education, for most students with or without disabilities, is to graduate from a degree or non-degree program and be prepared to enter the workforce. Meaningful employment with a decent pay in a productive career is one of the most consistent factors for community inclusion and independent living (Zhang et al., 2018). Being able to graduate from a postsecondary education program is often essential to acquire gainful employment. Therefore, regardless whether a student with a disability is in a degree program or a non-degree program, they need to understand the graduation requirements as soon as being admitted into the program, if not earlier. Once enrolled, it is essential for the student to plan his or her program of study based on these requirements.

Typical graduation requirements of degree programs. All degree programs have specific requirements for graduation. These include the general requirements by the college or university and specific requirements by the degree program. Typically, a student must successfully complete the postsecondary institution's core courses and earn enough credit hours in order to fulfill the degree or program requirements. The degree program within a specific department may divide its credit hour requirements into various categories. Required credit hours are derived from a combination of university-level required courses, program-level required courses, and field-based experiences. Under some specific conditions, certain required courses (e. g., foreign language courses) may be substituted with approved courses. Students need to learn all the rules and requirements in order to understand the pros and cons of course substitutions as these can be very specific to various institutions. In addition, based on the profession that the degree program prepares the student for, some may require the student to earn a professional certificate or other credential in order to graduate.

Many programs offer courses in a sequence based on students' class in the program (i.e., the year they enter the program and the year they expect to graduate). Students who enter the program in the same year typically take required core courses in the same sequence. It is always a good idea for the student with a disability to take these courses in the same sequence along with their peers in the same class. Advantages to following these schedules include on-time graduation and having a study group that can help one another. Taking courses in this sequence does not diminish a student's freedom of taking courses that meet their individual interests because each student can take different elective courses. A student who unexpectedly falls behind can certainly work with the academic advisor to modify course schedules to complete all required and elective courses as soon as possible. In many cases, falling behind in one or two core courses may not delay graduation if a modified schedule allows for completion of elective courses earlier and required core courses by the expected year of graduation. It is important to work with the academic advisor to identify and develop the best schedules each term.

Typical graduation requirements of non-degree programs for students with intellectual and developmental disabilities. In the past 10 years, there has been a significant increase of postsecondary education programs for individuals with intellectual and developmental disabilities (Grigal et al., 2012; Zhang et al., 2018). These programs vary in their overall goal, curriculum, and graduation requirements. These programs come in many lengths from one to four years, mirroring that of a traditional college experience.

A majority of these programs offer students a certificate or similar recognitions. As in the case for typical college students, students in one of these postsecondary education programs must complete a required number of credits in order to earn a certificate. The number of required credit and courses vary from program to program. For example, Project FOCUS at the University of Arizona is a 2-year program in which students who complete the program requirements earn a certificate in service learning. The required minimum credits is 25, including 3 credits from a course entitled, "Introduction to Service Learning and Meaningful Contributions to the Community," 15 credits from taking or auditing other academic courses, and a minimum of 7 internship credits.

Some postsecondary education programs for students with intellectual and developmental disabilities prepare students for a field or career with prescribed courses and internship experiences. For example, Texas A&M University offers a 1-year certificate program that prepares students for a career in human service in one of three tracks: direct support professionals, childcare professionals, and para-professionals. Students takes core courses specific to their track, enrichment courses, and practicum. Upon successful completion of these program requirements, students receive a certificate that will lead to employment in the corresponding field. The College of Arts in California offers students an opportunity to earn certificates of completion of individual courses. There are no specific requirements on the number of courses students must take, the length of time they must attend, or the number of times they may repeat courses. The 60-credit undergraduate course of study is available to students of all learning levels and instructional needs. There are no requirements for the number or type of courses an undergraduate student must take, attendance per week, or frequency of attendance. Students may repeat the undergraduate course of study as frequently as they like. Full or partial credit is granted based on the amount of experience, exposure, and participation in learning activities possible for each student during a given quarter, as demonstrated through class attendance and as reported by the instructor. The Marino Campus of Florida International University issues certificates to students who pass industry certifications through Microsoft, CompTIA, and the American Hotels and Lodging Association.

Job Development and Career Advancement for Individuals with Disabilities

In recent years, job development has been an emphasis for individuals with disabilities. To lead a self-determined life, employment is a crucial factor that influences how individuals with disabilities manage their lives (Zalewska, Migliore, & Butterworth, 2016). With income from a paid job, these individuals can learn budgeting and access to a good quality of life (Lindstrom, Hirano, McCarthy, & Alverson, 2014). In this section, the focus will shift to job development and career advancement.

Setting Academic Goals and Career Exploration

After entering postsecondary education, students need to set academic goals that lead to graduation and a future career. Setting an academic goal for oneself requires students to apply the self-determination skills they learned during high school, including choice-making, decision-making, and self-awareness (Getzel & Thoma, 2008). They need to consider their own interests, career direction, and aptitude first and then identify what they really like and dislike. They also need to understand program structures and graduation requirements. When students have clear academic goals, they can further explore their future career and job opportunities. Roberts (2010) proposed some guiding questions for students to consider in their setting academic and career goals. These guiding questions include:

• Is the desired career path employment-oriented or academic-oriented?

• What courses in a postsecondary education program support these career paths and interests?

Challenges Associated with Working in the Labor Market

Individuals with disabilities participating in a labor market is a cornerstone representing diversity, respect, and human rights in today's society. Working in a competitive employment market can provide financial benefits and social integration (Lindstrom et al., 2014). All people, including individuals with disabilities, desire to be included in a social group.

However, there are some challenges that employees with disabilities face in a workplace. The first challenge that draws a great deal of concern is limited job opportunities for individuals with disabilities (Lindstrom et al., 2014). Although these young adults have gone through career and interest exploration prior to finding a job, the jobs that meet their preferences and career goals may simply not exist. As a result, these individuals may take a job, but have difficulty maintaining employment. Moreover, most available jobs provide limited career advancement opportunities for employees with disabilities. The second challenge comes from other people's attitudes towards employees with disabilities. Toldrá and Santos (2013) investigated the working experiences of employees with disabilities and found that company culture and climate could be either a facilitator or a barrier to the employment of individuals with disabilities. If a corporate culture is inclusive in nature, it creates a nourishing environment in which employees with disabilities do not have to strive for the recognition of their professional abilities. An inclusive environment produces positive interpersonal relationships between employees with disabilities and coworkers. It facilitates teamwork, networking, and cooperation. However, if the working environment is full of discrimination and stigma, employees with disabilities need to spend extra time to adjust to this environment and struggle to receive the respect they deserve. The third challenge is physical accessibility. A lack of accessibility can be a barrier. Under this circumstance, reasonable accommodations or adjustments can increase job satisfaction. With a minor accommodation, employees with disabilities can complete assigned tasks and become a valuable contributor. Finally, meeting job requirements can be a big challenge for individuals with intellectual disability from the perspectives of employers because industries are transforming and the required skills and education levels are different compared to past decades (Kocman, Fischer, & Weber, 2018). Skill and education requirements influence retention decisions, which demonstrates a challenge for employees with disabilities to maintain a job for a long time.

Preparing for Employment

Skill development. Possessing necessary proficient skills is the main reason why an individual can find a job in a competitive job market. Some professional skills are basic requirements for jobs, which can be learned through postsecondary education or internship opportunities. Other skills, such as soft skills, need to be specifically taught when preparing individuals with disabilities for future jobs.

Scheef, Walker, and Barrio (2019) investigated desirable employment skills from the perspectives of job developers. They identified five soft skills that are important for individuals with disabilities, including attitude, dependability, stamina, communication, and flexibility. For attitude, job developers suggested that people with positive attitudes can adjust well in a workplace. In addition, personal traits such as being hard-working, being willing to learn, and taking initiative lead to positive work attitudes. For dependability, a dependable employee tends to have good attendance, punctuality, reliability, and loyalty. From the perspectives of job developers, although some employees with disabilities have less productivity, they are very reliable and coworkers and supervisors can trust them. Stamina is the ability to work for an expected amount of time by an employer. Employees who cannot work the entire shift might lose their job. Training individuals with disabilities to have the stamina to work will help them with job retention. For employees with disabilities, communication skills help them express what they need. If they work in service industries, they also need to learn how to communicate and interact with customers appropriately. Flexibility is the ability to adapt or complete many tasks. Individuals with disabilities were trained to complete one task at a time in school; however, in a workplace, multitasking is important because employees are expected to complete a variety of tasks. These soft skills help individuals with disabilities advance their careers.

Other skills, such as self-determination skills, are essential as well. Shogren et al. (2018) showed the relationship between self-determination and employment outcome, suggesting that increasing goal-directed behaviors could lead to integrated employment. Zalewska et al. (2016) found that psychological empowerment, a subscale of self-determination, was associated with employment outcome. If employees have psychological empowerment, they are more motivated to get involved with their work. Similarly, Lindsay, Adams, Sanford, McDougall, Kingsnorth, & Menna-Dack, (2014) explored desirable skills for entry-level positions from the perspectives of employers and employment counselors. They also identified soft skills as prerequisite skills for jobs.

Internship and employment preparation through postsecondary education programs. Postsecondary education programs have recently exerted an influence on employment preparation and increased opportunities for individuals with disabilities to live an independent life. Petcu, Chezan, and Van Horn (2015) investigated vocational-related services postsecondary education programs have employed to prepare individuals with disabilities for competitive employment. This study revealed that postsecondary education programs offer multiple and diverse training services, such as career counseling, person-centered planning, career assessment, career exploration, volunteering opportunities, and self-advocacy training. Among these services, volunteering and internship opportunities are most popular as they provide hands-on working experiences for individuals with disabilities. However, if employment preparation occurred only in classrooms, it may not build up the types of experiences that lead to employment (Lindstrom et al., 2014). It is important to include additional community work experiences because they bring such benefits as developing job skills and problem-solving skills. Zhang et al. (2018) also highlighted the importance of offering individuals with disabilities employment training in a one-year program, in which participants are provided with job-oriented training, opportunities to live a self-directed life, and internships in different settings (e.g., local schools, day care centers, or other residential settings). In addition, an intensive peer-mentoring system helps these individuals persist through a job setting. If they encounter challenges in a workplace, peer mentors provide them with immediate support to work through the problems. Similarly, Hendrickson et al. (2013) described an inclusive postsecondary education program in which individuals with disabilities engage in community activities through multiple internship opportunities. In this program, students take the core curriculum to improve their life skills, such as health and wellness skills. It also provides individualized advising, which focuses on student-centered goals and formulates a transition plan that leads to inclusive employment. Before students go into an internship, the program guides students to explore their career interests. Career exploration creates a connection between employment and personal goals and interests.

Familiarity with different kinds of assistive technology. Due to technological advancements, now more than ever before, individuals with disabilities use a variety of assistive technologies to assist them with task completions (Edyburn, 2010). Unfortunately, some assistive technologies students were used to during postsecondary education belong to the institution of higher education or another agency and cannot be taken to the new employment setting (Koch, 2017). Thus, individuals with disabilities should familiarize themselves with different kinds of assistive technologies so that they are prepared to use assistive technologies in the new employment environment. Plus, individuals with disabilities need to know what assistive technology devices they prefer and need to possess the ability to ask for these devices as a reasonable accommodation at their place of employment.

Other employment preparation strategies. In postsecondary education, the disabilities services office plays a pivotal role in preparing students with disabilities for future careers. Oswald, Huber, and Bonza (2015) investigated some practices that disabilities services offices have used to provide employment preparation for students with disabilities. Some effective strategies include:

• Enhancing communication skills. Students are encouraged to polish their internal and external communication skills. Once students get a job, communications skills often play a key role in job retention and promotions.

• Being aware of personal needs. Students need to understand how their disabilities influence their work performances and be prepared to communicate accommodation needs to the employer.

• Becoming involved with campus activities. Student organizations provide college students with rich opportunities to hone social skills and cultivate leadership abilities, many of which are skills employers look for. Students with disabilities should join these campus activities to enhance their preparation for employment.

• Understanding available resources. Students are encouraged to seek resources on campus and use these resources to assist with their employment preparation, such as developing a sound resume, practicing interview skills through mock interviews, and seeking networking opportunities. A postsecondary education institution usually has plenty of resources for students. Students need to actively gather information about these resources and seize every possibility.

• Applying high expectations to individuals with disabilities when preparing them for a future job opportunity (Lindstrom et al., 2014). Family plays an important role when it comes to expectations for young adults with disabilities. If the family shows confidence in their adult children's capabilities, they are more likely to complete schoolwork and daily tasks. In fact, parent expectation is a strong predictor of

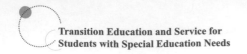
self-determination, employment, and independent living (Shogren, Villarreal, Dowsett, & Little, 2016).

Strategies for Transition between Jobs and Career Advancement

Due to the rapid development of technologies and modernization of industries, new career opportunities have become available to all individuals, including those with disabilities. Job changes are common in one's career. In addition, most people have opportunities to make upward progression in their careers, commonly referred to as career advancement. The skills needed for transition between jobs or for career advancement, however, are not adequately taught to students with disabilities (Grigal et al., 2012). Postsecondary education programs need to include trainings that prepare students for job changes and career advancements.

To prepare students with disabilities for finding a job, job changes, and career advancement, it is necessary to teach them basic employability skills. Employability skills are general and nontechnical competencies required for performing all jobs cut across all types and levels of jobs (Ju, Zhang, & Pacha, 2012). They are essential attributes that make an employee an asset to the employer (Buck & Barrick, 1987). Research has identified some employability skills employers expect all entry-level employees to possess. Examples of these include attitudes (e.g., dependability, staying with a task, getting along with others, and recognizing the importance of good health), communication, and basic knowledge (Baxter & Young, 1982). Casner-Lotto and Barrington (2006) identified professionalism or work ethic, teamwork or collaboration, oral communication, ethics or social responsibility, and reading comprehension as the five most important employability skills for new entry-level employees. Ju et al. (2012) identified four skills that are important for all employees. These are possessing integrity/honesty, following directions, showing respect for others, and having punctuality. Postsecondary education programs need to include coursework as well as on-the-job trainings that develop or enhance these basic employability skills, which will help individuals with disabilities make transitions between jobs because individuals with disabilities often lack these skills compared to people without disabilities (Lindsay et al., 2014).

To prepare students for career advancement, career-focused preparation is necessary so students learn the essential technical skills in the career of their choice. In addition, students need to pick a career that has growth opportunities. If a career does not have growth opportunities, it may become dull over time and even be terminated. Secondary and postsecondary education programs should recognize the limitations of certain careers when providing career advising and training to students. It is also important to teach students to recognize opportunities and find the criteria for promotions. Some of the skills needed for career advancement may include recognizing potential opportunities, seeking professional development opportunities, getting advice from a mentor, effective communication with supervisors, identifying job opportunities, and strategies for applying and interviewing for jobs. Communication skills are also important for someone who wants to further their career (Oswald et al., 2015).

References

Achieve. (2016). *Diplomas that matter: Ensuring equity of opportunity for students with disabilities*. Retrieved from https://www.achieve.org/files/Achieve_NCEO_111616.pdf

Agran, M., Sinclair, T., Alper, S., Cavin, M., Wehmeyer, M., & Hughes, C. (2005). Using self-monitoring to increase following direction skills of students with moderate to severe disabilities in general education. *Education and Training in Developmental Disabilities, 40*, 3-13.

American Psychiatric Association. (2013). *Diagnostic and statistical manual of mental disorders* (5th ed.). Washington, DC: Author.

Baker, K. Q., Boland, K., & Nowik, C. M. (2012). A campus survey of faculty and student perceptions of persons with disabilities. *Journal of Postsecondary Education & Disability, 25*, 309-329.

Baxter, M. B., & Young, J. L. (1982). What do employers expect from high school graduates? *NASSP Bulletin, 66*, 93-96.

Bruder, M. B., & Mogro-Wilson, C. (2010). Student and faculty awareness and attitudes about students with disabilities. *Review of Disability Studies: An International Journal, 6*, 3-13.

Buck, L. L., & Barrick, K. R. (1987). They're trained, but are they employable? *Vocational Education Journal, 62*, 29-31.

Burwell, N. R., Wessel, R. D., & Mulvihill, T. (2015). Attendant care for college students with physical disabilities using wheelchairs: Transition issues and experiences. *Journal of Postsecondary Education and Disability, 28*, 293-307.

Casner-Lotto, J., & Barrington, L. (2006). *Are they really ready to work? Employers' perspectives on the basic knowledge and applied skills of new entrants to the 21st century U.S. workforce*. Retrieved from http://www.conference-board.org/pdf_free/BED-06-Workforce.pdf

Committee on Equal Opportunities in Science and Engineering. (2006). *2005-2006 biennial report to Congress*. Arlington, VA: National Science Foundation.

Conner, D. J. (2012). Helping students with disabilities transition into college: 21 tips for students with LD or ADD/ADHD. *TEACHING Exceptional Children, 44*, 16-25.

Cullen, J. A. (2015). The needs of college students with autism spectrum disorders and Asperger's syndrome. *Journal of Postsecondary Education and Disability, 28*, 89-101.

Dallas, B. K., Sprong, M. E., & Kluesner, B. K. (2016). Multiuniversity comparison of faculty attitudes and use of universal design instructional techniques. *Rehabilitation Research, Policy & Education, 30*, 148-160.

Dowrick, P. W., Anderson, J., Heyer, K., & Acosta, J. (2005). Postsecondary education across the USA: Experiences of adults with disabilities. *Journal of Vocational Rehabilitation, 22*, 41-47.

Edyburn, D. (2010). Would you recognize universal design for learning if you saw it? Ten propositions for new directions for the second decade of UDL. *Learning Disability Quarterly, 33*, 33-41.

Engle, J. (2007). Post-secondary access and success for first-generation college students. *American Academic, 3*, 25-48.

Erickson, A. S. G., Noonan, P. M., Brussow, J. A., & Gilpin, B. J. (2014). The impact of IDEA indicator 13 compliance on postsecondary outcomes. *Career Development and Transition for Exceptional Individuals, 37*, 161-167.

Erickson, W., Lee, C., & von Schrader, S. (2016). *2015 disability status report: United States*. Retrieved from http://www.disabilitystatistics.org/StatusReports/2015-PDF/2015-StatusReport_US.pdf

Finnie, R., Wismer, A., & Mueller, R. E. (2015). Access and barriers to postsecondary education: Evidence from the youth in transition survey. *Canadian Journal of Higher Education, 45*, 229-262.

Flannery, K. B., Lombardi, A., & Kato, M. M. (2015). The impact of professional

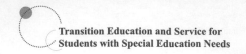
development on the quality of the transition components of IEPs. *Career Development and Transition for Exceptional Individuals, 38*, 14-24.

Fowler, C. H., Konrad, M., Walker, A. R., Test, D. W., & Wood, W. M. (2007). Self-determination interventions' effects on the academic performance of students with developmental disabilities. *Education and Training in Developmental Disabilities, 42*, 270-285.

Francis, G. L., Stride, A., & Reed, S. (2018). Transition strategies and recommendations: Perspectives of parents of young adults with disabilities. *British Journal of Special Education, 45*, 277-301.

Getzel, E. E., & Thoma, C. A. (2008). Experiences of college students with disabilities and the importance of self-determination in higher education settings. *Career Development for Exceptional Individuals, 31*, 77-84.

Giust, A. M., & Valle-Riestra, D. M. (2017). Supporting mentors working with students with intellectual disabilities in higher education. *Journal of Intellectual Disabilities, 21*, 144-157.

Griffin, M. M., Wendel, K. F., Day, T. L., & McMillan, E. D. (2016). Developing peer supports for college students with intellectual and developmental disabilities. *Journal of Postsecondary Education and Disability, 29*, 263-269.

Grigal, M., Hart, D., & Weir, C. (2012). A survey of postsecondary education programs for students with intellectual disabilities in the United States. *Journal of Policy and Practice in Intellectual Disabilities, 9*, 223-233.

Hart, D., Grigal, M., & Weir, C. (2010). Expanding the paradigm: Postsecondary education options for individuals with autism spectrum disorder and intellectual disabilities. *Focus on Autism and Other Developmental Disorders, 25*, 134-150.

Hendrickson, J. M., Carson, R., Woods-Groves, S., Mendenhall, J., & Scheidecker, B. (2013). UI REACH: A postsecondary program serving students with autism and intellectual disabilities. *Education & Treatment of Children, 36*, 169-194.

Institute for Community Inclusion. (2019). *What is a TPSID?* Retrieved from https://

thinkcollege.net/tpsid

Jackson, S. L. J., Hart, L., Brown, J. T., & Volkmar, F. R. (2018). Brief report: Self-reported academic, social, and mental health experiences of post-secondary students with autism spectrum disorder. *Journal of Autism and Developmental Disorders, 48*, 643-650.

Johnson, D. R., Stodden, R. A., Emanuel, E. J., Luecking, R., & Mack, M. (2002). Current challenges facing secondary education and transition services: What research tells us. *Exceptional Children, 68*, 519-531.

Ju, S., Zhang, D., & Pacha, J. (2012). Employability skills valued by employers as important for entry-level employees with and without disabilities. *Career Development for Exceptional Individuals, 35*, 29-38.

Katsiyannis, A., Zhang, D., Landmark, L., & Reber, A. (2009). Postsecondary education for individuals with disabilities: Legal and practice considerations. *Journal of Disability Policy Studies, 20*, 35-45.

Koch, K. (2017). Stay in the box! Embedded assistive technology improves access for students with disabilities. *Education Sciences, 7*, 1-8.

Kochhar-Bryant, C. A., & Bassett, D. S. (2002). *Aligning transition and standards-based education: Issues and strategies.* Arlington, VA: Council for Exceptional Children.

Kocman, A., Fischer, L., & Weber, G. (2018). The employers' perspective on barriers and facilitators to employment of people with intellectual disability: A differential mixed-method approach. *Journal of Applied Research in Intellectual Disabilities, 31*, 120-131.

Landmark College. (2019). *About Landmark College.* Retrieved from https://www.landmark.edu/about

Landmark, L. J., & Zhang, D. (2013). Compliance and best practices in transition planning: Effects of disability and ethnicity. *Remedial and Special Education, 34*, 113-125.

Lee, S. H., Wehmeyer, M. L., Palmer S. B., Soukup J. H., & Little T. D. (2008). Self-

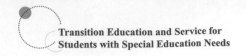
determination and access to the general education curriculum. *The Journal of Special Education, 42*, 91-107.

Lee, S. H., Wehmeyer, M. L., Soukup, J. H., & Palmer, S. B. (2010). Impact of curriculum modifications on access to the general education curriculum for students with disabilities. *Exceptional Children, 76*, 213-233.

Lee, Y., Wehmeyer, M., Palmer, S., Williams-Diehm, K., Davies, D., & Stock, S. (2010). Examining individual and instruction-related predictors of the self-determination of students with disabilities: Multiple regression analyses. *Remedial & Special Education, 33*, 150-161.

LeGary, R. A., Jr. (2017). College students with autism spectrum disorder: Perceptions of social supports that buffer college-related stress and facilitate academic success. *Journal of Postsecondary Education and Disability, 30*, 251-268.

Lindsay, S., Adams, T., Sanford, R., McDougall, C., Kingsnorth, S., & Menna-Dack, D. (2014). Employers' and employment counselors' perceptions of desirable skills for entry-level positions for adolescents: How does it differ for youth with disabilities? *Disability & Society, 29*, 953-967.

Lindsay, S., Cagliostro, E., & Carafa, G. (2018). A systematic review of barriers and facilitators of disability disclosure and accommodations for youth in post-secondary education. *International Journal of Disability, Development and Education, 65*, 526-556.

Lindstrom, L., Hirano, K. A., McCarthy, C., & Alverson, C. Y. (2014). "Just having a job": Career advancement for low-wage workers with intellectual and developmental disabilities. *Career Development and Transition for Exceptional Individuals, 37*, 40-49.

Lingo, M. E., Williams-Diehm, K. L., Martin, J. E., & McConnell, A. E. (2018). Teaching transition self-determination knowledge and skills using the ME! bell ringers. *Career Development and Transition for Exceptional Individuals, 4*, 185-189.

Lombardi, A. R., Murray, C., & Gerdes, H. (2011). College faculty and inclusive instruction: Self-reported attitudes and actions pertaining to universal design. *Journal of Diversity in Higher Education, 4*, 250-261.

Lyman, M., Beecher, M. E., Griner, D., Brooks, M., Call, J., & Jackson, A. (2016). What keeps students with disabilities from using accommodations in postsecondary education? *A Qualitative Review. Journal of Postsecondary Education and Disability, 29*, 131-140.

Martin, J. E., Mithaug, D. E., Cox, P., Peterson, L. Y., Van Dycke, J. L., & Cash, M. E. (2003). Increasing self-determination: Teaching students to plan, work, evaluate, and adjust. *Exceptional Children, 69*, 431-448.

McConnell, A. E., Martin, J. E., Juan, C. Y., Hennessey, M. N., Terry, R. A., el-Kazimi, N. A., Pannells, T. C., & Willis, D. M. (2013). Identifying nonacademic behaviors associated with post-school employment and education. *Career Development and Transition for Exceptional Individuals, 36*(3), 174-187.

Moriña, A. (2017). Inclusive education in higher education: Challenges and opportunities. *European Journal of Special Needs Education, 32*, 3-17.

National Council on Disability. (2000). *Transition and post-school outcomes for youth with disabilities: Closing the gaps to post-secondary education and employment.* Washington, DC: National Council on Disability. Retrieved from ERIC database. (ED450519)

National Secondary Transition Technical Assistance Center. (2012). *NSTTAC indicator 13 checklist form A.* Retrieved from https://www.transitionta.org/sites/default/files/transitionplanning/NSTTAC_Check listFormA.pdf

Newman, L. A., & Madaus, J. W. (2015). Reposted accommodations and supports provided to secondary and postsecondary students with disabilities: National perspective. *Career Development and Transition for Exceptional Individuals, 38*, 173-181.

Newman, L., Wagner, M., Cameto, R., Knokey, A. M., & Shaver, D. (2010). *Comparisons across time of the outcomes of youth with disabilities up to 4 years after high school: A report of findings from the National Longitudinal Transi-*

tion Study (NLTS) *and the National Longitudinal Transition Study-2* (NLTS-2) (NCSER 2010-3008). Menlo Park, CA: SRI International.

Newman, L., Wagner, M., Knokey, A. M., Marder, C., Nagle, K., Shaver, D., & Wei, X. (2011). *The post-high school outcomes of young adults with disabilities up to 8 years after high school: A report from the National Longitudinal Transition Study-2.* (NCSER 2011-3005). Washington, DC: National Center for Special Education Research.

Noonan, P. M., Erickson, A. G., & Morningstar, M. E. (2013). Effects of community transition teams on interagency collaboration for school and adult agency staff. *Career Development and Transition for Exceptional Individuals, 36*, 96-104.

Office for Civil Rights. (2011). *Students with disabilities preparing for postsecondary education: Know your rights and responsibilities.* Retrieved from https://www2.ed.gov/about/offices/list/ocr/transition.html

Oswald, G. R., Huber, M. J., & Bonza, A. (2015). Practice brief: Effective job-seeking preparation and employment services for college students with disabilities. *Journal of Postsecondary Education and Disability, 28*, 375-382.

Papay, C., Unger, D., Williams-Diehm, K., & Mitchell, V. (2015). Begin with the end in mind: Infusing transition planning and instruction into elementary classrooms. *Teaching Exceptional Children, 47, 310-318.*

Petcu, S. D., Chezan, L. C., & Van Horn, M. L. (2015). Employment support services for students with intellectual and developmental disabilities attending postsecondary education programs. *Journal of Postsecondary Education and Disability, 28*, 359-374.

Petcu, S. D., Van Horn, M. L., & Shogren, K. A. (2017). Self-determination and the enrollment in and completion of postsecondary education for students with disabilities. *Career Development and Transition for Exceptional Individuals, 40*, 225-234.

Prince, A. M. T., Plotner, A. J., & Yell, M. L. (2014). Postsecondary transition and the courts: An update. *Journal of Disability Policy Studies, 25,* 41-47.

Raue, K., & Lewis, L. (2011). *Students with disabilities at degree-granting postsecondary institutions* (NCES 2011-018). Retrieved from https://nces.ed.gov/pubs2011/2011018.pdf

Redpath, J., Kearney, P., Nicholl, P., Mulvenna, M., Wallace, J., & Martin, S. (2013). A qualitative study of the lived experiences of disabled post-transition students in higher education institutions in Northern Ireland. *Studies in Higher Education, 38*, 1334-1350.

Roberts, K. D. (2010). Topic areas to consider when planning transition from high school to postsecondary education for students with autism spectrum disorders. *Focus on Autism and Other Developmental Disabilities, 25*, 158-162.

Rojewski, J. W., Lee, I. H., & Gregg, N. (2015). Causal effects of inclusion on postsecondary education outcomes of individuals with high-incidence disabilities. *Journal of Disability Policy Studies, 25*, 210-210.

Rose, D. H., Harbour, W. S., Johnston, C. S., Daley, S. G., & Abarbanell, L. (2006). Universal design for learning in postsecondary education: reflections on principles and their application. *Journal of Postsecondary Education and Disability, 19*, 135-151.

Rosenbaum, J. E. (2018). Disabilities and degrees: Identifying health impairments that predict lower chances of college enrollment and graduation in a nationally representative sample. *Community College Review, 46*, 145-175.

Rowe, D. A., Alverson, C. Y., Unruh, D. K., Fowler, C. H., Kellems, R., & Test, D. W. (2014). A delphi study to operationalize evidence-based predictors in secondary transition. *Career Development and Transition for Exceptional Individuals, 38,* 113-126.

Scheef, A. R., Walker, Z. M., & Barrio, B. L. (2019). Salient employability skills for youth with intellectual and developmental disabilities in Singapore: The perspectives of job developers. *International Journal of Developmental Disabilities, 65*, 1-9.

Schneider, B., Broda, M., Judy, J., & Burkander, K. (2014). Pathways to college and

STEM careers: Enhancing the high school experience. *New Directions in Youth Development, 140*, 9-29.

Shaw, S. F. (2009). Transition to postsecondary education. *Focus on Exceptional Children, 42*, 1-16.

Shaw, S. F., & Dukes III, L. L. (2013). Transition to postsecondary education: A call for evidence-based practice. *Career Development and Transition for Exceptional Individuals, 36*, 51-57.

Shepler, D. K., & Woosley, S. A. (2012). Understanding the early integration experiences of college students with disabilities. *Journal of Postsecondary Education and Disability, 25*, 37-50.

Shogren, K. A., Burke, K. M., Anderson, M. H., Antosh, A. A., Wehmeyer, M. L., LaPlante, T., & Shaw, L. A. (2018). Evaluating the differential impact of interventions to promote self-determination and goal attainment for transition-age youth with intellectual disability. *Research and Practice for Persons with Severe Disabilities, 43*, 165-180.

Shogren, K. A., Villarreal, M. G., Dowsett, C., & Little, T. D. (2016). Exploring student, family, and school predictors of self-determination using NLTS2 data. *Career Development and Transition for Exceptional Individuals, 39*, 23-33.

Shogren, K. A., Wehmeyer, M. L., & Lane, K. L. (2016). Embedding interventions to promote self-determination within multitiered systems of supports. *Exceptionality, 24*, 213-224.

Sniatecki, J. L., Perry, H. B., & Snell, L. H. (2015). Faculty attitudes and knowledge regarding college students with disabilities. *Journal of Postsecondary Education & Disability, 28*, 259-275.

Snyder, T. D., & Dillow, S. A. (2010). *Digest of education statistics, 2009 (NCES 2010-013) (Table 231)*. Washington, DC: National Center for Education Statistics, Institute of Education Sciences, U.S. Department of Education.

Snyder, T. D., Brey, C. D., & Dillow, S. A. (2016). *Digest of education statistics, 2015 (NCES 2016-2014)*. Retrieved from https://nces.ed.gov/fastfacts/display.

asp?id=60

Squires, M. E., Burnell, B. A., McCarty, C., & Schnackenberg, H. (2018). Emerging adults: Perspectives of college students with disabilities. *Journal of Postsecondary Education and Disability, 31*, 121-134.

Stumbo, N. J., Hedrick, B. N., Weisman, C., & Martin, J. K. (2010/2011). An exploration into the barriers and facilitators experienced by university graduates with disabilities requiring personal assistance services. *Journal of Science Education for Students with Disabilities, 14*, 1-24.

Test, D. W., Mazzotti, V. L., Mustian, A. L., Fowler, C. H., Kortering, L., & Kohler, P. (2009). Evidence-based secondary transition predictors for improving postschool outcomes for students with disabilities. *Career Development for Exceptional Individuals, 32*, 160-181.

Texas Tech University. (2019). *CASE-connections for academic success and employment.* Retrieved from http://www.depts.ttu.edu/burkhartcenter/case/

Toldrá, R. C., & Santos, M. C. (2013). People with disabilities in the labor market: Facilitators and barriers. *Work, 45*, 553-563.

U.S. Bureau of Labor Statistics. (2014). *Employment projections.* Retrieved from http://www.bls.gov/emp/ep_chart_001.htm

U.S. Bureau of Labor Statistics. (2015). *Employment projections: 2014-24.* Retrieved from http://www.bls.gov/news.release/pdf/ecopro.pdf

Wehmeyer, M. L. (1999). A functional model of self-determination: Describing development and implementing instruction. *Focus on Autism and other Developmental Disabilities, 14*, 53-61.

Wehmeyer, M. L. (2006). Self-determination and individuals with severe disabilities: Re-examining meanings and misinterpretations. *Research and Practice for Persons with Severe Disabilities, 30*, 113-120.

Wehmeyer, M. L., & Little, T. D. (2009). Self-determination. In S. Lopez (Ed.), *The encyclopedia of positive psychology* (Vol. 2) (pp. 868-874). Boston, MA: Blackwell.

Wehmeyer, M. L., Palmer, S. B., Lee, Y., Williams-Diehm, K., & Shogren, K. A. (2011). A randomized-trial evaluation of the effect of whose future is it anyway? on self-determination. *Career Development for Exceptional Individuals, 34*, 45-56.

Wessel, R. D., Jones, J. A., Markle, L., & Westfall, C. (2009). Retention and graduation of students with disabilities: Facilitating student success. *Journal of Postsecondary Education and Disability, 21*, 116-125.

West, E. A., Novak, D., & Mueller, C. (2016). Inclusive instructional practices used and their perceived importance by instructors. *Journal of Postsecondary Education and Disability, 29*, 363-374.

Wood, W. M., Karvonen, M., Test, D. W., Browder, D., & Algozzine, B. (2004). Promoting student self-determination skills in IEP planning. *Teaching Exceptional Children, 36*, 8-16.

World Health Organization. (2004). *International statistical classification of diseases and related health problems* (10th revision ed.). Geneva, Switzerland: Author.

Yamamoto, K. K., Stodden, R. A., & Folk, E. D. R. (2014). Inclusive postsecondary education: Reimagining the transition trajectories of vocational rehabilitation clients with intellectual disabilities. *Journal of Vocational Rehabilitation, 40*, 59-71.

Zalewska, A., Migliore, A., & Butterworth, J. (2016). Self-determination, social skills, job search, and transportation: Is there a relationship with employment of young adults with autism? *Journal of Vocational Rehabilitation, 45*, 225-239. doi:10.3233/JVR-160825

Zeng, W., Ju, S., & Hord, C. (2018). A literature review of academic interventions for college students with learning disabilities. *Learning Disability Quarterly, 41*, 159-169.

Zhang, D., Grenwelge, C., & Petcu, S. (2018). Preparing individuals with disabilities for inclusive employment through the postsecondary access and training in human services (PATHS) program: Inclusive employment. *Inclusion, 6*, 224-233.

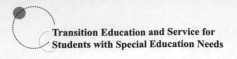

第五章 臺灣身心障礙學生轉銜至大專校院之實證分析

The Evidence-Based Analysis of Transition to Higher Education for Students with Disabilities in Taiwan

趙本強（Pen-Chiang Chao）、周宇琪（Yu-Chi Chou）、
鄭淑芬（Shu-Fen Cheng）

壹、緒論

我國特殊教育之實施含括學前教育、國民教育、高級中等教育、高等教育與成人教育等四個階段。根據《特殊教育法》第 31 條的規定：「為使各教育階段身心障礙學生服務需求得以銜接，各級學校應提供整體性與持續性轉銜輔導及服務……」（教育部，2019）。故由此可推知，學生自前一學習階段進入次一階段的歷程均可廣泛被視為是「轉銜」。就概念而言，轉銜兩字雖是國內特殊教育界慣用的名詞（如轉銜會議、生涯轉銜、轉銜輔導與服務等），但此名詞卻未被正式收錄於國語字（辭）典中，顯見其並非一般大眾常用的名詞。若根據分析哲學（analytic philosophy）的論述，當人們未能深究語言或文字深層的邏輯結構及意涵時，則往往容易被其表面意思誤導（Schwartz, 2012）。同理，若無法明瞭轉銜兩字的實質內涵，亦極有可能造成大眾對其誤解，故實有必要為轉銜做明確定義。根據《牛津英語詞典》（*Oxford English Dictionary*），「transition」被定義為「the process or a period of changing from one state or condition to another」，意謂從某種狀態或情況轉變至另一種狀態或情況的過程或期間。此番註解與國內《特殊教育法》的觀點頗為相符。但將轉銜置於實際教學場域探討時，則其並不僅單純侷限於身心障礙學生教育階段的轉換，更係指他們在

跨階段間的調整與適應（Connor, 2012; White et al., 2017）。特別是當這群學子從高中畢業後，轉換至高等教育機構或競爭性職場時所經歷之生活的改變、調適及經驗的習得與積累等更是典型的轉銜實例（Hendricks & Wehman, 2009; Wehman & Thoma, 2006）。綜言之，轉銜並非是一靜態的轉折點，而更屬動態的連續面，猶如由諸多轉銜服務的「點」構成的「面」。而由於「面」本身不具方向性，亦難以界定始點與終點，故頗能呼應前述《特殊教育法》第 31 條所言，學校提供的轉銜輔導與服務必須同時兼具整體性及連續性的特質。的確，誠如學界所倡導的無接縫轉銜（seamless transition）概念，主張從身心障礙學生在學期間即應提供其全方位的「轉銜服務」，以確保學生高中畢業後能順利銜接至大專校院求學或投入職場就業；而之後持續對學生在該新環境中所需的學習及生活適應給予協助，同樣亦是轉銜的一環（Certo, Luecking, Courey, Brown, Murphy, & Mautz, 2008; Certo et al., 2003; Luecking & Luecking, 2015; Test, 2009）。若以譬喻的方式來說明轉銜輔導與服務，則約莫可用大隊接力來比擬。即教師與專業人員組成選手群，身心障礙學生則像接力棒，在競賽過程中，選手奮力向前衝刺如同教師與專業人員戮力提供最佳的支援與服務，一棒接一棒則象徵著學生成長的歷程，從兒童至成年、從學校進入職場、從學生轉變為社會人士，不論處在哪個階段，均能獲得學校與社政單位的無接縫支援與服務。

至於轉銜輔導與服務的具體內容為何，《特殊教育法施行細則》（教育部，2013a）第 9 條第 5 款提及，該項輔導與服務的內容包括升學輔導、生活、就業、心理輔導、福利服務及其他相關專業服務等項目。另外，根據《特殊教育法》第 31 條而訂定的《各教育階段身心障礙學生轉銜輔導及服務辦法》（教育部，2000），則更具體闡明相關具體做法，包括應根據學生能力與需求訂定生涯轉銜計畫，且須將其納入個別化教育計畫（IEP）或特殊教育方案（適用大專以上學生）之中，以使學生能達成獨立生活、社會適應與參與、升學或就業等目標。此外，應針對就讀高級中等學校職業類科或特殊教育學校高職部學生，於其就讀高一、高二及高三時分別提供職能評估、職業教育／就業技能養成／職場實習，以及職業輔導評量等

服務。而對那些未繼續升學者則須提供其福利服務、職業重建，以及醫療或復健等服務，且原就讀學校應追蹤輔導 6 個月。若與轉銜教育執行成效頗佳的美國相較，則臺美雙方有多處共通點，例如：美國的《身心障礙者教育法》（IDEA, 2006）同樣亦規定，將學生的轉銜服務內容詳載於 IEP 中。而就內容而言，《身心障礙者教育法》（IDEA）則具體闡明轉銜服務乃一系列經妥善規劃之活動組成，其特色有三，包括：(1)轉銜活動強調成果導向的概念，藉由提升身心障礙學生在學業及生活能力的表現，以使其高中畢業後更能具備接受大專教育、技職教育、就業服務（包括支持性就業）、繼續及成人教育、成人生活服務、獨立生活或社區參與等能力；(2)活動的規劃與設計必須考量學生的需求、優勢、喜好及興趣等因素；(3)轉銜活動可藉由不同的形式呈現，例如：教學、專業服務、社區經驗、職涯發展，或其他與成人相關的生活服務等。而若有必要，基本生活技能訓練及功能性職業評估等亦屬轉銜活動的範疇。故由此可知，臺美雙方的轉銜服務實均強調升學與就業的輔導，以及伴隨學生蛻變為成年必須學習的獨立自主及社會參與能力。特別是《身心障礙者教育法》明訂，應針對 16 歲（即十一年級）以上學生擬定適切且可評量的畢業目標，該目標的訂定需參酌學生在教育、職業、生活技能等方面的轉銜評估結果，而目標的達成則有賴轉銜服務的協助。而若能讓學生直接參與此目標的訂定與執行，則更有助於其轉銜的成功（Konrad & Test, 2004; Test & Grossi, 2011）。

　　整體而言，高中階段身心障礙學生轉銜的目標主要可區分為升學與就業兩大類。但由於近年相關教育制度的改革，例如：國民教育權的觀念已由義務說轉為兼具義務與權利說的全球趨勢（教育部，2017a），故我國自 2014 年 8 月 1 日起開始實施十二年國民基本教育，冀望藉此推動國家整體教育之革新並提升國民素質。若身心障礙學生就讀高中的機會增加，則相對其未來繼續就讀大專校院的機率亦隨之增長。此外，除考試入學、個人申請入學及繁星推薦入學等一般管道外，「身心障礙學生升學大專校院甄試」及「大專校院辦理單獨招收身心障礙學生」兩者也提供身障生相對容易及適性的升學管道。其他有利身障生就讀大專的因素，包括：政府開放大專校院設立、大專階段的特教服務日益受重視，以及傳統升學／文憑主

義之觀念等。上述因素均直接或間接促使愈來愈多的身心障礙學生高中畢業後選擇繼續升學大專校院。根據王天苗（2014）的調查，我國 100 學年度高中身心障礙畢業生繼續升學大專校院的比例為 48.7%，此數據幾乎是美國 2005 年時高中身障生升大專比例（25%）（Wagner, Newman, Cameto, Garza, & Levine, 2005）的兩倍。雖然兩者的調查時間有約六年的落差，但不容否認地，我國身心障礙學生接受高等教育的情形已日趨普及。有鑑於如此的發展趨勢，大專身心障礙學生在學校的學習及生活適應狀況實值得吾人關注。國外研究指出，由於這群學子在生理與心理功能或能力之弱勢，故他們的學習適應情形通常不若其普通生同儕好（Stodden, 2005; Wagner et al., 2005）。國內的研究結果亦印證此論述，例如：視覺障礙、聽覺障礙及腦性麻痺三類大專校院身障生的學習適應情形並不理想，多數學生無法跟上教師授課進度且亦通常難以完成指定作業（許天威、蕭金土、吳訓生、林和姻、陳亭予，2002）。另外，陳麗如（2008）的研究亦發現，這群大專身心障礙學子面臨包括學習、心理、生理及生活等多樣性的生活困擾，其中以學習困擾的程度最大。不同背景變項身障生間的困擾程度亦有差異，包括男生較女生有更高度的學習與閱讀困擾；而三年級身障生則較一、二年級學生有更顯著的課堂限制困擾及生涯困擾。另感官障礙學生較肢體障礙學生有更高度的課堂限制、學習困擾、閱讀困擾及生活困擾等。上述大專校院身心障礙學生的學習適應不佳及各種困擾，或可解釋何以我國大專校院各類障別學生的平均休退學率約為 9.09%（林坤燦、羅清水、邱瀞瑩，2008）。為了更全面地了解我國高中階段身心障礙學生轉銜至大專校院的情形，包括其升學人數、升學管道、就讀學校型態、就讀科系或學門，以及學習與生活適應情形等，本章以《特殊教育統計年報》及「特殊教育長期追蹤資料庫」（Special Needs Education Longitudinal Study, SNELS）兩者的資料進行縱貫性與橫斷性分析，藉此檢視轉銜理論與實務間的差距。分析結果將可作為高中與大專教師、家長及相關專業人員提供身心障礙學生轉銜輔導與服務的參考依據。

▶貳、身心障礙學生就讀大專校院人數情形

根據 2009～2018 年《特殊教育統計年報》的資料（教育部，2009，2010，2011，2012，2013b，2014，2015，2016，2017c，2018）（如表 5-1 所示），自 2009 年起，身心障礙學生高中（職）畢業後就讀大專校院的總人數呈逐年增加趨勢，2009 年就學人數為 9,489 人，至 2018 年則增為 13,189 人，十年間的人數成長幅度達 39%。而該期間全國大專校院學生總人數（不含碩博士生）乃出現先成長（2009～2012 年）後衰退（2012～2018 年）的現象。但不受總人數逐年（近七年）遞減的影響，身障生在全國大專生的比例仍由 0.85% 成長至 1.26%。

就不同障別學生的就學情形而言，則各有不同的變化趨勢（如圖 5-1 所示）。若以 2009 及 2018 兩年作為比較的基準，資料顯示共有六種障別學生就讀大專的人數呈正成長趨勢，增加幅度由高至低依序為自閉症（758%）、智能障礙（361%）、學習障礙（310%）、情緒行為障礙（106%）、視覺障礙（5%）；另外，腦性麻痺為 2013 年新增障別，其在該年度及 2018 年的資料同樣亦呈正成長趨勢（178%）。反之，其餘障別學生的人數則呈遞減趨勢。減幅由高至低依序為其他障礙（-87%）、肢體障礙（-56%）、語言障礙（-34%）、多重障礙（-31%）、身體病弱（-12%）、聽覺障礙（-3%）。

整體而言，綜觀十年期間，數個障別學生人數的消長情形極為明顯，此也影響其在全體身障生中占的比例。具體言之，肢體障礙學生在 2009～2014 年間的人數均居各障別之冠，故所占比例亦皆為最高（最高峰時將近四成），至 2015～2016 年所占比例降至兩成以下，落居第二，2017～2018 年則更進一步排序第三。相反地，學習障礙學生人數因持續攀高，故其所占比例由最初的第四位，於 2010～2014 年間提升至第二位，2015 年起則連年皆是比例最高者。另外，自閉症學生人數亦是連年成長，故所占比例從排序倒數第二轉變為各障別中次高者，實是各障別中變化幅度最大者。此外，智能障礙學生人數的變化與前兩者相似，故所占比例連

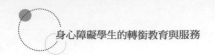

表 5-1 2009～2018 年身心障礙學生就讀大專校院人數及百分比統計

變項 （障別/ N/%）	年度									
	2009	2010	2011	2012	2013	2014	2015	2016	2017	2018
智能 障礙	268 （2.8）	375 （3.7）	483 （4.5）	610 （5.3）	739 （6.0）	855 （7.0）	923 （7.5）	1,065 （8.4）	1,159 （8.9）	1,235 （9.4）
視覺 障礙	661 （7.0）	696 （6.8）	666 （6.1）	675 （5.9）	668 （5.4）	723 （5.9）	793 （6.4）	809 （6.4）	738 （5.6）	692 （5.3）
聽覺 障礙	1,173 （12.4）	1,209 （11.8）	1,247 （11.5）	1,217 （10.6）	1,233 （10.0）	1,235 （10.1）	1,214 （9.8）	1,237 （9.8）	1,196 （9.1）	1,144 （8.7）
語言 障礙	149 （1.6）	172 （1.7）	167 （1.5）	171 （1.5）	177 （1.4）	162 （1.3）	146 （1.2）	140 （1.1）	119 （0.9）	98 （0.7）
肢體 障礙	3,420 （36.0）	3,403 （33.1）	3,284 （30.3）	3,014 （26.2）	2,826 （23.0）	2,562 （21.0）	2,256 （18.2）	2,023 （16.0）	1,798 （13.7）	1,514 （11.5）
腦性 麻痺	-	-	-	-	154 （1.3）	185 （1.5）	253 （2.0）	332 （2.6）	345 （2.6）	428 （3.3）
身體 病弱	917 （9.7）	992 （9.7）	1,059 （9.8）	1,247 （10.8）	1,320 （10.7）	1,344 （11.0）	1,174 （9.5）	1,019 （8.0）	939 （7.2）	808 （6.1）
情緒行 為障礙	593 （6.3）	631 （6.1）	670 （6.2）	705 （6.1）	759 （6.2）	851 （7.0）	953 （7.7）	999 （7.9）	1,106 （8.5）	1,224 （9.3）
學習 障礙	854 （9.0）	1,117 （10.9）	1,458 （13.4）	1,891 （16.4）	2,272 （18.5）	2,287 （18.8）	2,576 （20.8）	2,853 （22.5）	3,276 （25.0）	3,503 （26.6）
多重 障礙	422 （4.5）	456 （4.4）	438 （4.0）	424 （3.7）	398 （3.2）	384 （3.2）	367 （3.0）	358 （2.8）	346 （2.6）	291 （2.2）
自閉症	250 （2.6）	321 （3.1）	459 （4.2）	596 （5.2）	769 （6.3）	1,055 （8.7）	1,292 （10.4）	1,614 （12.7）	1,881 （14.4）	2,146 （16.3）
其他 障礙	782 （8.2）	902 （8.8）	922 （8.5）	971 （8.4）	973 （7.9）	547 （4.5）	429 （3.5）	229 （1.8）	180 （1.4）	106 （0.8）
身障生 合計	9,489	10,274	10,853	11,521	12,288	12,190	12,376	12,678	13,083	13,189
全國大 專生	1,119,507	1,124,425	1,134,285	1,139,465	1,137,193	1,136,332	1,132,684	1,111,082	1,076,765	1,048,563
身障生 占全國 大專生 百分比	0.85	0.91	0.96	1.01	1.08	1.07	1.09	1.14	1.22	1.26

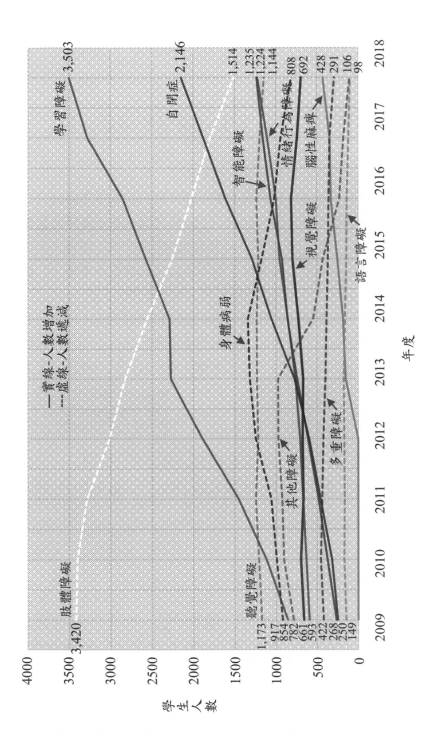

圖 5-1　2009～2018 年身心障礙學生就讀大專校院人數變化趨勢

年增加,至 2018 年時已成排序第三高者。另值得注意的是,由於其他障礙學生的人數持續減少,故其所占比例大幅遞減至不到 1%。其餘障別之人數比例變化幅度則相對較小。

參、大專校院身心障礙學生就讀學校型態分析

本章分別從學校屬性(公立或私立)及類型(一般大學或技專校院)兩層面進行分析。就屬性而言,在過去十年期間,身心障礙學生就讀公立大專校院的人數占全體身障生比例均介於二至三成之間,且呈逐年遞減趨勢(除 2012～2013 年外),十年期間人數比例減幅約為 7%(如表 5-2 所示)。相反地,身障生就讀私立大專校院的人數則呈連續成長趨勢(同樣除 2012～2013 年外),其人數比例由最初的 72%增加至 79%,此 7%的成長幅度即為就讀公立學校人數減少的比例。若參酌同期全國所有大專生的就學情形來看,則其就讀公私立學校的人數比例與身障生差異不大,但呈現的趨勢則略有不同。在 2009～2018 年間,全國大專生就讀公立學校的人數比例呈小幅成長趨勢(約 3%),就讀私立大專的人數比例則小幅衰退 3%。身心障礙大專生與全國大專生就讀公私立學校詳細人數分布情形,如表 5-2 所示。

表5-2　身心障礙大專生及全國大專生就讀公私立學校之人數及百分比統計

學生	學校屬性	年度									
		2009	2010	2011	2012	2013	2014	2015	2016	2017	2018
身障大專學生	公立	2,657 (28.0)	2,733 (26.6)	2,662 (24.5)	2,470 (21.4)	2,680 (21.8)	2,647 (21.7)	2,.671 (21.6)	2,733 (21.6)	2,789 (21.3)	2,808 (21.3)
	私立	6,832 (72.0)	7,541 (73.4)	8.191 (75.5)	9,051 (78.6)	9,608 (78.2)	9,543 (78.3)	9,705 (78.4)	9,945 (78.4)	10,294 (78.7)	10,381 (78.7)
	合計	9,489 (100.0)	10,274 (100.0)	10,853 (100.0)	11,521 (100.0)	12,288 (100.0)	12,190 (100.0)	12,376 (100.0)	12,678 (100.0)	13,083 (100.0)	13,189 (100.0)
全國大專學生	公立	284,121 (25.4)	288,021 (25.6)	289,749 (25.5)	291,125 (25.5)	292,743 (25.7)	295,068 (26.0)	297,756 (26.3)	299,671 (27.0)	300,094 (27.9)	299,004 (28.5)
	私立	835,386 (74.6)	836,404 (74.4)	844,536 (74.5)	848,340 (74.5)	844,450 (74.3)	841,264 (74.0)	834,928 (73.7)	811,411 (73.0)	776,671 (72.1)	749,559 (71.5)
	合計	1,119,507 (100.0)	1,124,425 (100.0)	1,134,285 (100.0)	1,139,465 (100.0)	1,137,193 (100.0)	1,136,332 (100.0)	1,132,684 (100.0)	1,111,082 (100.0)	1,076,765 (100.0)	1,048,563 (100.0)

　　進一步針對大專身障生就讀學校之類型進行分析時則發現，公立與私立學校兩者有頗大的差異（如表 5-3 所示）。具體言之，在就讀公立大專校院的身障生中，其就讀一般大學與技專校院的人數比例約為 7：3。相反地，若就在私立大專就讀的身障生而言，其就讀一般大學與技專校院的比例則約為 3：7。綜言之，就人數多寡而言，在過去十年期間，就讀私立技專校院的身障生人數皆為最高者，就讀私立一般大學的人數則居次，之後則分別是就讀公立一般大學者及公立技專校院者。圖 5-2 呈現此就讀此四類學校身障生人數的變化趨勢。

表 5-3　身心障礙學生就讀公私立大專校院中不同類型學校之人數及百分比統計

學校屬性	類型	年度									
		2009	2010	2011	2012	2013	2014	2015	2016	2017	2018
公立	一般大學	1,839 (69.2)	2,094 (76.6)	2,017 (75.8)	1,780 (72.1)	1,925 (71.8)	1,919 (72.5)	1,938 (72.6)	1,987 (72.7)	2,056 (73.7)	2,055 (73.2)
	技專校院	818 (30.8)	639 (23.4)	645 (24.2)	690 (27.9)	755 (28.2)	728 (27.5)	733 (27.4)	746 (27.3)	733 (26.3)	753 (26.8)
	合計	2,657 (100.0)	2,733 (100.0)	2,662 (100.0)	2,470 (100.0)	2,680 (100.0)	2,647 (100.0)	2,671 (100.0)	2,733 (100.0)	2,789 (100.0)	2,808 (100.0)
私立	一般大學	2,090 (30.6)	2,317 (30.7)	2,486 (30.4)	2,688 (29.7)	2,750 (28.6)	2,715 (28.5)	2,690 (27.7)	2,776 (27.9)	2,873 (27.9)	2,834 (27.3)
	技專校院	4,742 (69.4)	5,224 (69.3)	5,705 (69.6)	6,363 (70.3)	6,858 (71.4)	6,828 (71.5)	7,015 (72.3)	7,169 (72.1)	7,421 (72.1)	7,547 (72.7)
	合計	6,832 (100.0)	7,541 (100.0)	8,191 (100.0)	9,051 (100.0)	9,608 (100.0)	9,543 (100.0)	9,705 (100.0)	9,945 (100.0)	10,294 (100.0)	10,381 (100.0)

註：技專校院含技術學院及科技大學。

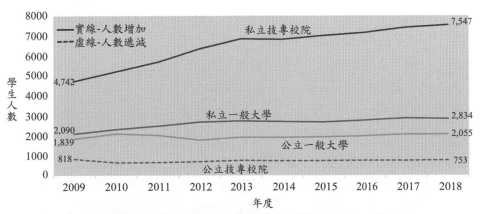

圖 5-2　大專校院身心障礙學生就讀不同學校類型人數變化趨勢　　167

肆、大專校院身心障礙學生就讀學門概況分析

根據《中華民國學科標準分類》（第五次修正版）（教育部，2017b），大專校院學科、系、所或學位學程可歸類為 27 個學門（如表 5-4 所示）。考量此版之分類係採用新的分類原則、架構及用詞等，故本章僅分析大專身心障礙學生近三年（2016～2018 年）的資料。此外，亦同時呈現該期間全國大專生的資料，以比較兩群體學生在專業學習領域的選擇是否有差異。首先，就身心障礙學生而言，表 5-4 中的資料顯示，該群學子在近三年就讀各學門的人數比例並無明顯變化。各年度皆以就讀「餐旅及民生服務」學門的人數比例最高（約 20%）。另「商業及管理」及「工程及工程業」是排序第二或第三的熱門學門，每年皆約12～14%的學生就讀。然選擇「商業及管理」學門的人數比例呈逐年降低趨勢，選讀「工程及工程業」學門的人數比例則連續微幅成長。基本上，就讀上述三個學門的人數幾近占各年度全體身障生的半數。此外，「人文」及「語文」兩學門亦有相對較多的學生選擇，每年約 7～9%的學生就讀，人數比例排序第四或第五高。修讀「資訊通訊科技」學門的人數比例原本頗高，但因連續二年選讀人數減少，故落居前五熱門學門之外。另值得注意的是，大專身障生每年約有 5%的學生選讀「醫藥衛生」及「社會福利」兩學門。其他學門的就讀人數比例則皆在 5%以下，其中「製造及加工」、「林業」、「漁業」及「衛生及職業衛生服務」等四個學門則無任何身障生就讀。

就全國所有大專生而言，在分析的三個年度中，就讀人數比例前五高的學門類別不但相同且排序亦未變，包括「商業及管理」（約17%）、「工程及工程業」（約15%）、「餐旅及民生服務」（約13%）、「醫藥衛生」（約10%）及「藝術」（約 9%）等五個學門。此外，「語文」及「資訊通訊科技」兩學門亦分別有約8%及7%的學生選讀。其他學門的就讀人數比例則皆在 3%以下。比較身心障礙大專生與全國大專生在各學門就讀人數比例可知，差異較大之處包括，每年身障生在「人文」及「餐旅及民生服務」學門的就讀人數比例均約高於全國大專生 7%，在「農業」及「社會福利」

表 5-4　2016～2018 年大專身心障礙學生與全國大專生各學門就讀人數及百分比統計

學門	2016		2017		2018	
	身障大專生	全國大專生	身障大專生	全國大專生	身障大專生	全國大專生
教育	307 (2.4)	19,926 (1.8)	323 (2.5)	20,132 (1.9)	312 (2.4)	19,813 (1.9)
藝術	323 (2.5)	94,588 (8.5)[5]	346 (2.6)	93,201 (8.7)[5]	379 (2.9)	92,717 (8.8)[5]
人文	1,093 (8.6)[5]	11,453 (1.0)	1,104 (8.4)[4]	11,217 (1.0)	1,160 (8.8)[4]	10,488 (1.0)
語文	999 (7.9)	84,500 (7.6)	1,091 (8.3)[5]	81,821 (7.6)	1,094 (8.3)[5]	79,075 (7.5)
社會及行為科學	498 (3.9)	28,734 (2.6)	478 (3.7)	28,137 (2.6)	441 (3.3)	28,656 (2.7)
新聞學及圖書資訊	184 (1.5)	17,524 (1.6)	191 (1.5)	17,019 (1.6)	172 (1.3)	15,630 (1.5)
商業及管理	1,723 (13.6)[2]	195,370 (17.6)[1]	1,730 (13.2)[3]	186,028 (17.3)[1]	1,654 (12.5)[3]	177,311 (16.9)[1]
法律	158 (1.2)	13,766 (1.2)	146 (1.1)	13,585 (1.3)	136 (1.0)	13,455 (1.3)
生命科學	160 (1.3)	21,866 (2.0)	166 (1.3)	21,037 (2.0)	161 (1.2)	20,023 (1.9)
環境	38 (0.3)	2,516 (0.2)	32 (0.2)	2,344 (0.2)	26 (0.2)	1,858 (0.2)
物理、化學及地球科學	101 (0.8)	15,208 (1.4)	118 (0.9)	14,903 (1.4)	135 (1.0)	14,895 (1.4)
數學及統計	115 (0.9)	11,726 (1.1)	112 (0.9)	11,435 (1.1)	113 (0.9)	10,993 (1.0)
資訊通訊科技	1,095 (8.6)[4]	73,597 (6.6)	972 (7.4)	68,892 (6.4)	844 (6.4)	70,527 (6.7)
工程及工程業	1,606 (12.7)[3]	171,100 (15.4)[2]	1,737 (13.3)[2]	166,057 (15.4)[2]	1,880 (14.3)[2]	160,761 (15.3)[2]
製造及加工	0	8,669 (0.8)	0	8,456 (0.8)	0	8,435 (0.8)
建築及營建工程	99 (0.8)	26,929 (2.4)	90 (0.7)	25,536 (2.4)	92 (0.7)	24,996 (2.4)
農業	330 (2.6)	7,650 (0.7)	353 (2.7)	7,616 (0.7)	362 (2.7)	7,787 (0.7)

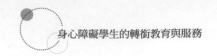

表 5-4　2016～2018 年大專身心障礙學生與全國大專生各學門就讀人數及百分比統計（續）

學門	2016		2017		2018	
	身障大專生	全國大專生	身障大專生	全國大專生	身障大專生	全國大專生
林業	0	2,037 (0.2)	0	2,030 (0.2)	0	1,976 (0.2)
漁業	0	2,001 (0.2)	0	1,958 (0.2)	0	2,158 (0.2)
獸醫	11 (0.1)	1,516 (0.1)	11 (0.1)	1,617 (0.2)	8 (0.1)	1,657 (0.2)
醫藥衛生	604 (4.8)	108,741 (9.8)[4]	667 (5.1)	109,676 (10.2)[4]	729 (5.5)	110,138 (10.5)[4]
社會福利	638 (5.0)	29,884 (2.7)	649 (5.0)	28,946 (2.7)	676 (5.1)	27,628 (2.6)
餐旅及民生服務	2,521 (19.9)[1]	149,726 (13.5)[3]	2,689 (20.6)[1]	142,692 (13.3)[3]	2,717 (20.6)[1]	135,269 (12.9)[3]
衛生及職業衛生服務	0	1,062 (0.1)	0	1,078 (0.1)	0	1,436 (0.1)
安全服務	5 (0.1)	1,010 (0.1)	6 (0.1)	1,542 (0.1)	13 (0.1)	1,275 (0.1)
運輸服務	35 (0.3)	8,950 (0.8)	44 (0.3)	8,796 (0.8)	56 (0.4)	8,453 (0.8)
其他	35 (0.3)	1,033 (0.1)	28 (0.2)	1,014 (0.1)	29 (0.2)	1,153 (0.1)
合計	12,678	1,111,082	13,083	1,076,765	13,189	1,048,563

註：上標數字代表該年度某學門就讀人數比例之排序。

學門則約高 2%。相反地，每年全國大專生則在「藝術」、「商業及管理」及「醫藥衛生」等三個學門的人數比例分別高於身障生約 6%、4%及 5%。兩群體學生在其他學門的人數比例差異則較不明顯。

▶ 伍、大專身心障礙學生升學管道分析

　　本章利用 SNELS 的資料分析身心障礙學生升學大專校院的管道。資料顯示（如表 5-5 所示），在使用加權值的模式下，參與研究之全體高中階段

表 5-5　各類身心障礙學生透過不同管道升學大專校院之人數及百分比統計

障礙類別	樣本人數	升學管道							
		申請入學	保送入學	考試分發	身心障礙學生升學大專校院甄試	學校單獨招生	繁星計畫	其他（產學合作、運動績優甄試）	不知道
智能障礙	25	3 (13.3)	0	5 (20.0)	7 (26.7)	5 (20.0)	0	5 (20.0)	0
視覺障礙	21	1 (6.0)	0 (2.0)	3 (14.0)	15 (70.0)	1 (6.0)	0	0 (2.0)	0
聽覺障礙	47	3 (5.7)	1 (1.9)	3 (7.6)	37 (78.1)	3 (6.7)	0	0	0
語言障礙	7	2 (28.6)	0	1 (14.3)	3 (42.9)	1 (14.3)	0	0	0
肢體障礙	79	15 (18.3)	2 (2.8)	12 (15.6)	43 (55.0)	7 (8.3)	0	0	0
身體病弱	59	11 (19.4)	0	8 (13.9)	28 (47.2)	11 (18.1)	0	0	1 (1.4)
情緒行為	43	7 (16.7)	2 (4.8)	5 (11.9)	15 (33.3)	12 (28.6)	0	2 (4.8)	0
學習障礙	270	27 (10.0)	0	39 (14.4)	150 (55.6)	42 (15.6)	0	6 (2.2)	6 (2.2)
多重障礙	6	0	0	1 (12.0)	3 (52.0)	1 (12.0)	0	1 (12.0)	0
自閉症	41	7 (17.9)	1 (1.9)	7 (17.9)	18 (42.5)	6 (15.1)	1 (1.9)	1 (2.8)	0
其他障礙	27	8 (29.6)	1 (3.7)	5 (18.5)	12 (44.4)	1 (3.7)	0	0	0
合計	624	84 (13.5)	7 (1.2)	90 (14.4)	329 (52.7)	90 (14.4)	1 (0.1)	15 (2.4)	7 (1.2)

註：表中數字係學生人數及其在某障別所占比例。學生人數為加權後數值，因採四捨五入計算原則，故可能出現細格人數的加總不等於樣本人數之情形。

身心障礙學生（$N = 624$）在其畢業該年（2012 年 7 月），有超過五成（52.7%）以上的學生係藉由「身心障礙學生升學大專校院甄試」進入大專校院就讀。另藉由「申請入學」、「考試分發」及「學校單獨招生」等三

種方式升學的學生人數亦各約占 14%。換言之，以此四種管道升學之高中階段身心障礙畢業生合計高達九成以上。除此之外，少數學生係藉由「保送入學」（1.2%）或「繁星計畫」（0.1%）管道升學。另亦有 2.4%的學生是透過其他管道（包括產學合作、運動績優甄試）進入大專校院就讀。在所有受訪學生中，有 1.2%的學生無法明確陳述其升學的管道。

進一步比較各不同障別學生的升學情形，可歸納出以下八個特點：(1)各障別學生皆以利用「身心障礙學生升學大專校院甄試」此管道升學者占最大宗；(2)智能障礙學生透過「身心障礙學生升學大專校院甄試」升學的比例與其他障別相較明顯偏低，其升學方式約略均分於考試分發、學校單獨招生或其他管道等；(3)視覺與聽覺障礙兩類學生分別有七成及約八成學生透過「身心障礙學生升學大專校院甄試」管道升學，其是這兩組學生最主要的升學途徑；(4)約三成的情緒行為障礙學生是透過「學校單獨招生」方式入學，居各障別之冠；(5)各障別中僅有 1 名自閉症學生能藉由「繁星計畫」管道升學；(6)多重障礙學生是唯一未能利用「申請入學」方式升學者；(7)各障別學生藉由「保送入學」方式升學的比例均低（少於 5%），且僅侷限於其中半數障別之學生；(8)有極少數身體病弱及學習障礙學生無法陳述其升學方式。

陸、大專身心障礙學生就讀之學校類型分析

有別於前述《特殊教育統計年報》呈現的資料，SNELS 的資料僅針對三種學校類型進行調查。資料顯示（如表 5-6 所示），我國高中階段身心障礙學生畢業後以就讀大學／技術學院者占絕對多數（96.5%），僅有極少數的學生係選擇進入二年制專科學校（3.2%）或空中大學（0.3%）就讀。針對就讀大學／技術學院之學生而言，其中 133 人就讀公立學校、469 人就讀私立學校，兩者比例接近 1：4。就讀公立與私立二專的人數比例則為 2：3。空中大學則皆屬公立學校。

進一步比較各不同障別學生就讀的學校類型可歸納出以下七項特點：(1)僅就大學／技術學院該類型學校而言，各障別皆為就讀私立學校的人數

表 5-6　各類身心障礙學生就讀不同學校類型之人數分布及百分比統計

| 障礙類別 | 樣本人數 | 大學／技術學院 | | 二年制專科學校 | | 空中大學 |
		公立	私立	公立	私立	公立
智能障礙	25	2（8.0）	21（84.0）	0	0	2（8.0）
視覺障礙	21	10（47.6）	11（52.4）	0	0	0
聽覺障礙	47	21（46.2）	25（53.8）	0	0	0
語言障礙	7	3（42.9）	4（57.1）	0	0	0
肢體障礙	79	22（27.8）	56（70.9）	1（1.3）	0	0
身體病弱	59	17（28.8）	41（69.5）	0	1（1.4）	0
情緒行為障礙	43	9（21.4）	29（69.0）	1（2.4）	3（7.1）	0
學習障礙	270	36（13.3）	222（82.2）	6（2.2）	6（2.2）	0
多重障礙	6	1（14.3）	5（71.4）	0	1（14.3）	0
自閉症	41	9（22.0）	31（75.6）	0	1（2.4）	0
其他障礙	27	4（14.8）	23（85.2）	0	0	0
合計	624	133（21.3）	469（75.2）	8（1.3）	12（1.9）	2（0.3）

註：表中數字係學生人數及其在某障別所占比例。學生人數為加權後數值，因採四捨五入計算原則，故可能出現細格人數的加總不等於樣本人數之情形。

比例較高；(2)智能障礙學生就讀公立大學／技術學院的人數比例最低（不到一成），有高達八成五的學生就讀私立學校；(3)視覺、聽覺及語言等三類感官／生理障礙學生的就學型態相似，即均沒有學生就讀二專或空中大學。另外，三者就讀公私立大學／技術學院的人數比例接近（約各占半數），尤其是視障與聽障兩者的數據非常接近；(4)肢體障礙及身體病弱兩者是另一個相似組，兩者皆有 1%的學生就讀二專，且就讀公私立大學／技術學院的人數比列均約為 3：7；(5)情緒行為障礙學生中有約 10%的學生選擇就讀二專，係各障別中次高者。另其就讀公私立大學／技術學院的人數比例則皆約為 2：7；(6)多重障礙學生就讀二專的人數比例居各障別之冠，約占一成五；(7)學習障礙、自閉症與其他障礙等三者皆以就讀私立大學／技術學院者占相對多數，介於七成五至八成五之間。

柒、大專校院身心障礙學生需要學校提供協助之情形

SNELS 針對大專校院身心障礙學生在就學期間需要學校協助情形進行調查。首先，就全體身障生而言，分析結果顯示（如表 5-7 所示），在調查的九個項目中，大專身障生需要工讀機會／獎助學金所占的人數比例最高，約六成的學生表達有此需求。其次，需求人數比例相對較高的項目尚包括課業協助、安排社交活動、電腦能力訓練、心理／生涯輔導等方面的協助；各項目的需求人數比例相當，均介於三至四成之間。另外，亦有28%的學生表達需要學校提供其生活協助。輔具設備、無障礙設施、醫療協助等三者則相對需求人數比例較低，僅約 11～16% 的學生有需求。

就各障礙類別學生而言，分析結果可歸納出以下九項特點：(1)各障別學生均以有工讀機會／獎助學金需求的人數比例占最高。其中視覺、聽覺及肢體障礙等三類學生的需求比例相對較高，視障生的需求比例甚至高達84%，居各障別之冠；(2)除語言障礙學生之外，其他障別學生均需要校方提供課業協助，特別是智能、視覺、聽覺及多重障礙等四類學生均有超過半數的學生需要協助。另自閉症學生亦有接近五成的學生表達有此需求；(3)有半數的視障學生表達有生活協助的需要，人數比例居各障別之冠。另有四成的聽障學生亦有此需求；(4)語言障礙學生除工讀機會／獎助學金的需求人數比例較高外，在其餘項目的需求均僅約一成左右。在課業協助、生活協助、安排社交活動及無障礙設施等四個項目甚至無人需要協助；(6)多重障礙與自閉症學生中均有超過半數需要學校提供其心理／生涯輔導；(7)有六成的智能障礙學生需要學校協助安排社交活動，人數比例居各障別首位。另視覺、聽覺與多重障礙及自閉症等四類學生亦有約五成的學生需要安排社交活動之協助；(8)有六成的視覺障礙學生需要輔具設備之協助，人數比例居各障別之冠。另多重障礙學生中有此需求者亦高達五成六；(9)肢體與多重障礙學生需要無障礙設施的人數比例相對最高，各約占三成。另後者亦有相同的人數比例需要學校提供其醫療協助。

表5-7　大專校院身心障礙學生需要學校提供之協助調查結果（人數及百分比）

障礙類別	樣本人數	項目								
		課業協助	生活協助	工讀機會／獎助學金	電腦能力訓練	心理／生涯輔導	安排社交活動	輔具設備	無障礙設施	醫療協助
智能障礙	25	13 (53.3)	8 (33.3)	15 (60.0)	12 (46.7)	12 (46.7)	15 (60.0)	5 (20.0)	5 (20.0)	7 (26.7)
視覺障礙	21	13 (64.0)	10 (50.0)	17 (84.0)	9 (44.0)	7 (36.0)	10 (50.0)	12 (60.0)	6 (28.0)	5 (26.0)
聽覺障礙	47	30 (63.8)	21 (43.8)	33 (71.4)	22 (46.7)	20 (41.9)	25 (52.4)	15 (32.4)	7 (15.2)	10 (21.0)
語言障礙	7	0	0	3 (42.9)	1 (14.3)	1 (14.3)	0	1 (14.3)	0	1 (14.3)
肢體障礙	79	31 (39.4)	26 (33.0)	55 (70.6)	30 (37.6)	30 (37.6)	30 (37.6)	20 (25.7)	27 (33.9)	12 (14.7)
身體病弱	59	17 (29.2)	16 (27.8)	36 (61.1)	14 (23.6)	18 (30.6)	17 (29.2)	6 (9.7)	5 (8.3)	12 (19.4)
情緒行為障礙	43	15 (35.7)	8 (19.0)	23 (54.8)	15 (35.7)	17 (40.5)	9 (21.4)	2 (4.8)	1 (2.4)	2 (4.8)
學習障礙	270	90 (33.3)	60 (22.2)	138 (51.1)	90 (33.3)	75 (27.8)	90 (33.3)	27 (10.0)	15 (5.6)	30 (11.1)
多重障礙	6	3 (56.0)	2 (36.0)	3 (56.0)	2 (36.0)	3 (56.0)	3 (56.0)	3 (56.0)	2 (36.0)	2 (36.0)
自閉症	41	20 (49.1)	12 (28.3)	27 (65.1)	17 (41.5)	22 (52.8)	22 (52.8)	4 (9.4)	3 (6.6)	5 (13.2)
其他障礙	27	3 (11.1)	8 (29.6)	18 (66.7)	6 (22.2)	4 (14.8)	6 (22.2)	1 (3.7)	1 (3.7)	4 (14.8)
合計	624	237 (37.9)	172 (27.5)	370 (59.3)	218 (34.9)	208 (33.4)	226 (36.3)	96 (15.5)	72 (11.5)	90 (14.4)

註：表中數字係學生人數及其在某障別所占比例。學生人數為加權後數值，因採四捨五入計算原則，故可能出現細格人數的加總不等於樣本人數之情形。

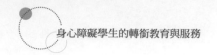

捌、大專校院資源教室教師提供身心障礙 學生協助之情形

　　除了調查大專身障生需要的協助外，SNELS 亦進一步檢視資源教室輔導教師提供這些協助的情形（如表 5-8 所示）。整體而言，根據身障生自身的感受，半數以上（53%）的學生認為輔導教師有提供其課業及安排社交活動兩種協助。排序在此兩者之後的是提供學生心理／生涯輔導、生活協助、工讀機會／獎助學金等協助，三者的人數比例約占四至五成之間。此外，有介於二至三成的學生認為教師有提供其輔具設備、無障礙設施、電腦能力訓練等協助；認為教師有提供醫療協助者的比例最低，僅占 18.6%。

　　跨障礙類別的分析結果呈現以下七項特點：(1)輔導教師提供視障與聽障學生課業協助的人數比例最高，介於七至八成之間。但智能與情緒行為障礙學生接受此協助的比例則僅約兩成多，為各障別中最低者；(2)教師提供視覺、聽覺、肢體及多重障礙等四類學生生活及工讀機會／獎助學金兩方面協助的人數比例相對最高，前項協助介於六至七成之間，後項協助則介於五至六成之間；(3)教師未提供語言障礙學生任何的電腦能力訓練、輔具設備及無障礙設施等三項協助；(4)情緒行為障礙學生不論在課業、生活、工讀機會／獎助學金、心理／生涯輔導、安排社交活動、醫療等項目上，獲得教師協助的比例皆為各障別中最低者；(5)身體病弱學生中有六成的人接受教師提供安排社交活動協助，比例相對是各項目中最高者；(6)學習障礙學生則以接受課業協助的人數比例相對最高（約五成三）；(7)教師提供自閉症學生的協助中，以安排社交活動及心理／生涯輔導的比例最高，有超過半數的學生均接受此協助；另亦有四成五的學生接受課業協助。

　　將表 5-7 與表 5-8 兩者的人數資料進行交叉比對後可知，大專身障生獲得協助的情形可歸納為三大類，包括學校／教師提供協助的人數少於有需求的人數、等於有需求的人數、高於有需求的人數，三者代表的意義分別

表5-8　大專校院資源教室教師提供身心障礙學生之協助調查結果（人數及百分比）

障礙類別	樣本人數	項目								
		課業協助	生活協助	工讀機會／獎助學金	電腦能力訓練	心理／生涯輔導	安排社交活動	輔具設備	無障礙設施	醫療協助
智能障礙	25	7 (26.7) △	7 (26.7) △	3 (13.3) △	7 (26.7) △	7 (26.7) △	7 (26.7) △	5 (20.0) ○	5 (20.0) ○	5 (20.0) △
視覺障礙	21	15 (72.0) ◎	14 (68.0) ◎	11 (54.0) △	8 (38.0) △	13 (62.0) ◎	16 (78.0) ◎	15 (74.0) ◎	11 (52.0) ◎	6 (28.0) ◎
聽覺障礙	47	37 (79.0) ◎	30 (63.8) ◎	28 (59.0) △	16 (34.3) △	28 (60.0) ◎	35 (75.2) ◎	27 (58.1) ◎	19 (41.0) ◎	12 (26.7) ◎
語言障礙	7	2 (28.6) ◎	3 (42.9) ◎	3 (42.9) ○	0△	3 (42.9) ◎	3 (42.9) ◎	0△	0○	1 (14.3) ○
肢體障礙	79	53 (67.9) ◎	52 (66.1) ◎	46 (58.7) △	18 (22.9) △	48 (60.6) ◎	55 (69.7) ◎	40 (51.4) ◎	40 (51.4) ◎	22 (28.4) ◎
身體病弱	59	27 (45.8) ◎	26 (44.4) ◎	27 (45.8) △	12 (20.8) △	29 (48.6) ◎	35 (59.7) ◎	16 (26.4) ◎	17 (29.2) ◎	16 (26.4) ◎
情緒行為障礙	43	10 (23.8) △	11 (26.2) ◎	4 (9.5) △	3 (7.1) △	9 (21.4) △	10 (23.8) ◎	6 (14.3) ◎	4 (9.5) ◎	3 (7.1) ◎
學習障礙	270	144 (53.3) ◎	93 (34.4) ◎	99 (36.7) △	54 (20.0) △	108 (40.0) ◎	126 (46.7) ◎	63 (23.3) ◎	54 (20.0) ◎	39 (14.4) ◎
多重障礙	6	4 (64.0) ◎	4 (64.0) ◎	3 (52.0) ○	2 (32.0) ○	4 (64.0) ◎	4 (64.0) ◎	3 (52.0) ○	3 (52.0) ◎	1 (24.0) △
自閉症	41	19 (45.3) △	14 (34.0) ◎	13 (32.1) △	9 (21.7) △	24 (57.5) ◎	26 (62.3) ◎	6 (14.2) ◎	6 (14.2) ◎	5 (13.2) ○
其他障礙	27	11 (40.7) ◎	11 (40.7) ◎	10 (37.0) △	7 (25.9) ◎	10 (37.0) ◎	15 (55.6) ◎	5 (18.5) ◎	7 (25.9) ◎	5 (18.5) ◎
合計	624	329 (52.7) ◎	264 (42.4) ◎	248 (39.7) △	136 (21.8) △	282 (45.2) ◎	332 (53.2) ◎	186 (29.9) ◎	166 (26.7) ◎	116 (18.6) ◎

註：△=協助未能滿足需求、○=協助符合需求、◎=協助高於需求。

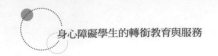

是協助不足、適中、充裕（如表 5-8 中的註記）。具體言之，在所有障別學生之各類需求項目中（共 99 個），教師協助不足的有 28 個（占 28.3%）、適中的有 9 個（占 9.1%）、充裕的則有 62 個（占 62.6%）。就協助不足之處而言，教師提供智能障礙學生協助中，有高達 7 個項目的協助是不足的，情緒行為障礙學生有 4 項，自閉症學生則有 3 項，其餘障別學生則僅有 1～2 項目的協助不足（如表 5-9 所示）。

表 5-9　資源教室教師提供大專身心障礙學生的協助低於需求的項目

障別	協助不足項目數	項目
智能障礙	7	課業、生活、工讀機會／獎助學金、電腦能力訓練、心理／生涯輔導、安排社交活動、醫療
視覺障礙	2	工讀機會／獎助學金、電腦能力訓練
聽覺障礙	2	工讀機會／獎助學金、電腦能力訓練
語言障礙	2	電腦能力訓練、輔具設備
肢體障礙	2	工讀機會／獎助學金、電腦能力訓練
身體病弱	2	工讀機會／獎助學金、電腦能力訓練
情緒行為障礙	4	課業、工讀機會／獎助學金、電腦能力訓練、心理／生涯輔導
學習障礙	2	工讀機會／獎助學金、電腦能力訓練
多重障礙	1	醫療
自閉症	3	課業、工讀機會／獎助學金、電腦能力訓練
其他障礙	1	工讀機會／獎助學金

玖、身心障礙學生就讀大專校院時遭遇的問題與困難

SNELS 列舉 11 項問題與困難並允許學生以複選方式選擇。分析結果顯示（如表 5-10 所示），就全體身心障礙學生而言，以有學習方面問題與困難者占的人數比例相對較高，其中有約三成四的學生有課業學習困難。此外，不適應大學學習方式、就讀科系與興趣不合及老師的教法不適合自己

表 5-10　大專校院身心障礙學生就學時遇到的問題與困難情形（可複選）

障礙類別	樣本人數	問題／困難										
		就讀科系與興趣不合	課業學習困難	和同學相處困難	獨立生活困難	老師的教法不適合自己	和老師相處有問題	不適應大學學習方式	無障礙設施不夠	輔具或設備不夠	經濟困難	校園大，跑教室或行動困難
智能障礙	25	2 (6.7)	13 (53.3)	7 (26.7)	2 (6.7)	2 (6.7)	3 (13.3)	2 (6.7)	0	0	2 (6.7)	0
視覺障礙	21	2 (10.0)	4 (20.0)	2 (8.0)	2 (8.0)	2 (12.0)	2 (12.0)	3 (16.0)	2 (10.0)	2 (10.0)	2 (10.0)	2 (10.0)
聽覺障礙	47	4 (9.5)	24 (50.5)	11 (22.9)	3 (6.7)	9 (19.0)	2 (3.8)	14 (29.5)	0 (1.0)	0 (1.0)	5 (10.5)	3 (6.7)
語言障礙	7	1 (14.3)	2 (28.6)	0	1 (14.3)	0	0	1 (14.3)	0	1 (14.3)	1 (14.3)	0
肢體障礙	79	14 (17.4)	16 (20.2)	7 (9.2)	4 (5.5)	6 (7.3)	1 (0.9)	12 (14.7)	6 (7.3)	0	6 (8.3)	11 (13.8)
身體病弱	59	6 (9.7)	9 (15.3)	7 (11.1)	2 (4.2)	4 (6.9)	2 (4.2)	6 (9.7)	1 (1.4)	0	5 (8.3)	4 (6.9)
情緒行為障礙	43	7 (16.7)	17 (40.5)	9 (21.4)	0	5 (11.9)	3 (7.1)	13 (31.0)	0	0	5 (11.9)	1 (2.4)
學習障礙	270	30 (11.1)	96 (35.6)	33 (12.2)	15 (5.6)	18 (6.7)	12 (4.4)	39 (14.4)	3 (1.1)	3 (1.1)	57 (21.1)	9 (3.3)
多重障礙	6	1 (20.0)	3 (44.0)	1 (24.0)	1 (12.0)	1 (12.0)	0	1 (16.0)	1 (12.0)	0	1 (16.0)	1 (16.0)
自閉症	41	7 (17.9)	21 (50.0)	14 (33.0)	4 (9.4)	9 (22.6)	3 (6.6)	11 (25.5)	0	0 (0.9)	6 (15.1)	1 (2.8)
其他障礙	27	4 (14.8)	6 (22.2)	0	1 (3.7)	1 (3.7)	0	4 (14.8)	1 (3.7)	1 (3.7)	6 (22.2)	0
合計	624	78 (12.6)	210 (33.7)	90 (14.4)	35 (5.6)	57 (9.2)	29 (4.6)	105 (16.8)	14 (2.2)	8 (1.3)	96 (15.4)	32 (5.2)

註：表中數字係學生人數及其在某障別所占比例。學生人數為加權後數值，因採四捨五入計算原則，故可能出現細格人數的加總不等於樣本人數之情形。

的人數比例分別為 17%、13% 及 9%。有經濟困難及和同學相處困難的人數比例亦屬相對較高，兩者皆約為 15%。有其他問題或困難的人數比例則相

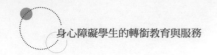

對較低，介於 1～6%之間。

就各障別學生的分析結果而言，可歸納出以下七項特點：(1)半數以上的智能障礙學生有課業學習困難，人數比例（53%）居各障別之冠；(2)視覺、語言及肢體障礙等三類學生有相似的結果，即皆以有課業學習困難者占相對多數，唯人數比例並不高，僅占二至三成；(3)有五成的聽覺障礙學生有課業學習困難，人數比例在各障別中排序第二。另有約三成的學生不適應大學學習方式，人數比例同樣亦屬次高；(4)情緒行為障礙學生中除了有四成的學生表達有課業學習困難外，另亦有三成的學生不適應大學學習方式，此人數比例為所有障別中最高者；(5)學習障礙學生以有課業學習困難的人數比例最高，其次為有經濟困難，所占人數比例分別為36%及21%；(6)多重障礙學生中有四成以上有學業學習困難；(7)半數的自閉症學生有課業學習困難，此外，有約 26%的學生不適應大學學習方式；另認為教師教法不適合自己的占23%，此比例為各障別中最高者。

拾、大專校院身心障礙學生在校生活情形

SNELS 更具體地針對大專身心障礙學生在就學期間的人際互動、生活快樂程度、是否參與社團、打工、翹課及學習滿意情形等進行調查。分析結果顯示（如表 5-11 及 5-12 所示），就全體學生而言，他們對在學校與同學相處情形抱持正向看法（即很好或還可以）的比例高達九成六，僅極少數的學生認為他們與同學的關係是不太好或很不好。與此結果一致，同樣亦有九成六的學生認為其大學生活很快樂或還可以，僅 4%的學生認為他們不太快樂或很不快樂。另就參加社團而言，半數以上的學生有參加社團，但亦有四成七的學生未參與社團。大專身障生有打工與未打工的比例約為 3：7。就翹課情形而言，有將近一半的學生未曾翹過課，約三成的學生很少翹課，一成五有時翹課，常常翹課者僅占 2%。整體而言，約二成的學生對自己在校的學習情形感到很滿意，約六成五覺得還算滿意，不太滿意和很不滿意者相對較少，人數比例分別為 15%與 2%。

就各障別學生的情形而言，可歸納出下列九項特點：(1)智能障礙學生

表 5-11　大專校院身心障礙學生在學校生活情形

障別	樣本人數	在學校和同學相處得好嗎		覺得大學生活很快樂嗎		在大學參加社團嗎		上大學後，打過工嗎	
		很好／還可以	不太好／很不好	很快樂／還可以	不太快樂／很不快樂	有	沒有	有	沒有
智能障礙	25	22 (86.6)	4 (13.4)	23 (93.3)	2 (6.7)	12 (46.7)	13 (53.3)	3 (13.3)	21 (86.7)
視覺障礙	21	20 (96.0)	1 (4.0)	20 (94.0)	1 (6.0)	14 (66.0)	7 (34.0)	4 (20.0)	17 (80.0)
聽覺障礙	47	44 (95.2)	2 (4.8)	45 (96.2)	2 (3.8)	29 (61.9)	18 (38.1)	15 (31.4)	32 (68.6)
語言障礙	7	7 (100.0)	0	7 (100.0)	0	2 (28.6)	5 (71.4)	1 (14.3)	6 (85.7)
肢體障礙	79	77 (98.2)	1 (1.8)	76 (96.3)	3 (3.7)	37 (46.8)	42 (53.2)	21 (26.6)	58 (73.4)
身體病弱	59	56 (94.4)	3 (5.6)	56 (94.4)	3 (5.6)	31 (52.8)	28 (47.2)	19 (31.9)	40 (68.1)
情緒行為障礙	43	39 (92.8)	3 (7.2)	39 (92.8)	3 (7.2)	20 (47.6)	22 (52.4)	14 (33.3)	28 (66.7)
學習障礙	270	261 (96.7)	9 (3.3)	264 (97.8)	6 (2.2)	144 (53.3)	126 (46.7)	93 (34.4)	177 (65.6)
多重障礙	6	6 (96.0)	0 (4.0)	6 (92.0)	0 (8.0)	2 (36.0)	4 (64.0)	2 (32.0)	4 (68.0)
自閉症	41	39 (93.4)	2 (6.6)	37 (90.6)	4 (9.4)	20 (47.2)	22 (52.8)	9 (20.8)	33 (79.2)
其他障礙	27	27 (100.0)	0	27 (100.0)	0	21 (77.8)	6 (22.2)	4 (14.8)	23 (85.2)
合計	624	597 (95.8)	26 (4.2)	599 (96.1)	24 (3.9)	331 (53.1)	293 (46.9)	185 (29.6)	439 (70.4)

註：表中數字係學生人數及其在某障別所占比例。學生人數為加權後數值，因採四捨五入計算原則，故可能出現細格人數的加總不等於樣本人數之情形。

與同學相處很好／還可以的比例相對最高（87%），有無參與社團的比例約各半，打工比例最低（13%），從來不翹課的比例則最高（67%）。另排除2個遺漏值後，100%的學生對自己的學習情形感到還算滿意或很滿意；(2) 視覺與聽覺兩障別學生情況類似，其人際互動佳與生活快樂者的比例皆高

表 5-12　大專校院身心障礙學生在學校學習情形

障別	樣本人數	你上大學後，有沒有翹過課				滿意自己在學校的學習情形嗎			
		從來沒有	很少	有時候	常常	很滿意	還算滿意	不太滿意	很不滿意
智能障礙	25	17 (66.7)	7 (26.7)	0	0	13 (53.3)	10 (40.0)	0	0
視覺障礙	21	9 (44.0)	10 (48.0)	1 (6.0)	0 (2.0)	3 (16.0)	13 (62.0)	3 (16.0)	1 (6.0)
聽覺障礙	47	24 (51.4)	14 (29.5)	8 (18.1)	0 (1.0)	7 (14.3)	32 (68.6)	8 (16.2)	0 (1.0)
語言障礙	7	2 (28.6)	2 (28.6)	3 (42.9)	0	1 (14.3)	3 (42.9)	3 (42.9)	0
肢體障礙	79	37 (46.8)	25 (32.1)	14 (18.3)	2 (2.8)	12 (14.7)	55 (69.7)	12 (14.7)	1 (0.9)
身體病弱	59	29 (48.6)	20 (33.3)	10 (16.7)	1 (1.4)	9 (15.3)	42 (70.8)	7 (11.1)	2 (2.8)
情緒行為障礙	43	14 (33.3)	21 (50.0)	6 (14.3)	1 (2.4)	6 (14.3)	26 (61.9)	8 (19.0)	2 (4.8)
學習障礙	270	138 (51.1)	93 (34.5)	33 (12.2)	6 (2.2)	54 (20.0)	168 (62.2)	45 (16.7)	3 (1.1)
多重障礙	6	3 (44.0)	2 (40.0)	1 (12.0)	0 (4.0)	1 (24.0)	4 (64.0)	0 (8.0)	0 (4.0)
自閉症	41	25 (60.4)	11 (25.5)	5 (12.3)	1 (1.9)	9 (20.8)	25 (60.4)	7 (17.9)	0 (0.9)
其他障礙	27	8 (29.6)	10 (37.1)	9 (33.3)	0	3 (11.1)	20 (74.1)	3 (11.1)	1 (3.7)
合計	624	305 (48.9)	214 (34.4)	91 (14.5)	12 (1.9)	118 (18.9)	398 (63.7)	96 (15.4)	11 (1.7)

註：表中數字係學生人數及其在某障別所占比例。學生人數為加權後數值，因採四
　　捨五入計算原則，故可能出現細格人數的加總不等於樣本人數之情形。智能障
　　礙組中有 2 個遺漏值。

達九成以上，社團參與比例則分屬第二與第三高。兩者皆以沒有打工者占
主要多數。上課情形頗佳，分別有四成五及五成的學生從未翹過課。兩者
皆約八成的學生滿意其學習情形，但值得注意的是兩障別亦皆有 16%的學
生不太滿意自己的學習情形；(3)語言障礙學生人際關係佳且生活屬快樂者

皆達 100%。另其未參與社團的比例最高（71%）。從未翹課的比例為各障別中最低（29%），但對自己學習情形感到不太滿意者為 43%，高居各障別之冠；(4)肢體障礙與身體病弱兩者的情況類似，九成以上學生與同學相處情形佳且覺得大學生活快樂，兩者參加社團的比例皆約各半，沒有打工者約占七成，約半數的學生從未翹課。約八成五以上的學生均滿意其在校的學習情形；(5)情緒行為與學習障礙兩類學生則是另一對類似的組別，兩者人際關係佳且快樂者皆達九成以上，情障生未參與社團者略高於參與者，學障生則相反，兩者皆以沒有打工者占相對多數。半數學障生從未翹課，情障生則僅三成。情障與學障生兩者對自己在校學習屬還算滿意或很滿意者分別為 76%與 82%；(7)多重障礙學生九成以上人際關係佳且覺得大學生活快樂，有參與社團或打工者皆各占三成，從未翹課者占四成五，對自己整體學習情形感到滿意者約九成；(8)自閉症學生中九成以上有良好的人際關係且覺得大學生活快樂，有無參與社團的比例約各半，未打工者則占八成，曾未有翹課的比例高達六成，為各障別中次高者，八成的學生滿意自己在校的學習；(9)其他障礙學生是另一人際關係佳且生活快樂皆達 100%的障別，有參與社團者約占八成，八成五的學生則未打工，有時翹課的比例約占三成，為各障別中次高者，八成五的學生對自己的學習情形感到滿意。

▌拾壹、結語

　　綜觀上述的分析可知，我國高中階段學生轉銜至大專校院的人數呈逐年增加的趨勢，且此股趨勢並未受到少子化現象的影響。各障別中尤以認知障礙類高中生升學大專的成長趨勢最明顯，此情況與美國頗為類似，例如：該國自閉症學生就讀大專的人數不斷成長（Francis, Duke, Kliethermes, Demetro, & Graff, 2018; Kuder & Accardo, 2018），情緒行為障礙學生的轉銜結果亦是如此（Cooper & Pruitt, 2005; Newman et al., 2011）。另外，學習障礙學生進入大專就讀的成長趨勢則更是顯著（Hadley, 2018），讀大學已成為該障別高中畢業生最主要的選擇進路（Madaus & Shaw, 2006）。根據一份

全國性的調查，32.7%的學障生於高中畢業三至五年後會進入大專校院就讀（Wagner et al., 2005），若將時間拉長至畢業六年內，則就學比例大幅增加至 60.9%（Sanford, Newman, Wagner, Cameto, Knokey, & Shaver, 2011）。此外，就智能障礙學生而言，其大專就學人數亦是呈成長趨勢（Grigal, Hart, & Migliore, 2011），主要可歸因於法律的保障，特別是《高等教育機會法》（Higher Education Opportunity Act, HEOA, 2008），該法不但提供學生就學獎助金，亦補助更多大專校院成立專為智能障礙學生設立的高等教育（Postsecondary Education, PSE）方案。而此 PSE 方案實提供大專智能障礙學生更多接受高等教育或進階生活技能訓練的機會，有助於該群學子未來過自主的生活（Kelley & Westling, 2013; Neubert & Moon, 2006; Plotner & Marshall, 2015）。礙於篇幅限制，本章無法詳述 PSE 的類型與內容，然此方案頗值得我國參考。畢竟根據《特殊教育統計年報》的資料（教育部，2018），高中智能障礙學生占該階段所有身障生之比例為 24.7%，但在大專階段之比例則僅為 9.7%。一份以 SNELS 資料庫樣本為分析對象的研究顯示，智能障礙學生高中職畢業後，繼續升大學者僅占 6.3%，另雖有 41.1%的學生投入職場就業，但亦有 52.6%的學生待在家中（Chao, Chou, & Cheng, 2019）。如何提供這群既未升學亦未就業的國民其所需的福利服務、職業重建、醫療或復健等服務，實值得吾人關注。

　　雖然身心障礙學生就讀公私立大專校院的比例與全國大專生的比例未有顯著的落差，但不可否認地，身障生就讀公立學校的比例在過去十年已減少7%，此即代表就讀私立大學的人數比例上升7%，而其中人數成長的部分更主要聚集於私立技術學院或科技大學。雖說該類型學校多數為辦學績優的學校，但近年亦有極少數學校因相關主、客觀因素而退場，包括：高鳳數位內容學院（2014 年）、永達技術學院（2014 年）、高美醫護管理專科學校（2018 年）、亞太創意技術學院（2018 年）等。故提供高中階段身心障礙學生充分且正確的升學資訊，是教師在提供轉銜輔導與服務過程中重要的工作事項，以確保身障生畢業後能繼續接受有品質的高等教育。而就身心障礙學生升學方式而言，超過半數的學生是藉由專為身障生辦理的「身心障礙學生升學大專校院甄試」管道升學，若再加上「學校單獨招

生」管道，有將近七成的身障生可因此獲得高等教育受教權，此結果實令人感到欣慰。但不可諱言的，「身心障礙學生升學大專校院甄試」仍有其不足之處，例如：公立學校的招生名額遠低於私立學校，而且並非所有科系均提供身障生名額，僅特別針對部分障別學生（包括視覺障礙、聽覺障礙、腦性麻痺、自閉症、學習障礙等五類）提供招生名額，其餘障別學生則均歸類至其他障礙生此類別，或者大學組第四類組科系僅提供名額給聽覺障礙及學習障礙兩類學生等。而有關「學校單獨招生」較不足之處則是，提供此入學管道的大專校院僅侷限於部分學校（如 108 學年度僅 35 校），並未廣泛普及於各個大專校院。身障生進入大專校院後，相對多數的學生（約五分之一）選擇就讀餐旅及民生服務學門，此比例約高於全國大專生的比例 7%。如此的結果令人憂喜參半，喜的是該學門所屬科系（如生活應用與保健系、美容系、化妝品應用系、餐旅管理系、運動競技系、觀光暨休閒遊憩學系、娛樂事業管理系等）均強調具實用性之專業知識與技能的教導，此對學生未來謀職與就業有極大的助益；但憂的是不知此發展趨勢究竟是出於學生自主決定後的結果，抑或是教育制度刻意規劃出的結果，實值得未來政策制定者深思。

　　如前所述，轉銜輔導與服務的內容包括升學輔導、生活、就業、心理輔導、福利服務及其他相關專業服務等。綜觀本章前述的分析結果可知，我國大專校院身障生在校期間的學習與生活適應情形大致尚屬良好。超過九成以上的身障生不論在人際互動或生活快樂程度等項目均為正向結果，且此結果可同時類推至各不同障別學生。此外，多數大專身障生很少或從不翹課，唯語言障礙與其他障礙兩類學生偶爾翹課的比例分別高達四成與三成，另聽覺障礙、肢體障礙及自閉症等三類學生亦有約二成的學生有此情形。這群學生的行為動機值得教師進一步探究，以期能在行為問題惡化前進行介入與輔導，畢竟大專身障生的平均休退學率高達 9%（林坤燦等人，2008）。此外，從身障生的需求面來看，雖然各障別學生有其不同的需求項目及人數，但令人訝異的是，需要學校提供工讀機會／獎助學金是所有障別學生共同的心聲，且在各障別中有此需求的學生人數均占最多。由於 SNELS 將工讀機會與獎助學金兩者合併為一道問題，故要了解身障

真正的想法頗不容易，但若同時參酌身障生是否打工的分析結果來看（僅三成學生有打工），或可合理歸納出大專身障生有獎助學金的需求更甚於工讀機會的結論。當然，我們也不能排除學生因課業繁忙而無法參與打工的可能性。綜言之，大專身障生有明顯經濟需求的結果或可歸因於他們多數來自於社經地位相對較低的家庭，而若再考量這群學子中有近八成的人係就讀學費較昂貴的私立大專，故確實有可能造成其沉重的經濟負擔。因此如何幫助這群學子減輕其在經濟上的負荷，以使其能專心向學實是當前高等教育中重要的議題之一。除此之外，智能障礙、情緒行為障礙及自閉症等三者顯然也需要資源教室教師提供更充裕的輔導與協助，因為這群學子在多個項目的需求均無法獲得充分的協助。特別是智能障礙學生在課業、生活、工讀機會／獎助學金、電腦能力訓練、心理／生涯輔導、安排社交活動、醫療等七個項目的需求，均未能獲得有效協助，實為各障別中相對最弱勢的一群。總結而言，超過八成的大專身障生對自己在校的學習情形感到滿意，如此結果亦突顯我國目前針對高中階段身心障礙學生轉銜至大專校院的輔導與服務工作已初具成效，然而未來如何能進一步提供這群學生在大專校院求學與生活中所需的各項輔導與服務，並協助其畢業後順利轉銜至職場就業與成人生活，則是另一個特殊教育必須關注的議題。

參考文獻

中文部分

王天苗（2014 年 5 月 25 日）。**特殊教育長期追蹤資料庫之建置與運用**。發表於 2014 年 SNELS 次級資料分析工作坊。中原大學，桃園縣。

林坤燦、羅清水、邱瀞瑩（2008）。臺灣地區大專校院身心障礙學生休退學現況調查研究。**東臺灣特殊教育學報，10，1-19**。

教育部（2000）。**各教育階段身心障礙學生轉銜輔導及服務辦法**。臺北市：作者。

教育部（2009）。**特殊教育統計年報**。臺北市：作者。

教育部（2010）。**特殊教育統計年報**。臺北市：作者。

教育部（2011）。**特殊教育統計年報**。臺北市：作者。

教育部（2012）。**特殊教育統計年報**。臺北市：作者。

教育部（2013a）。**特殊教育法施行細則**。臺北市：作者。

教育部（2013b）。**特殊教育統計年報**。臺北市：作者。

教育部（2014）。**特殊教育統計年報**。臺北市：作者。

教育部（2015）。**特殊教育統計年報**。臺北市：作者。

教育部（2016）。**特殊教育統計年報**。臺北市：作者。

教育部（2017a）。**十二年國民基本教育實施計畫**。臺北市：作者。

教育部（2017b）。**中華民國學科標準分類**（第五次修正版）。臺北市：作者。

教育部（2017c）。**特殊教育統計年報**。臺北市：作者。

教育部（2018）。**特殊教育統計年報**。臺北市：作者。

教育部（2019）。**特殊教育法**。臺北市：作者。

許天威、蕭金土、吳訓生、林和姻、陳亭予（2002）。大專校院身心障礙學生學校適應狀況之研究。**特殊教育學報，16，159-198**。

陳麗如（2008）。大專校院身心障礙學生轉銜生活與轉銜行為之研究。**特殊教育學報，28**，57-96。

英文部分

Certo, N. J., Luecking, R. G., Courey, S., Brown, L., Murphy, S., & Mautz, D. (2008). Plugging the policy gap at the point of transition for individuals with severe intellectual disabilities: An argument for a seamless transition and federal entitlement to long-term support. *Research and Practice for Persons with Severe Disabilities, 33*, 85-95.

Certo, N. J., Mautz, D., Pumpian, I., Sax, C., Smalley, K., Wade, H. A., ...Batterman, N. (2003). Review and discussion of a model for seamless transition to adulthood. *Education and Training in Developmental Disabilities, 38*, 3-17.

Chao, P. C., Chou, Y. C., & Cheng, S. F. (2019). Self-determination and transition outcomes of youth with disabilities: Findings from the Special Needs Education Longitudinal Study. *Advances in Neurodevelopmental Disorders, 3*, 129-137.

Connor, D. J. (2012). Helping students with disabilities transition to college. *Teaching Exceptional Children, 44*, 16-25.

Cooper, J., & Pruitt, B. A. (2005). Creating opportunities for success in college settings for students with emotional and behavioral disorders. *Beyond Behavior, 14*, 23-26.

Francis, G. L., Duke, J. M., Kliethermes, A., Demetro, K., & Graff, H. (2018). Apps to support a successful transition to college for students with ASD. *Teaching Exceptional Children, 51*, 111-124.

Grigal, M., Hart, D., & Migliore, A. (2011). Comparing the transition planning, postsecondary education, and employment outcomes of students with intellectual and other disabilities. *Career Development for Exceptional Individuals, 34*, 4-17.

Hadley, W. (2018). Students with learning disabilities transitioning from college: A one-year study. *College Student Journal, 52*, 421-430.

Hendricks, D. R., & Wehman, P. (2009). Transition from school to adulthood for youth with autism spectrum disorders: Review and recommendations. *Focus on Autism and Other Developmental Disabilities, 24*, 77-88.

Higher Education Opportunity Act of 2008, Pub. L. No. 110-315. § 122 STAT. 3078 (2008).

Individuals With Disabilities Education Act, 20 U.S.C § 1400 *et seq.* (2006).

Kelley, K., & Westling, D. L. (2013). A focus on natural supports in postsecondary education for students with intellectual disabilities at Western Carolina University. *Journal of Vocational Rehabilitation, 38*, 67-76.

Konrad, M., & Test, D. W. (2004). Teaching middle-school students with disabilities to use an IEP template. *Career Development for Exceptional Individuals, 27*, 101-124.

Kuder, J. S., & Accardo, A. (2018). What works for college students with autism spectrum disorder. *Journal of Autism and Developmental Disorders, 48*, 722-731.

Luecking, D. M., & Luecking, R. G. (2015). Translating research into a seamless transition model. *Career Development and Transition for Exceptional Individuals, 38*, 4-13.

Madaus, J. W., & Shaw, S. F. (2006). The impact of the IDEA 2004 on transition to college for students with learning disabilities. *Learning Disabilities Research and Practice, 21*, 273-281.

Neubert, D. A., & Moon, M. S. (2006). Postsecondary settings and transition services for students with intellectual disabilities: Models and research. *Focus on Exceptional Children, 39*, 1-8.

Newman, L., Wagner, M., Knokey, A., Marder, C., Nagle, K., Shaver, D., & Wei, X. (2011). *The post-high school outcomes of young adults with disabilities up to 8 years after high school. A report from the National Longitudinal Transition*

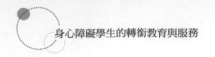

Study-2 (NLTS2). Menlo Park, CA: SRI International.

Plotner, A. J., & Marshall, K. J. (2015). Postsecondary education programs for students with intellectual disability: Facilitators and barriers to implementation. *Intellectual and Developmental Disabilities, 53*, 58-69.

Sanford, C., Newman, L., Wagner, M., Cameto, R., Knokey, A. M., & Shaver, D. (2011). *The post-high school outcomes of young adults with disabilities up to 6 years after high school: Key findings from the National Longitudinal Transition Study-2 (NLTS2)*. Menlo Park, CA: SRI International.

Schwartz, S. P. (2012). *A brief history of analytic philosophy: From Russell to Rawls*. Chichester, West Sussex: Wiley-Blackwell.

Stodden, R. A. (2005). The status of persons with disabilities in postsecondary education. *TASH Connections, 2*, 4-5.

Test, D. W. (2009). Seamless transition for all. *Research and Practice for Persons with Severe Disabilities, 33*, 98-99.

Test, D. W., & Grossi, T. (2011). Transition planning and evidence-based research. *Journal of Vocational Rehabilitation, 35*, 173-175.

Wagner, M., Newman, L., Cameto, R., Garza, N., & Levine, P. (2005). *After high school: A first look at the postschool experiences of youth with disabilities. A report from the National Longitudinal Transition Study-2 (NLTS2)*. Menlo Park, CA: SRI International.

Wehman, P., & Thoma, C. A. (2006). Teaching for transition. In P. Wehman (Ed.), *Life beyond the classroom: Transition strategies for young people with disabilities* (4th ed.) (pp. 201-236). Baltimore, MD: Paul H. Brookes.

White, S. W., Elias, R., Capriola-Hall, N. N., Smith, I. C., Conner, C. M., Asselin, S. B., ...Mazefsky, C. A. (2017). Development of a college transition and support program for students with autism spectrum disorder. *Journal of Autism and Developmental Disorders, 47*, 3072-3078.

第六章　轉銜評量
Transition Assessment

張大倫（Dalun Zhang）、Leena Jo Landmark、
鞠頌（Song Ju）、李依帆（Yi-Fan Li）
中文摘錄：李依帆

中文重點摘錄

▶壹、緒論

　　轉銜評量為身心障礙學生轉銜計畫與服務的根基，學者定義轉銜評量為：「一連續的過程，引導參與者了解學生對於未來工作、教育、社區社交生活之需要、偏好及興趣。個別教育計畫中的轉銜目標及服務應以轉銜評量為基礎」（Thoma, Held, & Tamura, 2001, pp. 70-71）。

　　從以上的定義來看，轉銜評量是一「連續」的行動，並且以「學生本人」為中心，轉銜評量同時也需要教師、家長，以及其他專業人員合作進行。以往轉銜評量以就業導向為原則，但轉銜評量及計畫漸漸擴展至其他領域，包含：獨立生活技能、休閒娛樂安排、社交技巧、交通安排，以及其他功能性技能，如此多領域之評量，更加突顯專業人員合作的必要性（Thoma et al., 2001, p. 248）。

　　轉銜評量與一般的傳統性評量有所差別。首先，轉銜評量是以學生為中心（person-centered），評量的目的即是要了解學生對於未來生活規劃的各個層面。其次，轉銜評量是一連續的過程，同時是視學生需要（need-based）進行評量，並非每一種領域都要進行測量，在決定測量之前，評量者最好能提供測量的理由再決定是否施測。轉銜評量同時也發生在不同的場域，如教室、社區及工作場所。綜合以上特點，使得轉銜評量扮演特殊的

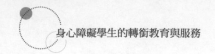

角色,也與傳統性評量有所區別。

貳、轉銜評量的目的

　　轉銜評量是擬定轉銜計畫的基礎。首先,轉銜評量的目的即是要幫助身心障礙學生了解自己的生涯規劃並且做出明智的選擇。在評量的過程中,身心障礙學生更加認識自己的需要、偏好及興趣,進一步設定未來的就業、教育以及社區生活的目標。其次,轉銜評量也幫助身心障礙學生銜接社區資源及服務。最後,轉銜評量協助身心障礙學生加強自我決策的技能,在評量的過程中,學生為主動參與者,專業人員扮演協助的角色。學生也根據自己的需要及興趣,設定長短程目標,如此一連串的過程加強學生自我決策的能力。以下討論轉銜評量的評量內容及測驗類型。

一、測量偏好與興趣

　　測量身心障礙學生對特定領域的偏好與興趣,是轉銜評量的第一步驟。了解學生的偏好與興趣,往往可反映出學生的價值觀以及對生活方式賦予的意義。偏好與興趣評量可以從不同領域方面著手,如未來升學、生涯職業目標、居住安排、社區活動等。評量也可以透過各種方式進行,例如:訪談學生及家人、非正式問卷調查,以及正式的興趣評量。Collier、Griffin與Wei(2016)發展一份非正式的問卷評量,此問卷評量包含38道問題,每一個問題代表轉銜相關的活動與規劃,受試者可依據這38道問題表達看法與觀點,進而初步掌握受試者的興趣與偏好。另一種評量方式則是使用影片的方式調查學生的職涯興趣,可參見如 CareerOneStop 網站(U.S. Department of Labor, 2019)、Texas OnCourse 網站(University of Texas, 2018)。透過影片呈現各行各業的概況,不僅能掌握學生對職業的興趣與選擇,同時也提供學生職涯探索的機會。

二、測量優勢及需求

　　轉銜評量應是以優勢本位為主的評量。透過評量，評量者能描繪出身心障礙學生擅長的技能，不論這技能是使用在課業學習、社區生活及職涯工作（Carter, Trainor, Sun, & Owens, 2009），生涯目標的發展應以優勢能力為基礎。此重要性也反映美國 IDEA（2004）的規定，身心障礙學生之個別化教育計畫與轉銜計畫應考量學生的優勢技能。

　　測量優勢能力及需求的方式同樣也很多元，評量者可使用影片及說故事的方式，讓學生表達自己的需求及擅長的技能；評量者也可使用問卷的方式，邀請學生本人、家長及教師填寫問卷，了解學生擅長的活動。優弱勢評量也包含正式的評量，如「轉銜計畫量表」（第二版）（Transition Planning Inventory, 2nd ed., TPI-2），此評量包含十種領域的優勢技能及興趣調查，並分為教師版、家長版及學生版。TPI-2 現已有翻譯成中文版及其他語言。

　　針對職涯方面的優勢技能及需求評量，以「生活中心生涯教育課程」（Life-Centered Career Education）（Brolin, 1992）模式為例，此一課程本位評量描繪身心障礙學生對生涯知識與技能的能力。其他職涯方面的評量，如 BRIGANCE Diagnostic Employability Skills Inventory（Brigance, 1995）、Responsibility and Independence Scale for Adolescents（Salvia, Neisworth, & Schmidt, 1990）。自我決策方面的評量則包含：AIR Self-determination Scale 以及 ARC Self-determination Scale。兩種自我決策的評量皆可在 Zarrow Center for Learning Enrichment, University of Oklahoma（2019）網站中找到。

三、轉銜評量的類型

　　轉銜評量的類型可分為正式評量跟非正式評量。正式評量指的是標準化測驗，測驗具備良好的信度與效度。評量者使用正式評量之前，需先了解測驗的性質及施測對象，根據施測對象的需要挑選適合的測驗。正式評量的內容不一定與轉銜領域相關，如成就測驗、智力測驗及適應行為評量，但測驗的結果可以為個別化教育計畫的一部分，也可以成為發展轉銜

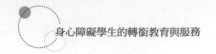

計畫的參考依據。

非正式評量包含的範圍相當廣泛，如結構式訪談、環境分析、觀察測驗、課程本位評量、功能性行為調查等。如同正式評量，非正式評量可以提供重要的訊息，例如：評量者使用正式評量施測，發現受試者對零售業感興趣，但正式評量可能無法測量受試者完成零售業工作任務的表現，評量者需透過工作分析，觀察受試者是否能獨立完成零售業的工作任務。透過正式評量與非正式評量提供的資訊，評量者方可綜合分析並且研判受試者目前的優勢技能及需求。

另一種評量為「功能性職業技能分析」（Functional Vocational Evaluation）。功能性職業技能分析可包含正式評量或非正式評量，透過各種評量的分析，觀察、描述以及預測身心障礙學生的職業潛能，此評量的特色強調在真實工作環境中的表現。

功能性職業技能分析提供「功能性」的資訊，例如：透過職業興趣評量可能無法掌握學生對職業技能的習得程度，但透過在真實工作環境中的實際操作，評量者觀察學生的工作表現，產生功能性的資訊，此資訊可協助後續轉銜目標的擬定與轉銜服務的安排。

此評量能為各專業人員（如職業輔導員、教師、家長等）提供功能性職業技能分析結果，且重點是能提供身心障礙學生在不同環境中的工作表現，進而讓各專業人員能綜合研判身心障礙學生目前的優勢能力及需要學習的技能。

▍參、轉銜評量與決定轉銜目標

一、發展未來願景

如同前述，轉銜評量為決定轉銜目標及服務的基礎。當各專業人員透過轉銜評量蒐集足夠的訊息，即可協助身心障礙學生發展未來願景。

未來的願景將描繪高中職畢業後，身心障礙學生如何經營生活及職涯安排。然而，或許是考量到未來要面臨的挑戰，身心障礙學生對未來的願

景常常被旁人忽略。專家建議，協助身心障礙學生陳述未來的願景，可以思考以下的要素：學生高中職畢業後想做的事、學生的優勢技能、學生需要的協助，以及將來的居住安排。可參考下面兩個例子（Loo, 2019）：

Troy 畢業後想進入 ABCD 大學就讀科學相關科系，他夢想在野外的自然保護區工作。Troy 和他的家人認為，Troy 在大學就學時需要讀書技巧及考試調整的支持服務。Troy 上大學後，仍會持續與媽媽同住，但一旦他完成學業，並且有了穩定的工作，他想要搬進一間公寓裡。

Lisa 在高中職畢業後，需要就業輔導協助她找到理想的工作。她似乎比較喜歡從事可以跟人互動的工作。過去 Lisa 曾經有相當成功的工作經驗，她之前在超市及快餐店工作。Lisa 的媽媽希望 Lisa 能加入社區居住方案，與女性的同儕一同學習獨立生活。Lisa需要學習在獨處的時候能從事適當的休閒娛樂，同時也需要學習如何照顧自己，以及其他獨立生活的技能。

二、決定適當的轉銜服務

根據評量的結果，了解身心障礙學生目前的能力以及未來的願景，個別化教育專業計畫的各專業人員可協助身心障礙學生發展未來的轉銜目標與預期成果。專業人員可從以下領域進行考量：高中職後的教育方案、就業、社區生活、居住安排、休閒娛樂、經濟收入安排、家事學習、社區資源銜接、交通、機構及法律資源、健康服務、人際關係等。一旦決定轉銜的目標與預期成果，各專業人員將協助身心障礙學生與家庭決定需要提供的服務，以及指定專業人員負責服務項目，以此進行跨專業的整合。

三、發展教育計畫

如同前述，轉銜計畫的發展是一連串的行動，並且也是一個整合各專業的過程。從發展願景、制定轉銜目標與預期成果、到決定服務與行動，這些將融入個別化教育計畫當中，成為學校提供教學與服務的依據。跨專業的整合相當重要，每一個專業人員的角色缺一不可，例如：教導身心障

礙學生記帳的技能，除了可以在生活技巧課上學習，也可融合在應用數學課裡，這表示生活技巧課的老師及應用數學課的老師可進行合作，提供學生專業整合的學習。

四、身心障礙學生本人與家長參與

轉銜計畫與服務的發展必須以學生及家長為中心，專業人員從旁協助給予支持。學生的參與必須從轉銜評量開始，評量者可以與學生一同討論評量結果並且詢問學生是否同意評量結果，學生也可以提出問題，透過雙方詢問、對話與討論，學生將會更了解自己，並且為自己設定合理的期待與目標。若學生不同意評量結果，評量者可以協助學生使用其他額外的評量方式再進行評量。

同樣地，家庭參與也是轉銜過程中重要的核心。如同每一位身心障礙學生是獨特的，家庭也呈現各個不同的樣貌。當專業人員制定轉銜計畫時，可參考家庭當中各個成員的意見與看法，並且了解家庭互動的模式。對於障礙程度較重、需要長期家庭支持的身心障礙者而言，了解家庭的功能特別重要。專業人員需要使用彈性的方式鼓勵家庭參與轉銜計畫的擬定，一開始專業人員需要解釋轉銜的目的，並且考量家庭參與的方式，例如：對於忙碌的家庭，教師可以考慮使用郵寄的方式，將轉銜評量寄至家中，並且附上回郵信封，讓家庭可將轉銜評量再寄回學校。Scheef 與 Johnson（2017）考量到現在為網路發達的時代，專業人員可以使用 Google 文件的方式或其他網路平臺與家庭合作。對於需要長期支持的身心障礙者，建議可以使用個人中心規劃（person-centered planning）。個人中心規劃強調各專業人員以問題解決的方式，協助身心障礙學生發展優勢技能，並且視學生的需要提供服務，而不是要求學生適應現有的服務，所有提供的服務將依照學生的需要進行調整。 家庭成員以及親友也將會是重要的支持，共同為身心障礙學生未來的願景進行規劃。

Transition Assessment

Dalun Zhang, Leena Jo Landmark, Song Ju & Yi-Fan Li

How does transition assessment work in the transition planning process? Let's see an example. John is a 21-year-old young man with Down syndrome and a low average IQ under WAIS-IV. The adaptive behavior and functioning assessment (Vineland-3) show a relative strength in communication, but weaknesses in daily living skills and socialization. John attends school regularly and has access to adapted curricula as well as modified coursework tailored to his learning needs. He enjoys swimming, watching movies, going out to eat, and traveling. He loves working with animals and has always wanted to work at a zoo.

In high school, John participates in various transition programs and receives transition services, including in-school work study, community-based work study, community access experiences, on-the-job training/education, and community volunteering experiences. John's ongoing age-appropriate transition assessments include:

- Academic and functional behavior skills assessment.
- Surveys, questionnaires, and interviews completed by his family and teachers about his skills, interests, preferences, needs, and supports.
- Life skills assessment.
- Employability skills assessment.
- Career assessment.
- Environmental or situational assessment completed during job exploration.
- Observations and evaluations on job performance.

Based on his transition assessment results, John's Individualized Education Program (IEP) team decides he will be participating in a post-school employment training program and getting a part-time job at a pet store after graduation. John is also interested in living on his own, so he will be living in an apartment with some support from his parents. His current training and coursework focus on employability skills, daily living skills, self-determination, and related job skills.

John attends work study programs in school and the community. In school, he receives job training in the school cafeteria. He also participates in a work-study job in a local grocery store to assist in bagging and cleaning. Through these activities, he receives training on following directions, problem-solving, self-advocacy, and communication. His strengths and needs are constantly assessed during the process. With the help from his teachers and family, John gets an internship in a local zoo to further explore his career interest. Career assessment and informal assessments are conducted to address his needs and goals. In addition to job-related trainings, John also receives training on community and daily living skills from school and his family, such as transportation, safety, financing skills, etc., where ongoing assessments are conducted through formal evaluations and informal observations. Through the local adult service agency and the support from the family, John will be admitted to a local employment training program after graduation and have a part-time job in a pet store. In this case, transition assessments have been implemented throughout transition planning to support John to identify postsecondary goals and develop plans to move toward achieving those goals.

Transition assessment is defined by the Division on Career Development and Transition (DCDT) of the Council for Exceptional Children as an "ongoing process of collecting data on the individual's needs, preferences, and interests as they relate to the demands of current and future working, educational, living, and personal and social environments. Assessment data serve as the common thread in the transition process and form the basis for defining goals and services to be included in the Individualized Education Program (IEP)" (Thoma, Held, & Tamura, 2001, pp. 70-71). Transition assessment is an ongoing, student-centered, and coordinated process that encompasses a wide range of methods, including career assessment, vocational assessment, functional assessment, and curriculum-based assessment. "Transition assessment and planning has expanded its focus beyond employment and careers to include community living, daily living skills, recreation/leisure, social skills, transportation, and financial skills" (Thoma et al., 2001, p. 248).

Transition assessment differs from traditional assessment in special education in several ways. First, transition assessment is person-centered and individualized, which focuses on various individual characteristics (e.g., strengths, preferences, interests, needs, and future goals), whereas traditional assessment only focuses on academic performance and skills. Second, transition assessment is ongoing, consisting of numerous assessments implemented in different areas, and is need-based, whereas traditional assessment is typically conducted annually. Furthermore, transition assessment can be conducted in various places (e.g., classroom, community, and job sites), whereas traditional assessment usually occurs in the classroom. Finally, transition assessment focuses on longitudinal results, which allows for backward planning, whereas traditional assessment focuses on current skills and performance (Kochhar-Bryant & Greene, 2009).

Purpose of Transition Assessment

Transition assessment plays a critical role in the transition process, which provides foundational knowledge and information to students and families and assists in identifying transition needs, developing transition plans, and monitoring the transition process. First, transition assessment leads to a discovery process and helps students make informed decisions. Transition assessment allows students to identify individual strengths, interests, preferences, needs, and post-school goals in the areas of employment, postsecondary education or training, and community living. Second, transition assessment offers a basis for identifying a course of study, resources, programs, and services to achieve post-school goals. Finally, transition assessment promotes self-determination and enhances student involvement in the transition pro-

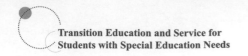

cess. It helps students understand their goals, take charge of the process, and make plans to achieve their goals (Test, Aspel, & Everson, 2006).

Process of Transition Assessment

The reason we engage in transition planning for students with disabilities is to help them figure out what they want to do after completing high school and how to get there. The plan should reflect the student's future vision, interests, and preferences while considering the student's strengths and weaknesses. Consequently, appropriate identification of these individual aspects is essential to ensure adequate planning. To do so, we need to engage in an ongoing process of transition assessment that systematically gathers and analyzes data to determine the student's strengths, interests, and needs relevant to employment, postsecondary education or training, and other adult life areas (Neubert, 2003). Based on the results of the assessment, school personnel can help the student set post-school goals and plan transition services to move toward achieving those goals.

Assessing Student Preferences and Interests

Lohrmann-O'Rourke and Gomez (2001) classified transition outcomes into four broad domains of living, working, playing, and learning. An individual needs to have certain competencies in a specific domain in order to take part in activities related to that domain. For example, domestic skills and accessing community resources are some competencies required of an individual for independent living in the community, and task-specific and employability skills are necessary for working in the community. However, whether or the extent to which an individual pursues those competencies in a specific domain is a personal choice of lifestyle. In other words, an individual student's personal preferences and interests dictate what types of post-school outcomes they want to work on during the transition process. Hence, understanding the student's interests and preferences is the initial focus of the transition assessment process.

Assessment of individual interests and preferences is particularly important because it provides value and meaning to the lifestyle of the individual. To gain a comprehensive understanding of these preferences, Lohrmann-O'Rourke and Gomez (2001) proposed to use a process of systematic preference assessment that involves four steps: (a) selecting options for sampling, (b) providing sampling opportunities, (c) observing the individual's response to the option, and (d) interpreting their response as an indicator of preference versus non-preference. Information about student interests and preferences may be collected in such adult life areas as postsecondary education, career goals, living arrangement, friendship, community access, and any others the student and their family consider important to plan for. There are many ways to collect data on student preferences, including interviews with the student and their family, asking the student to complete a questionnaire, or administering a formal assessment tool. Collier, Griffin, and Wei (2016) developed an informal assessment tool named "*Student Transition Questionnaire*," which was designed to obtain student perspectives on transition-related topics. Students rate themselves on 38 items that describe important transition-related activities. Another way of assessing student interests and preferences is for a student to watch online videos that show clusters of jobs and what people do on these jobs to give themselves an idea. One such example is the CareerOneStop website (U.S. Department of Labor, 2019). Another example is the Texas OnCourse website (University of Texas, 2018). In addition, many interest inventories are available for the school to use with students with disabilities for the purpose of identifying individual preferences in key transition areas. Some of these are free on the Internet; others can be purchased from a publisher. More specific and in-depth assessment tools are available to assess interests and preferences in independent living, self-determination, postsecondary education options, and careers.

Assessing Student Strengths and Needs

Student strengths are what the student is good at. These can be in any areas of student learning and personal traits in school and out-of-school environments. Transition assessment should be strengths-based (Carter, Trainor, Sun, & Owens, 2009). In order to help students choose appropriate future goals for adulthood, it is important to base the goals and intended outcomes in each goal area on the student's strengths because building on their existing strengths and skills can maximize their opportunity for success (Carter et al., 2009). This emphasis is further reinforced in U.S. Federal legislation in the Individuals with Disabilities Education Improvement Act (IDEA, 2004) when it requires the IEP team to consider the student's strengths when transition services are planned.

There are many ways to assess student strengths. One common way is a class activity that asks students to draw an "identity tree," where family and friends make up the roots, interests and strengths represent the trunk, and character and virtue become the leaves (Wejr, 2015). Other examples include a verbal or video introduction of themselves or a story book that tells others about their strengths. Surveys of the students and their close relatives or friends are also good ways to learn about what the student is good at. Wejr shared the *"Who Am I?" Flowchart* that was proposed by Leyton M. Schnellert (2011) for students to use to demonstrate their personal interests and what they do well or what they need help on. This flowchart is also a great way to help the students put some thoughts into knowing themselves. Understanding their own interests and needs is the basis for self-advocacy.

A more formal and comprehensive transition assessment tool is the *Transition Planning Inventory-Second Edition* (TPI-2) (Clark & Patton, 2014). This assessment tool is designed to gather data about student transition needs in terms of their preferences, interests, and strengths. It covers 10 planning areas: employment, further education/training, daily living, leisure activities, community participation, health, self-determination, communication, interpersonal relationships, and other. There are three forms: one for the student, one for parents, and one for educators. Each party completes one form to report student abilities and experiences. The assessment packet also includes 15 comprehensive case studies to provide examples for schools and teams regarding how to use the assessment and how to interpret data. The recent computerized version added two additional forms aimed to collect data on student interests and preferences. The computer version is more user friendly in data processing and interpretation. The TPI-2 has been translated into Chinese and other languages.

In addition to these assessments of student general strengths and needs, there is a need to assess their interests and strengths in some specific areas such as vocational and career, employability skills, social skills, independence, self-determination, and postsecondary education. The *Life Centered Career Education (LCCE): Competency Assessment Knowledge Batteries* (Brolin, 1992) is a curriculum-based assessment designed to assess career education knowledge and skills of students receiving special education services. The *Responsibility and Independence Scale for Adolescents* (Salvia, Neisworth, & Schmidt, 1990) assesses an adolescent's behavior in terms of taking responsibility and exercising independence. It is an individually administered, norm-referenced instrument intended to assess the adaptive behavior of adolescents between the ages of 12 and 19 years. It consists of 136 items that a parent or a spouse (if an older adolescent) answers *yes* or *no* to indicate whether the student performs the specific task. The *BRIGANCE Diagnostic Employability Skills Inventory* (Brigance, 1995) consists of 6 sub-tests and 1,400 items to assess student employability skills. The *AIR Self-determination Scale* and the *ARC Self-determination Scale* are comprehensive tools for gauging a student's level of self-determination. Both self-determination assessments are freely available at the Zarrow Center for Learning Enrichment, University of Oklahoma (2019) website.

Types of Transition Assessment

Transition assessment is used to determine a student's preferences, interests, strengths, and needs as pertaining to the student's post-school life. Transition assessment should occur before the development of the annual IEP because the rest of the IEP should be based upon the findings from the transition assessment and the student's postsecondary plans. Transition assessment should also be chronologically age-appropriate, as opposed to developmentally age-appropriate. In other words, the transition assessments one uses for an 18-year old student should not look like a transition assessment developed for a 12-year old student. When making decisions about age-appropriateness of transition assessments, it is helpful to consider what is appropriate for a same-aged peer who does not have a disability. This does not mean the transition assessment has to be written in language more difficult than the student can understand; it does mean that the assessor needs to consider what a person without a disability would be doing when planning for his/her future. For example, an 18-year old student does not need to be assessed in order to determine his/her high school course of study, because that decision should have been already made. Possible areas in which to assess for transition include academic skills, communication skills, employability skills, health and medical care needs, life skills, accommodations and other supports, work preferences, interests, and aptitudes. Transition assessments can be formal or informal. The IDEIA does not require the use of both formal and informal transition assessments; however, best practice is to use a combination of formal and informal assessments.

Formal Transition Assessment

Formal transition assessments are standardized instruments with standardized procedures that have been norm-referenced for a specific population. Formal transition assessments also provide evidence of validity and reliability when used with a sample from the population the assessment was normed. Thus, it is important to make sure the formal transition assessment is being administered to an individual who is from the population the instrument was normed. For example, there are formal transition assessments for students with developmental disabilities, intellectual disability, and learning disabilities.

Formal transition assessments are particularly useful when conducting the initial transition assessment for a student because these types of assessments can provide the IEP team with information to determine how the student compares to his/her same-aged peers with and without disabilities, depending on the assessment. Formal transition assessments are not always *transition-specific*, that is, other formal assessments that have been administered for the student's initial or reevaluation for special education services can serve as a transition assessment. Examples of these types of formal assessments (that can be considered formal transition assessments, too) include academic achievement tests, intelligence tests, and adaptive behavior scales (Clark, 2007). Although these types of assessments are not usually associated with transition, they can be considered transition assessments because of the valuable information they provide the IEP team. For example, results from an achievement test provide the IEP team with information about the strengths of the student that can be built upon or that need remediation before going to college. Additionally, there are formal transition assessments that are *transition-specific*. These transition assessments include interest inventories, self-determination scales, quality of life scales, social skills inventories, and vocational skills assessments (Clark, 2007). Some examples of formal transition assessments include:

- Armed Services Vocational Aptitude Battery (ASVAB)
- American Institutes for Research (AIR) Self-determination Scale
- Becker Reading Free Interest Inventory
- Brigance Life Skills Inventory
- O*NET Ability Profiler
- Stanford Achievement Test (SAT)
- The ARC's Self-determination Scale
- Transition Assessment and Goal Generator (TAGG)
- Transition Planning Inventory-2
- Vineland Adaptive Behavior Scales
- Wechsler Intelligence Scale for Adults

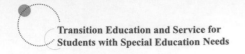
• Woodcock Johnson IV

Informal Transition Assessment

Informal transition assessments include all the other sources of information and assessments that are not standardized for a specific population. Informal transition assessments come in many forms including structured interviews, person-centered planning assessments, environmental or situational analysis, observations, rating scales, curriculum-based assessments, functional skill inventories, criterion-referenced checklists, and school performance measures such as grades and behavior reports, and more. As you can see, informal transition assessments are a broad group of assessments. However, informal transition assessments can provide the IEP team with valuable information that a standardized assessment may not be able to provide. For example, an educator may have learned from a formal assessment that a student has an interest in working in retail. However, when the student is actually training in a retail environment, the educator can use a task analysis form to determine the percentage of steps of a task the student is able to complete without prompts. This data is valuable because it informs the educator and IEP team of the instruction the student will need to be successful in that particular retail environment.

Functional Vocational Evaluation

In IDEIA, one of the possible transition services listed is the Functional Vocational Evaluation (FVE). The FVE is not defined in law, but the Vocational Evaluation and Career Assessment Professional Association (Castiglione et al., 2009) provides the following definition:

> Functional Vocational Evaluation (FVE) is a systematic assessment process used to identify practical useable career and employment-related information about an individual. FVE incorporates multiple formal and informal assessment techniques to observe, de-

scribe, measure, and predict vocational potential. A distinctive feature in all FVE's is that FVE includes (and may emphasize) individualized experiential and performance-based opportunities, in natural vocational or work environments. (p. 51)

There are three levels of vocational evaluation: screening, exploration, and vocational evaluation. The FVE is a part of the Level III vocational evaluation that is reserved for individuals who need help making postsecondary career goals, for whom the first two levels of vocational evaluation have not provided sufficient data for making vocational and subsequent instructional decisions, and for those who have more significant support needs due to their disability.

A key part of an FVE is the focus on *functional* data. Functional data in the FVE generally means observable data collected in simulated or real work environments. In other words, having the student complete an interest inventory by checking off characteristics of jobs they think they would like would not result in functional data. Conversely, observing a student in different work environments to determine their percentage of time on task in the environment would result in functional data. Although vocational rehabilitation counselors can conduct the FVE, educators are also able to conduct an FVE. Functional data can be obtained from multiple members of the IEP team, including the special educator, the transition specialist, the assessment professional, the career and technology educator, and related services providers. One educational professional, usually the special educator or transition specialist, would be responsible for analyzing the data already in existence and determining what other data needs to be obtained. Then, they would make a plan for obtaining the needed data.

Because an FVE is not *one* specific assessment, there are many possible data sources, assessments, and tools that could be used for an FVE. Data from related services professionals can be used for the FVE. As an example, an orientation and mobility specialist can provide data on how the student navigates their community. Com-

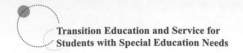
mon special education methods, such as task analysis and constant time delay, can be used to collect functional data. For example, computing the percentage of steps the student completes independently (or with what level of prompting they need) on a specific job task provides valuable information, as does determining the time interval a student takes before completing a task or needing a prompt. Environmental or situational analyses are other educational techniques that can be used to collect data for the FVE, and formal assessments, such as aptitude tests, can provide information that can be used for the FVE, too.

Transition Assessment to Determine Post-School Goals

Results from the transition assessment need to be analyzed and used to produce a student profile, which is a key document on which a transition plan is made. This profile can be generated in a form such as the TPI-2 profile form or in any other format that is easily understood by team members. The profile is the most important document for the IEP team to discuss the transition strengths and needs of a student. The profile is where the IEP team lists the assessments administered, dates they were administered, and summarizes the findings. When the IEP team meets, members need to go over the data and determine the student's strengths, weaknesses, and needs. If additional assessment is necessary, additional assessments can be scheduled. Sometimes, the team may find the results from formal assessments do not tell the full story about the student or the formal assessments may not fit the needs of students with more significant disabilities. In these situations, the team can recommend the administration of informal assessments.

When the team has enough information from the assessments, the next step is to move from assessment to planning. To assist the team in this change from assessment to planning, members can complete a note form or just taking notes of essential information to document key areas that are related to the student's future as an adult and areas that need transition planning and services. After this step, the team can focus on developing statements of present levels of performance and goals related to post-school transition.

Future Vision Statement

Obtaining the student's future vision helps everyone feel more comfortable and confident as they share and plan one of the most important rites of passage in a young adult's life. This is often done by collecting a future vision statement from the student and their family. The vision statement is a description of what the student will do after completing high school and what supports they may need in order to engage in those post-school activities. However, obtaining a future vision statement is often overlooked in the transition assessment process because it is not a required component of the IEP. But, it is one of the most important steps in person-centered planning practices (Lohrmann-O'Rourke & Gomez, 2001; Miner & Bates, 1997; Whitney-Thomas, Shaw, Honey, & Butterworth, 1998). Writing a future vision statement with the student and their family is also a good way to help them think about the future because many parents of children and youth with disabilities find it difficult to think about the future as they are overwhelmed with the challenges at hand (Graves & Graves, 2019).

Writing a Future Vision Statement

A future vision statement for the purpose of transition planning typically includes four elements: what the student wants to do after high school, strengths for what they envision to do, supports needed, and living arrangement considerations. Loo (2019) developed a worksheet for writing a future vision statement for transition planning, and the following examples of future vision statements are based upon that work:

• Troy wants to enter ABCD University and study science. He dreams of working in the field of wildlife and land conservation. Troy and his family are concerned he will need help structuring his study habits and need testing accommoda-

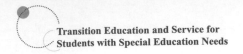

tions to be a successful college student. He plans to live at home with his mother while attending college, but he would like to live in an apartment once he finishes school and gets a job.

• Lisa will need supported employment services to obtain and maintain a job. She seems to prefer working around people. She has had enjoyable experiences in a grocery store as a bagger and as a lobby attendant in a fast food restaurant. Lisa's mother would like to see her living with a group of other young women in a community home or an apartment program. Lisa needs to learn some recreational activities she can initiate when she is alone. She also needs to learn some personal care skills and homemaking skills with a higher level of independence.

Determining Transition Services

Based on the student's present levels of performance and future vision statement, the IEP team can work with the student and family to specify post-school outcomes. This can be done by going through the life domains for transition planning and determining what outcomes the student wants to achieve in each area. There can be more than one outcome in each area; however, outcomes must be based on assessment data (i.e., student's strengths, interests, and preferences) and the future vision. Life domains the team may need to consider include:

- Postsecondary education
- Employment
- Community-based access
- Living arrangements
- Recreation/leisure
- Income/financial needs
- Domestic
- Community living
- Advocacy/legal
- Transportation

- Health and medical services
- Relationships

Once outcomes are specified, the IEP team needs to identify specific action steps and assign them to each party. In other words, all members of the IEP team need to have some responsibilities of taking on specific actions to help the student achieve the outcomes in the academic year following the IEP meeting. For example, teachers need to incorporate the specified outcomes into instruction to teach the student the necessary skills for independent living such as finance and budgeting. Vocational rehabilitation counselors may need to help the student plan off-campus or summer employment opportunities. It is important every action step has a timeline attached to it so there is assurance the action is completed on time.

Developing the Student's Educational Program

The action steps outlined by the IEP team that are pertaining to school need to be incorporated into the student's IEP and implemented. This is the best way for schools to provide instruction and support services that systematically prepare the student to achieve the desired outcomes. If the actions for schools are not embedded into instruction or school support services, the transition planning effort would be lost. It is important for the special education teacher who serves on the IEP team to work with other teachers, including the general education teacher if the student takes classes in the general education classroom, to see what courses address the needed knowledge and skills and who can teach those knowledge and skills if they are not already addressed in the course. Working as a team to operationalize the desired outcomes and action steps is key for breaking down goals into specific learning activities.

The school's action steps pertaining to instruction of life skills can be infused into subject matter instruction (Patton, Cronin, & Wood, 1999). For example, the life skill of keeping basic financial records can be infused into a consumer mathematics course or similar courses that cover applied mathematics skills. Infusion of this life

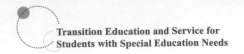

skill can take the following steps: (a) discuss record-keeping systems needed for managing family finances (e.g., maintaining a budget, preparing and paying taxes), (b) examine occupations that require financial record-keeping skills (e.g., seeking and securing a job), and (c) examine various types of community involvement that involve financial record-keeping skills (e.g., creating change in the community through volunteer work on a community fundraiser). However, for infusion of life skills to happen, the IEP team needs to make sure specific action steps are included in the transition plan.

Student and Family Involvement in Transition Assessment

Unlike other types of educational evaluations, student and parent roles in transition evaluation and assessment are expanded from completing assessments given to them by educational professionals to being an actual part of the evaluation decision-making and interpretation processes. Because transition assessments are used to plan and prepare for a student's future, the student and their family have critical roles. Person-centered practices are useful in obtaining information that can be used to develop truly individualized plans to facilitate the student's transition to adulthood.

Student Roles in Transition Assessment

The student is at the center of transition assessment. After all, how can educators plan for a student's future after school without the input of that student? Just like with the rest of the IEP, transition assessment should be individualized to the student, and the student should have genuine input. Participating in the transition assessment process may be another way to develop student self-determination (Collier et al., 2016), and student self-determination is associated with better post-school outcomes (Landmark, Ju, & Zhang, 2010).

Student input in the transition assessment process can include the student taking transition assessments, administering informal transition assessments, and analyzing transition assessment results with the educator's assistance. Educators are likely most familiar with having the student taking transition assessments in the form of answering questions about the student's future or completing surveys of their interests. However, students can also administer some transition assessments. For example, a student could use an informal transition assessment on identifying his/her strengths to interview his/her parents about what his/her parents believe are the student's strengths. Not only would the student be involved in collecting the data, but the student would also be able to have a conversation with his/her parents about how his/her parents sees strengths in the student. This type of transition assessment not only provides the educator with information about the student, but it also gives the student an opportunity to develop his/her self-efficacy. Finally, the student can help the educator with analyzing the transition assessment results. The educator would need to do some preliminary analysis, but could then present the student with the findings. The educator could ask the student if the student agrees with the findings, and then ask the student to support his/her agreement or disagreement with examples. If the student does not fully agree with the educator's initial assessment, then the educator and student can come up with a plan to obtain more data through additional transition assessment.

Family Roles in Transition Assessment

Just like every student is different, so too is every family. When conducting transition assessment, educators can obtain information from various family members including the student's parents, grandparents, siblings, and other family members who may be responsible for the student in the future. It is very important to understand the dynamics of the family, especially when transition planning for students who have more complex support needs and will need the support of their family for the rest of their lives. In some families, parents may be the decision-makers, but in other families, an elder in the family may be the decision-maker. Sometimes parents may expect their other children to take responsibility in the future for their child with a disability, or the child without a disability expects to play a significant role in their sibling with a disability's adult life. In these situations, the special education case manager should encourage the family to include the sibling without a disability, when age-appropriate, in the transition planning for the child with the disability (Hagiwara, Palmer, Hancock, & Shogren, 2019). The educator needs to understand these potentialities and seeks to obtain transition assessment data from the individuals who will be responsible for the individual with a disability in the future.

Family members can be involved in the transition assessment process in several ways. However, it is important for the educator to explain the purpose of transition assessment and subsequent planning before asking family members to complete transition assessments. Simple to complete transition assessments can be sent home to parents for completion and return to the school. However, it may be easier for the educator to convert the transition assessment to an electronic version that can be emailed to texted to a parent to complete. For example, Scheef and Johnson (2017) suggest creating a Google form from a transition assessment and sending the link to the family member to complete. The responses from the family member are then immediately available to the teacher without having to rely on the child or parent to send the transition assessment to school. If the teacher is using a transition assessment in the form of an interview, the teacher may call the family member and obtain the information over the phone or alternately set up a meeting with the family member in order to administer the transition assessment.

For students with disabilities who will require significant support needs as an adult, person-centered planning is a great way to collect data (and make a plan) from the individuals who will support the student as an adult. There are multiple formats of person-centered planning including Planning Alternative Tomorrows with Hope (PATH), Making Action Plans (MAPs), Personal Futures Planning, and more. No matter the method of person-centered planning one chooses to use as a transition assessment, all person-centered planning methods have commonalities. Person-centered planning involves the individual with a disability and a group of people who will support the person and problem-solve with the group to help the individual achieve a desirable life. The group of people who support the individual with a disability is not limited to immediate family members; indeed, family friends may be a part of this group of supporters. During the person-centered planning process, the group usually has a facilitator that guides the discussion to determine what is important to the individual with a disability and what is important for the individual with a disability when planning for the person's future life.

Conclusions

The transition from school to adulthood is a complex process that involves many agencies and individuals. Good transition planning based on adequate transition assessment and is data-driven. In order for all individuals to work together and plan adequate transition services for a student, they need to have a good understanding of the student's interests and strengths and the future goals are based on the student's individual needs. Conducting appropriate transition assessment is one of the first steps necessary for transition planning. Sharing transition assessment among all those who support the student is also important so that all are on the same page. The student and family must be an integral part of the transition assessment because they know the student better than anyone else. Working in collaborations is key to successful transition planning.

References

Brigance, A. H. (1995). *BRIGANCE diagnostic employability skills inventory*. North
Billerica, MA: Curriculum Associates.

Brolin, D. E. (1992). *Life centered career education: Competency assessment batteries*. Reston, VA: Council for Exceptional Children.

Carter, E. K., Trainor, A. A., Sun, Y., & Owens, L. (2009). Assessing the transition-related strengths and needs of adolescents with high-incidence disabilities. *Exceptional Children, 76*, 74-94.

Castiglione, S., Ashley, J. M., Hamilton, M., Leconte, P. J., McConnell, J., O'Brien, M., & Juliana, D. (2009). VECAP white paper on functional vocational evaluation (in support of IDEIA). *Vocational Evaluation and Career Assessment Journal, 6*(1), 49-58.

Clark, G. M. (2007). *Assessment for transitions planning* (2nd ed.). Austin, TX: Pro-ed.

Clark, G. M., & Patton, J. R. (2014). *Transition planning inventory* (2nd ed.) (TPI-2). Austin, TX: Pro-ed.

Collier, M. L., Griffin, M. M., & Wei, Y. (2016). Facilitating student involvement in transition assessment: A pilot study of the Student Transition Questionnaire. *Career Development and Transition for Exceptional Individuals, 39*, 175-184. doi:10.1177/2165143414556746

Graves, J. C., & Graves, C. (2019). *Writing a strong vision statement*. Retrieved from https://www.makespecialeducationwork.com/writing-strong-vision-statement

Hagiwara, M., Palmer, S. B., Hancock, C. L., & Shogren, K. A. (2019). Sibling roles in family-school partnerships for students with disabilities during transition planning. *Career Development and Transition for Exceptional Individuals, 42*, 194-200. doi:10.1177/2165143418792045

Individuals with Disabilities Education Act (IDEA), 20 U.S.C. § 1400 (2004).

Kochhar-Bryant, C., & Greene, G. (2009). *Pathways to successful transition for youth with disabilities: A developmental process* (2nd ed.). Englewood, NJ: Prentice-Hall.

Landmark, L. J., Ju, S., & Zhang, D. (2010). Substantiated best practices in transition: Fifteen plus years later. *Career Development for Exceptional Individuals, 33*, 165-176. doi:10.1177/0885728810376410

Lohrmann-O'Rourke, S., & Gomez, O. (2001). Integrating preference assessment within the transition process to create meaningful school-to-life outcomes. *Exceptionality, 9*, 157-174.

Loo, S. (2019). *Vision statement worksheets for transition planning*. Retrieved from https://www.aane.org/transition-planning-worksheet

Miner, C. A., & Bates, P. E. (1997). The effect of person centered activities on the IEP/transition planning process. *Education and Training in Mental Retardation and Developmental Disabilities, 32*, 105-112.

Neubert, D. A. (2003). The role of assessment in the transition to adult life process for students with disabilities. *Exceptionality, 11*, 63-75. doi:10.1207/S15327035EX1102_02

Patton, J. R., Cronin, M. E., & Wood, S. J. (1999). *Infusing real-life topics into existing curricula: Recommended procedures and instructional examples for the elementary, middle, and high school levels*. Austin, TX: Pro-ed.

Salvia, J., Neisworth, J. T., & Schmidt, M. W. (1990). *Responsibility and independence scale for adolescents*. Itasca, IL: Riverside Insights.

Scheef, A. R., & Johnson, C. J. (2017). The power of the cloud: Google forms for transition assessment. *Career Development and Transition for Exceptional Individuals, 40*, 250-255. doi:10.1177/2165143417700844

Schnellert, L. M. (2011). *Collaborative inquiry: Teacher professional development as situated, responsive co-construction of practice and learning* (Unpublished doctoral dissertation). University of British Columbia, Vancouver, Canada.

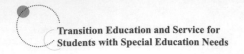
Test, D., Aspel, N. P., & Everson, J. M. (2006). *Transition methods for youth with disabilities*. Upper Saddle River, NJ: Pearson.

Thoma, C. A., Held, M., & Tamura, R. (2001). An overview of transition assessment: A person-centered approach to supporting student's choices for life. *2000 TASH Conference Yearbook*. Baltimore, MD: TASH.

U.S. Department of Labor. (2019). *CareerOneStop: Video library*. Retrieved from https://www.careeronestop.org/Videos/video-library.aspx

University of Texas. (2018). *Texas OnCourse*. Retrieved from https://texasoncourse.org/

Wejr, C. (2015). 10 ways to determine the strengths of our students. Retrieved from http://chriswejr.com/2015/04/19/10-ways-to-determine-the-strengths-of-our-students/

Whitney-Thomas, J., Shaw, D., Honey, K., & Butterworth, J. (1998). Building a future: A study of student participation in person-centered planning. *The Journal of the Association for Persons With Severe Handicaps, 23*, 119-133.

Zarrow Center for Learning Enrichment, University of Oklahoma. (2019). *Self-determination assessment tools*. Retrieved from http://www.ou.edu/education/centers-and-partnerships/zarrow/self-determination-assessment-tools

第七章　臺灣高中階段身心障礙學生之學校本位轉銜輔導模式

The School-Based Transition Model for High School in Taiwan

林素貞（Su-jan Lin）

　　轉銜的概念是指從一個情境跨越到另一個情境的轉換過程，它可以巨觀地指個人一生的生涯階段垂直性轉換，它也可以微觀地指個人在同一階段內的平行性不同情境或角色的轉換。以巨觀角度而言，生涯乃是探討在個人生命的全程中，如何成長與經歷不同階段的發展轉換歷程（林宏熾，1999；林幸台，2019；陳靜江、鈕文英，2008）。以微觀角度而言，轉銜也可以指個人在某一個階段內的角色和情境的轉換，例如：學生的轉學，或是托兒所或幼兒園內幼兒面對一些活動形式的轉換都是轉銜（Thomas, 2019）。然而，不管垂直性和平行性轉銜變化都是生涯發展的重要議題，教育領域則希望透過生涯教育能協助個人有更佳的生涯發展和成效，生涯教育倡導從幼兒階段起即有系統性實施整合性課程和活動，包括生涯覺知（career awareness）、生涯探索（career exploration）、志工活動、職業訓練、就業訓練、學徒制方案，以及非職業性角色體驗等，以統合個人於家庭、學校、社區中所有的學習活動，期使個人能實現自我潛能，終其一生在家庭、學校、社區、公民、經濟、休閒等各種的成人生活領域中取得適當發展（林幸台，2019；Brolin, 1995; Halpern, 1991; Levinson, 1998; Sitlington, Neubert, & Clark, 2010）。

壹、高中階段轉銜理念與實施之發展

　　從生涯教育的歷史發展觀之，生涯教育最初始發展即是從高中階段出發。1971 年，當時的美國教育部長 Sidney P. Marland 在休士頓對美國中學校

長協會所作的一篇講稿中，強烈呼籲中學階段教育必須重視學生畢業後的發展，此一觀點的提出乃基於三項背景：當時社會情勢的刺激、實用教育理念的發展，以及社會對教育改革的呼籲。此一時期 D. E. Brolin 也提出生涯教育的四大循序漸進的發展方向，包含：(1)生涯覺知（career awareness）；(2)生涯探索（career exploration）；(3)生涯準備（career preparation）；(4)生涯同化（career assimilation）——係指個人畢業離開高中後，轉接至就業或是接受高等教育的社會化過程；基於教育實施的需求，Brolin 也設計出「生活中心生涯教育課程」（life centered career education, LCCE），此生涯教育課程將同樣適用於一般學生和身心障礙學生（Brolin, 1995）。

　　若以生涯發展的不同階段目標觀之，個人最重要的轉銜關鍵大約於14～16 歲的青春期，也就是臺灣學生在國中要升上高中職之時，或是高中職階段，因為這個時期個人的生涯抉擇將會影響其一生的生涯發展，尤其在成人期的工作職業上發展（Trainor, 2017）。若從美國的轉銜服務的相關法規觀之，亦可了解青春期轉銜議題的重要性，以及其對身心障礙學生生涯發展的關鍵性。美國在 1990 年於《身心障礙者教育法》（IDEA）修訂中，第一次於法規中正式要求必須提供身心障礙學生的「轉銜計畫」（Transition Plan）。當時此法規針對轉銜議題乃有下列兩項要求：一是要求在 3 歲左右幼兒的「個別化家庭服務計畫」（Individual Family Service Plan, IFSP）中必須包含「轉銜計畫」，期待透過此轉銜計畫，可以幫助身心障礙幼兒從早期療育機構平順地銜接到學前教育機構或後續的教育環境；二是最遲在 16 歲，所有接受特殊教育的學生都必須要有「轉銜計畫」；它可以視個案狀況獨立擬定為「個別化轉銜計畫」（Individual Transition Plan, ITP），亦可以納入學生的「個別化教育計畫」（IEP）之中（Flexer, Baer, Luft, & Simmons, 2013）。隨後，美國在 1997 年修訂的《身心障礙者教育 1997 年修正法》中，則更明確採用了「轉銜服務」（transition service）一詞，此轉銜服務指為身心障礙學生所設計，強調學校需以結果為導向（outcome-oriented）提供一系列整合性活動給身心障礙學生；這系列性的活動將促進學生可由學校順利過渡到學校畢業後的生活，系列性活動

的內涵，包括高中畢業後的教育、職業訓練、整合式就業（包括支持性就業）、成人繼續教育、成人服務、成人獨立生活、社區參與。法規要求學校在規劃轉銜服務的相關教學活動必須考量：(1)根基於學生個別的需要，考慮學生的偏好與興趣；(2)包括教學、社區經驗、就業準備，以及其他離校後成人生活所應具備能力的相關活動；如果可能或必須的話，教學活動尚包含日常生活技能與功能性評量。美國 1997 年的修訂法案相較於 1990 年的法案對於轉銜議題之規定，乃有兩項重要變革：(1)規定身心障礙學生提早至年屆 14 歲時，教學機構必須每年於其個別化教育計畫（IEP）的不同內容項目下，適當地陳述及記載該學生有關「職業教育」、「進階安置課程」的轉銜服務需求；(2)在身心障礙學生年屆各州所規定法定年齡之最遲前一年，教學機構必須於其 IEP 中，適當地陳述及記載該學生已被告知，達到各州法定年齡的相關權益（林素貞，2007）。

現行美國 2004 年修訂的《身心障礙者教育 2004 年修正法》（IDEA, 2004）中，更重申轉銜服務是以學生離開學校後之「以成果為導向」（result-oriented）的整合性教學活動歷程，這個定義改變了之前 1997 年修訂法案的「以結果為導向」（outcome-oriented）轉銜理念。結果與成果的意義本質相似，但是結果（outcome）通常指事情經過長時間發展之後的後果，而這些後果比較難以預料和掌握；成果（result）則是指某些事件直接引起的後果，而這些後果比較可以掌握和預測。Halpern、Yovanoff、Doren 與 Benz（1995）、Heal、Rusch（1995）以及 Trainor（2017）都提出針對身心障礙學生所提供的轉銜服務過程中，必須強調考量學生未來就業和成人社區生活需求的教學介入之必要性和重要性。亦即是轉銜服務必須重視學生學習之後對於其未來升學、就業或生活的成效，不再僅是「有」提供學生學習的機會，更要提出對學生後續成人生活有助益的具體成效。美國 2004 年《身心障礙者教育 2004 年修正法》再對轉銜服務提出非常清楚且明確的定義：轉銜服務意指為身心障礙學生所統整的一系列活動，包含：(1)以成果為導向的歷程；強調提升身心障礙學生在學科學習和實用性技能的能力，以有助於他們從高中學校教育到學校畢業後的生活與環境適應。學生高中畢業後的環境可能包括繼續接受高等教育、參與職業訓練、廣泛性就

業（包含支持性就業）、成人繼續教育、成人服務、獨立生活和社區參
與；(2)轉銜服務乃是基於學生的個別需求而設計，其考量應包含學生的優
勢能力、偏好和興趣；(3)轉銜服務設計應基於多元評估，其內容應涵蓋教
學、相關專業服務、社區經驗、就業發展、成人生活目標、日常生活技
能、功能性職業的評估（IDEA, 2004）。

　　如前所述，轉銜的理念發展脈絡乃延伸自生涯發展與教育、職業教育
以及轉銜教育（Sitlington et al., 2010; Wehman, 2013），從美國特殊教育法規
對轉銜的定義和內容的轉變，可以得知他們非常重視中學階段身心障礙學
生的轉銜計畫；轉銜的理念在特殊教育的發展與應用，也隨著社會和教育
理念的變遷以及法規修訂的變遷不斷做調整，現階段美國特殊教育乃通用
「轉銜服務」（transition service）一詞，臺灣則是使用「轉銜輔導與服務」
一詞。我國在特殊教育法規出現轉銜的理念，則起始於 2009 年公告的《特
殊教育法》第 31 條：「為使各教育階段身心障礙學生服務需求得以銜接，
各級學校應提供整體性與持續性轉銜輔導及服務；其轉銜輔導及服務之辦
法，由中央主管機關定之」（教育部，2019），此乃明確指出各教育階段
針對身心障礙學生的轉銜輔導與服務的重要性和必要性；教育部更於 2010
年依據此條款公告《各教育階段身心障礙學生轉銜輔導及服務辦法》（教
育部，2010），此辦法成為我國實施轉銜輔導與服務的最高指導原則。依
據此辦法，我國轉銜輔導與服務的目標應為協助學生達成獨立生活、社會
適應與參與、升學或就業等，亦對於執行轉銜輔導服務的時程有明確的規
範，此辦法乃指出教育階段需進行的轉銜輔導與服務之內容，例如：各級
學校應評估身心障礙學生個別能力與轉銜需求，再訂定出適切之生涯轉銜
計畫，並協調社政、勞工及衛生主管機關，提供學生整體性與持續性轉銜
輔導及服務。此外高級中等以下學校應將生涯轉銜計畫納入學生個別化教
育計畫，專科以上學校應納入學生的個別化支持計畫。

▌貳、成功轉銜的重要影響因素

　　美國從 1970 年代開始，教育界不斷重視與研究對身心障礙學生的轉銜

計畫和服務的模式，再搭配特殊教育相關法規的要求，轉銜服務成為高中階段身心障礙學生的重要核心議題（Halpern et al., 1995; Morgan & Riesen, 2016; Test, Aspel, & Everson, 2006; Wehman, 2013），也因此相關研究豐盛，可作為實務執行轉銜服務之參考。Kohler（1993, 1996, 1998）以及 Kohler 與 Field（2003）曾經提出了身心障礙學生高中畢業後能轉銜成功的學校實務執行的五項重要向度，Kohler、Gothberg、Fowler 與 Coyle（2016）更提出完整的「轉銜方案向度 2.0 版」（Taxonomy for Transition Programming 2.0），以作為轉銜服務的參考。此五類內容分述如下：(1)以學生為主的規劃（含個別化教育計畫、執行計畫的策略、學生的參與）；(2)考量學生的發展（含評估、基本學科能力、生活社交和情緒處理能力、職業技能和就業能力、學生所需的支持、教學上的需求）；(3)整合相關單位的合作（含合作的機制、相關服務的銜接）；(4)家庭的參與（含家庭的參與、家庭的賦權、家庭的準備度）；(5)學校有系統的規劃相關活動（含計畫的內容、計畫的評估、計畫的策略、實施辦法和程序、相關支援的配套措施、學校的氛圍）。Wehman（2013）也提出有關高中階段身心障礙學生成功轉銜教育的六項重要議題：(1)學生的職業能力以及對就業的想法與準備；(2)自我決策（self-determination）與自我倡權（self-advocacy）；(3)社交能力（social competence）；(4)學校和社區的融合經驗；(5)父母的參與；(6)高中畢業後的持續教育機會；他認為此六項議題的完整運作，方能造就身心障礙學生從高中畢業之後無接縫轉銜至成人的生活，包含升學、就業、支持性就業、職業訓練、社區參與和獨立生活等。以上相關研究者所提出的身心障礙學生的成功轉銜模式，已經成為教育實務工作者努力的方向。

國立轉銜技術協助中心（NTACT）乃是美國為了提升身心障礙學生中學畢業後能有成功發展的長期研究計畫，這項計畫由美國教育部特殊教育司（OSEP）以及復健行政部門提供經費補助，此計畫主要為以研究成果幫助各州政府的教育部門、各學區教育局、各州職業復健機構，如何協助身心障礙學生可以在高中畢業後成功銜接繼續升學大專校院或是就業，協助方式乃為提供有效的學校介入指標以及實務運作方案，成功的預測指標包含身心障礙學生可以完成嚴格的學科課程，以及參與各項生涯發展相關課

程。這些有效的預測指標乃經由實證研究支持、研究支持和實務經驗支持的三種評估層次所組合而成，此中心目前已經提出 20 項可以有效預測身心障礙學生高中畢業後成功發展的教育介入指標（National Technical Assistance Center on Transition [NTACT], 2019），此 20 項學校所提供介入的預測指標和學生高中畢業後的升學高等教育、就業或獨立生活等重要成果的配對，如表 7-1 所示，此 20 項學校所提供的課程或活動之預測指標，全部和學生未來的就業有關，其中 13 項則和學生未來是否升學高等教育有關，只有 5 項和學生成人的獨立生活能力有關。該中心亦彙整每一項成功轉銜實務運作預測指標下具體的實施課程與教學或方案，以提供實務工作者參考，此中心的網址為 https://transitionta.org/about，有興趣者可以進一步了解其詳細內容。

　　國立轉銜技術協助中心（NTACT）為了有效評估學校的教育介入對身心障礙學生高中畢業後成功發展的成效，也研發可以讓學區教育局和學校針對轉銜輔導與服務進行自我評鑑的模式，此評鑑結果共有四種等級：目前未執行、斷斷續續執行、剛開始執行和目前已經執行，四種等級中的「目前未執行」指學區或校內有 0 至 25% 的學生偶爾或未持續學習此一預測指標的敘述內容；「斷斷續續執行」指學區或校內有 25 至 50% 的學生偶爾或未持續學習此一預測指標的敘述內容；「剛開始執行」指學區或學校想要落實執行此項指標，目前學區或學校內有 50 至 75% 的學生持續有學習此一預測指標的敘述內容；「目前已經執行」指學區或校內已經有 75 至 100% 的學生持續性有學習此一預測指標的敘述內容。此自我評鑑為量化的評鑑模式，評鑑標準所得分數共分有四類：「沒有證據」是 0 分；「證據薄弱」是 1 分；「證據中度」是 2 分；「證據充足」是 3 分。每一個評鑑標準都要求有具體描述性資料，例如：最佳之 3 分的「證據充足」乃指學區或學校必須提出：(1)各項計畫或課程的實施歷程資料（含教案或活動設計）、相關的表格和實施紀錄，以及學生在各單元或單課的成績評量；(2)學生的學習成果、學生的回家作業；(3)各項計畫或課程的執行評鑑資料。全國轉銜技術協助中心已建立非常嚴謹且具體的轉銜輔導與服務之評鑑系統，其以完整的大量佐證資料評估學校轉銜的重要介入指標之實施成果，確實可以作為學校自我評鑑，或是教育行政單位評鑑學校之重要參考工具。

表 7-1　轉銜成效之學校介入預測指標與學生畢業後成效對照表

在學校的預測指標／畢業後成果	升學高等教育	就業	獨立生活
生涯覺知課程		×	
社區經驗		×	
通過高中畢業考試和要求／取得高中畢業資格		×	
設定目標	×	×	
在普通學校接受融合教育	×	×	×
跨機構合作	×	×	
個別化職涯探索課程	×	×	
有薪水的工作經驗	×	×	×
家長期待子女高中畢業後能繼續升學大學或就業	×	×	×
家長／家庭參與		×	
基本學科或實用性學科課程		×	
自我倡權／自我決策	×	×	
自我照顧／獨立生活技能	×	×	×
能與他人溝通和合作的態度和行為之社交技能課程	×	×	
學生的支持網絡（家庭、朋友、教師和社福人員）	×	×	×
中學階段為畢業後成人生活預做準備的轉銜計畫	×	×	
使用交通工具到不同地方的能力		×	
特定技能的職業教育	×	×	
發展工作態度和基本工作能力課程		×	
青年自主／自己做決定	×	×	

參、我國近二十年高中階段轉銜研究趨勢

　　1990 年開始，美國的法規要求學校要實施身心障礙學生的轉銜服務，我國對於轉銜輔導與服務的法規要求則始於 2010 年，法規對於教育實施轉銜服務乃有其重要影響力，然而臺灣的實務界和學術界亦早有相關的研究成果，針對高中職階段身心障礙學生的轉銜輔導與服務的相關研究，本文利用國家圖書館所設立的「臺灣博碩士論文知識加值系統」搜尋 2000 至 2019 年之間的臺灣所發表的碩博士論文，先以「轉銜」一詞進行搜尋，再一一檢視選取以高中職階段身心障礙學生為研究對象的論文，結果共有 47 篇碩博士論文，請參見本章參考文獻，其中有 3 篇為博士論文研究（李玉錦，2014；周玫君，2018；蘇皇妃，2008），其餘 44 篇為碩士論文（尤淑君，2008；石筱郁，2007；吳季純，2008；吳明燕，2015；吳宣鋒，2009；吳政寰，2019；宋采霓，2016；李建德，2012；李淑君，2003；李雯琪，2010；林和姻，2003；林炯承，2011；邱志鴻，2013；胡曼莉，2013；張嘉容，2016；許明儀，2006；許芳瑜，2009；許家璇，2003；許雅婷，2008；郭嫦燕，2014；陳怡錦，2014；陳冠伶，2011；陳映如，2009；陳維婷，2013；陳靜怡，2006；陳韻年，2013；黃小婷，2009；黃蕙蓮，2006；黃靜宜，2006；黃璽璇，2005；楊岱蓉，2016；楊純斐，2011；楊琇雅，2011；葉盈均，2014；劉玉婷，2001；歐怡君，2003；潘佳伶，2017；蕭漢寧，2014；鍾和村，2013；簡美蘭，2010；蘇盈宇，2003；蘇湘甯，2014；蘇微真，2015；龔瑪婷，2013）。本文依據研究方法、研究對象、特殊教育安置型態和研究區域四個向度，綜合分析我國高中職階段轉銜議題的研究趨勢。此 47 篇論文的研究方法主要為問卷調查、訪談、行動研究、主題分析法，以及回溯型世代研究；研究對象主要乃以集中式特教班（綜合職能科）的智能障礙學生為主，其他障礙類別學生包含學習障礙、自閉症、視覺障礙、聽覺障礙、肢障障礙、多重障礙學生；學生的安置型態則包含一般高中職資源班、集中式特教班和特殊學校高職部；研究區域則主要以全臺灣為研究場域，少部分以單一縣市為主。

在此 47 篇碩士論文研究中，本文發現其可分類為五個範疇進行討論，包含職業準備與就業、升學、成人生活、轉銜計畫和評估、家長參與轉銜計畫。此二十年間學位論文研究首先最常使用的研究主題是職業準備與就業轉銜，占全體研究篇數的 36%，研究內容包括職業試探、職業能力之評量、職業輔導評量、就業轉銜的學校課程安排與教學、職場實習課程、就業安置及追蹤輔導、職業準備與就業開發、就業準備之學生參與、相關專業間互動合作、個別化轉銜計畫的擬定。

其次是生涯轉銜模式與評量的議題，占全體之 27%，例如：有研究者發展「轉銜服務量表」，探討包含自我照顧、心理健康／自我決定、功能性學科能力、人際互動、居家生活、社區／休閒生活的基礎轉銜能力。亦有研究者發展評估學生「規劃下一階段的轉銜能力」，包含升學、職業訓練、就業、獨立生活的安排、社會互動、婚姻和家庭計畫等。也有研究者探討轉銜需求量表，包括「職業生活期望」、「社區適應期望」、「生活照顧期望」、「醫療復健期望」和「教育學習期望」五個向度內容。

第三個研究議題是家長參與其子女轉銜服務的研究，占全體之 24%，涵蓋就業轉銜的親師合作與家長參與、家長參與轉銜服務的現況、家長參與轉銜服務的期望等。最後兩個轉銜研究議題則是探討升學以及成人生活，各占 6.5%。高中職階段的生活轉銜議題包含休閒娛樂的需求、身心障礙學生的自我決策、居家服務、機構服務，也有研究者探討成人的社會適應與成年生活、健康管理與心理衛生，以及財務規劃與居家安排問題。升學轉銜議題則包括了解身心障礙學生在升學上的學習技能、獨立生活技能、自我倡權及了解入學資訊和條件的準備度，以及如何協助身心障礙高中職學生順利升學與完成大專校院學業之需求等。

由上述 2000 至 2019 年之間我國高中職階段轉銜的研究趨勢可知，近年來我國仍將此一階段的轉銜議題關注焦點放在職業與就業轉銜，成人的獨立生活和升學議題則相對弱化，若以前述美國多年來所探討出身心障礙者成功轉銜需涵蓋就業、升學和獨立生活之全面性概念而言，我國現階段對於轉銜的研究與實務應用，宜再廣化與深化對身心障礙學生之升學和未來獨立生活議題的教育；但是可喜的現象，應該可看出我國家長已將參與其

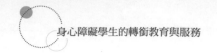

子女的轉銜規劃和決策當成重要的議題。

肆、我國高中階段學校本位轉銜實驗模式雛議

如前所述，我國學術界和實務界對於高中階段轉銜已逐漸累積足夠的成果，然而如相關的研究所指出，轉銜的實施乃是強調以由學校本位出發建構學生的升學、就業和社區經驗的運作（Polloway, Patton, Serna, & Bailey, 2018a; Test, Mazzotti, Mustian, Fowler, Kortering, & Kohler, 2009; Trainor, 2017; Wehman, 2013），因此本文作者乃於 2016 年進行研究探討我國高中職身心障礙學生的轉銜輔導與服務現況和發展（林素貞、詹孟琦、陳玉娟，2016），主要研究目的為了解我國技術型高中執行轉銜輔導與服務現況，以及提出相關人員的合作模式。美國在身心障礙學生之轉銜計畫的實施已經有近三十年的歷史，他們的實務經驗之運作模式確實值得我們借鏡與參考（Clark, Synatschk, Patton, & Steel, 2012; Polloway et al., 2018a）。本研究的學校轉銜運作模式主要參考美國 Patton 與 Clark（2014）以來兩位學者所發展的轉銜計畫模式（transition planning model）（如圖 7-1 所示），此模式乃是兩位學者依據美國特殊教育法規要求，再配合美國的學校實際運作方式發展而成。此模式包含兩個階段：第一個階段是學生整體轉銜需求評估；第二階段則是學生轉銜計畫的擬定。此模式在第一階段為了協助教育工作者的診斷評估工作進行，亦發展出「偏好、興趣和優勢量表」（Career Interests, Preferences, and Strengths Inventory, CIPSI）以及「轉銜計畫量表」（第二版）（Transition Planning Inventory, 2nd ed., TPI-2），以了解學生在轉銜輔導過程中，適應未來離開學校後所需要的工作、學習和生活能力的需求。第二階段的轉銜計畫則包含兩部分：一是身心障礙學生未來在工作、學習和生活能力之知識和技能的訓練；二是如何連結身心障礙學生未來在大學校園或工作職場所需要的相關支援和資源；此模式提出學生的相關知識和技能的訓練，乃有賴學校教師、輔導人員和相關人員透過正式課程以進行教學。

本研究先參考美國學者 Patton & Clark 於 2014 年所提出的轉銜計畫歷程

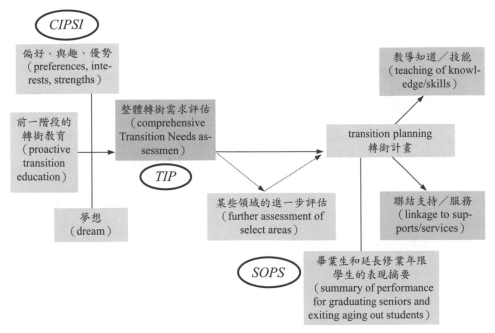

圖 7-1　Patton & Clark 的轉銜計畫歷程模式

資料來源：Patton 與 Clark（2014）

模式，再依據臺灣轉銜相關法規要求，以公立和私立各一所高級職業學校為研究對象，以人員訪談和實地訪視方式，了解兩所技術型高中的轉銜輔導與服務之運作實務，從而發展出學校本位轉銜輔導與服務執行步驟為：(1)需求評估；(2)擬定轉銜計畫；(3)召開轉銜會議；(4)分工執行；(5)成效評估；(6)追蹤輔導；本研究所欲建構的學校本位身心障礙學生轉銜輔導及服務運作歷程模式，如圖 7-2 所示。

依據 Kohler 等人（2016）所提出身心障礙學生高中畢業後能轉銜成功的五項重要類別之一的「整合相關單位的合作機制」，本研究模式針對校內相關人員的分工合作，乃先界定出學校的直接相關人員。此兩所實驗學校皆設有特殊教育組，學校內皆設有集中式特教班（綜合職能科）和資源班，除了資源班的特殊教育教師，此二校亦聘有資源教室輔導員和職業輔導員。本研究選取技術型高中為實驗學校，主要乃考量其同時設有集中式

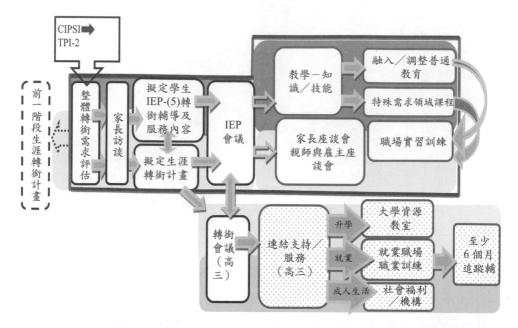

圖 7-2　臺灣技術型高中身心障礙學生轉銜輔導及服務運作模式

特教班和資源班，集中式特教班的身心障礙學生畢業後的轉銜乃以就業為主，分散式資源班的學生則以升學轉銜為主，選擇技術型高中為實驗學校則可以兼顧我國高中階段身心障礙學生轉銜需輔導與服務的多元性，同時因為此兩所實驗學校皆編制有多位特殊教育班教師，一位資源教師、一位資源教室輔導員、一位職業輔導員。因此以一所技術型高中為例，轉銜輔導與服務將可整合特殊教育教師、普通教育教師、學校輔導教師、職業輔導員和資源教室輔導員。

　　本研究的甲實驗學校全校日夜間部共有 17 科 216 個班級，學生總數為 9,737 人，其中身心障礙學生人數為 370 人，分布於集中式特教班（綜合職能科）共有 6 班，學生人數約為 90 人；就讀於普通班而接受資源教室服務的身心障礙學生則有 280 人。乙實驗學校全校共有 9 科 65 個班級，學生總數為 2,302 人，其中身心障礙學生人數為 77 人，集中式特教班（綜合職能科）共有 3 班，學生人數約為 45 人；就讀於普通班而接受資源班服務的身心障礙學生約有 32 人。

　　目前，美國有些州在高中為了執行身心障礙學生的轉銜輔導與服務，亦在學校聘用轉銜輔導員（transition specialist），以利學生轉銜服務相關工作的運作，此輔導員亦非教師，主要以行政協調溝通和學生個案管理員為主要工作職責。我國高中職資源班（教室）的發展歷史是所有教育階段最緩慢的一環，目前我國高中職各校的資源教師都是一至兩位教師，卻必須承擔全校所有身心障礙學學生的教學與輔導、和普通班教師的協調溝通，以及特殊教育的相關行政工作等，包含身心障礙學生之轉銜輔導與服務，以及大學校園的升學資源連結（林素貞，2014），確實超過負荷，已經影響教學職責和成效。我國的國民與學前教育署已於 2014 年起，於公私立高中職設立資源教室輔導員，其聘用標準為公立高中職全校有 40 位以上身心障礙學生，而私立高中職全校有 20 位以上身心障礙學生；值至 2015 年度全國已經有 103 所高中職各聘有一位資源教室輔導員，相信後續將會繼續增加校數與輔導員人數。國民與學前教育署聘用非具教師資格之資源教室輔導員，以協助各校的特殊教育相關業務之推行，以減輕各校資源教師須執行教學、特殊教育行政和學生資源整合的工作負荷。事實上，高中職資源教室輔導員特質和大專校院資源教室輔導員的角色非常相似，大專校院資源教室輔導員乃以學生個案管理與資源整合職務為主，也包含了身心障礙大學生的轉銜輔導工作（林素貞，2014）。如前所述，我國高中職資源教室輔導員也將和美國高中轉銜輔導員一樣，具有相同的職責。因此目前在資源教師以教學為主，資源教室輔導員以個案管理員和行政協助為主的工作職務前提下，本研究欲以資源教室輔導員為主的轉銜輔導職責規劃，配合資源教師和職業輔導員，規劃執行高中階段資源班（教室）學生的轉銜計畫模式，以利我國高中職資源班（教室）推動身心障礙學生轉銜輔導與服務的運作。

　　本研究透過實地訪視了解兩所實驗學校的轉銜運作方式，再以行動研究和兩所學校一起建構出高中階段學校本位轉銜輔導與服務的可行模式，以下針對此模式的執行步驟逐一說明。第一項執行步驟為：需求評估。本研究實驗學校乃採用「轉銜計畫量表」（第二版）（TPI-2）與「偏好、興趣和優勢量表」（CIPSI）兩項轉銜評估工具，以及教師自編之「職業能力

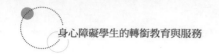

評估」和「我喜歡做的事」問卷以了解學生的轉銜需求。

國內陳靜江、鈕文英（2008）曾經發展「高中職階段身心障礙者轉銜能力評量表」，以作為身心障礙學生擬定轉銜計畫之依據；此評量表乃是參考 Clark 與 Patton 於 1997 所編製之「轉銜計畫量表」（TPI）而成，而此「轉銜計畫量表」（TPI）在 2014 年已經修訂為第二版（TPI-2），其目的是提供學校人員一個可接受、可信賴的方法，以全面性地決定所察覺到學生的轉銜需求，也因此此評估表相同題目內容共有三個版本：學生、學校和家庭，學生版由學生自行填寫，學校版則由熟悉學生的教師或輔導人員填寫，家庭版則是由家長填寫，因為涉及美國的多元文化背景，家庭版除了英語還有拉丁文、中文、韓文等，所以臺灣的使用者即可以直接使用此評估表的中文版。「轉銜計畫量表」（第二版）（TPI-2）的內容共有 57題，分屬工作、學習和生活三個領域，工作領域包含生涯抉擇、就業的知識與技能兩個次領域；學習領域包含未來的教育、功能性溝通和自我決策三個次領域；生活領域則包含獨立生活、金錢管理、社區參與、休閒、健康和人際關係六個次領域。教師或輔導人員將從學生本身、學校人員和家長的填答中，找出學生是否在工作、學習和生活的 11 個次領域中，有轉銜輔導與服務的需求。

美國 2004 年修訂的《身心障礙者教育 2004 年修正法》中要求轉銜計畫，必須基於學生的個別需求，包含學生的優勢能力、偏好和興趣而加以設計，Clark 等人（2012）為了因應美國特殊教育法規的要求，協助教育工作者能評估身心障礙學生此轉銜上的需求，而發展出「偏好、興趣和優勢量表」（CIPSI）。此量表為網路線上評量，共包含四個向度：一般偏好、個人興趣、個人優勢和職業興趣，每一個向度設計有不同問題讓填答者回答，填答者完成題目後，此量表會完成資料分析，填答者可以立即印出結果報表，教師或輔導人員可以協助學生考量其他相關條件，再做個人生涯抉擇的整體分析。

第二項與第三項執行步驟分別為：擬定轉銜計畫與召開轉銜會議。兩所實驗學校皆在學生由國中升學高中職的暑假，先召開新生轉銜會議，邀請新生及其家長、國中端教師、高職端輔導教師共同參與會議，初步了解

每個新生的特質、興趣與學習需求等。而從高一上學期到高三下學期，每一學期開學前學校皆會為身心障礙學生召開個別化教育計畫會議，以及個別化教育計畫的期末檢討會議。高中職階段身心障礙學生的轉銜計畫，通常會納入其個別化教育計畫內容的第五項：學生之轉銜輔導及服務內容。參與會議的人員通常包含：導師、任課教師、輔導教師、特教專業團隊等相關人員、家長或學生本人，大家共同討論學生學習的目標與需求，提供適切之學習目標及彈性評量。每一學期末的個別化教育計畫會議主要為檢核、評估或調整每一位身心障礙學生的整體學習成效。

　　第四項執行步驟為：分工執行。本研究彙整兩所實驗學校，依照時間軸發展，區分集中式特教班（如表 7-2 所示）和分散式資源班（如表 7-3 所示），從國中升高一暑假開始運作。以下分述從高一到高三每一學期，學校針對轉銜所實施的各種教學、活動或會議，以作為分工執行轉銜輔導與服務的具體措施。

表 7-2　集中式特教班一至三年級轉銜輔導與服務活動一覽表

年級	會議／活動名稱	形式	辦理內容	辦理單位
國中升高一暑假	新生適性輔導安置座談會	個別	1. 辦理當年度新生適性輔導轉銜會議，邀請新生及其家長、國中端教師、高職端輔導教師共同參與會談，初步了解新生個別特質、興趣、學習需求等。 2. 實施職業能力評估，確認新生職業類，以及學習上所需輔具及無障礙設施等。	輔導教師特教班教師
	新生始業輔導活動	團體	由學務處辦理當年度所有入學學生之始業輔導，內容包含認識各處室及其服務項目、認識校園、校園守則等。	學務處新生班導師（含普通教師及特教教師）
	家訪	個別	針對安置新生，由綜職科教師分組進行家訪，了解學生個人特質、生態環境評估、家庭功能概況、職業興趣傾向，實施「我喜歡做的事」問卷。	特教班教師

表 7-2　集中式特教班一至三年級轉銜輔導與服務活動一覽表（續）

年級	會議／活動名稱	形式	辦理內容	辦理單位
高一上學期	親職講座	團體	邀請特殊教育類親職教育專家蒞校分享：親子教養、親子溝通、生命教育等講題，增進家長正向教養技巧與態度，鼓勵依孩子優勢能力與特質，引導適切生涯發展方向。	輔導教師特教班教師
	親師溝通家訪或電訪	個別	導師視需要進行家訪或電訪，協助家長了解學生學習現況、職業教育課程學習內容，研討未來生涯轉銜發展可行方向，鼓勵準備丙級專業技能培訓。	特教班教師
高一下學期	親師溝通家訪或電訪	個別	導師視需要進行家訪或電訪，協助家長了解學生學習現況、職業教育課程學習內容，研討未來生涯轉銜發展可行方向，鼓勵準備丙級專業技能培訓。	特教班教師
	親職講座	團體	邀請特殊教育類親職教育專家蒞校分享：親子教養、親子溝通、生命教育等講題，增進家長正向教養技巧與態度，鼓勵依孩子優勢能力與特質，引導適切生涯發展方向。	特教班教師
	親師溝通家訪或電訪	個別	導師視需要進行家訪或電訪，協助家長了解學生學習現況、職業教育課程學習內容，研討未來生涯轉銜發展可行方向，鼓勵準備丙級專業技能考照。	特教班教師
高一下學期	職場見習	團體	1. 依學生興趣性向及職業能力評估分組，配合職業教育課程每週一天至相關職場見習實作，深入了解職場現況及所需能力，以為三年級校外實習做準備。 2. 由各職場輔導教師帶隊前往實習職場，認識工作環境、工作人員、工作內容等相關事項，以做好職場實習前之準備。	特教組長特教班導師各任課教師職業輔導員
	職場參訪	團體	參訪相關職場，讓學生了解不同職場之工作內容與職場需求。	輔導教師特教班教師
	職場實習前置會議	團體	學生於職場實習前召開，邀請廠商、家長、學生及職場輔導教師出席會議，共同認識彼此，並討論職場實習之相關注意事項。	特教組長特教班導師職場輔導教師職業輔導員

表 7-2 集中式特教班一至三年級轉銜輔導與服務活動一覽表（續）

年級	會議／活動名稱	形式	辦理內容	辦理單位
高一下學期	校外實習	個別	安排校外職場實習，依學生之能力、職業性向，以及考量跨職類之多元學習，進行校外職場實習安排，實際於業界進行工作與學習（高二每週 1 天、高三每週 3 天）。	特教組長 特教班導師 職場輔導教師 職業輔導員
	職業輔導評量會議	個別	邀請勞工局個案管理員，為職業性向不明確、就業能力和特質不明確等之學生，辦理職業輔導評量評估。	特教組長 特教班導師 職業輔導員
高二下學期	親師溝通家訪或電訪	個別	導師視需要進行家訪或電訪，協助家長了解學生學習現況、職業教育課程學習內容，研討未來生涯轉銜發展可行方向，鼓勵準備丙級專業技能培訓。	特教班教師
	職場見習	團體	依學生興趣性向及職業能力評估分組，配合職業教育課程每週一天至相關職場見習實作，建立職場概念，以為三年級校外職場實習做準備。	輔導教師 特教班教師
	職場參訪	團體	參訪相關職場，讓學生了解不同職場之工作內容與職場需求。	輔導教師 特教班教師
	校外實習	個別	安排校外職場實習，依學生之能力、職業性向，以及考量跨職類之多元學習，進行校外職場實習安排，實際於業界進行工作與學習（高二每週 1 天）。	特教組長 特教班導師 職場輔導教師 職業輔導員
	職場實習檢討會議	團體	邀請廠商、家長、學生及職場輔導教師出席會議，分享及討論一年來學生實習之表現，感謝職場之協助外，建議事項也將作為未來努力之方向。	特教組長 特教班導師 職場輔導教師 職業輔導員
高三上學期	職場實習	個別	依學生興趣性向及職業能力，於學生住家生活社區，媒合實習職場，由現場主管、自然支持者、巡廠老師與家長，共同指導學生工作技能、職場適應、交通訓練、人際互動等，以期學生畢業後順利就業轉銜。	職場輔導教師 特教班教師
	高三家長多元入學說明會	團體	邀請有意升學之家長及學生蒞校，說明身心障礙大專甄試及四技二專相關升學訊息，以利家長引導學生未來生涯進路規劃。	輔導教師 特教班教師
	職場參訪	團體	參訪相關職場，讓學生了解不同職場之工作內容與職場需求。	輔導教師 特教班教師

表 7-2　集中式特教班一至三年級轉銜輔導與服務活動一覽表（續）

年級	會議／活動名稱	形式	辦理內容	辦理單位
高三上學期	職場實習前置會議	團體	於職場實習前召開，邀請廠商、家長、學生及職場輔導教師出席會議，共同認識彼此，並討論職場實習之相關注意事項。	特教組長 特教班導師 職場輔導教師 職業輔導員
	個別化職業轉銜會議	個別	邀請勞工局個案管理員，為高三具就業意願及符合勞工局服務資格之學生，進行個案現況討論及就業評估。	特教組長 特教班導師 職業輔導員
	校外實習	個別	安排校外職場實習，依學生之能力、職業性向，以及考量跨職類之多元學習，進行校外職場實習安排，實際於業界進行工作與學習（高三每週 3 天）。	特教組長 特教班導師 職場輔導教師 職業輔導員
	親師座談會	團體	由學務處辦理全校之親師座談會活動，活動包含專題演講及親師溝通時間等。	學務處 各班導師（含普教及特教）
高三下學期	親師溝通家訪或電訪	個別	導師視需要進行家訪或電訪，協助家長了解學生校外實習現況，共同協助學生適應職場環境，為未來就業做好準備。	特教班教師
	職場實習	個別	依學生興趣性向及職業能力，於學生住家生活社區，媒合實習職場，由現場主管、自然支持者、巡廠老師與家長，共同指導學生工作技能、職場適應、交通訓練、人際互動等，以期學生畢業後順利就業轉銜。	職場輔導教師 特教班教師
	職場參訪	團體	參訪相關職場，讓學生了解不同職場之工作內容與職場需求。	輔導教師 特教班教師
	親師雇主座談會	團體	邀請職場實習雇主、巡場老師與學生家長，共同討論學生在職場上已具備之工作能力或尚需調整之工作態度與專業技能等。	輔導教師 特教班教師
	生涯轉銜輔導座談會	個別	邀請勞工局職業重建人員、地區職業輔導員，蒞校與學生及家長個別座談，討論未來轉銜安置單位之建議。	輔導教師 特教班教師
	親師雇主暨實習檢討座談會	團體	介紹社會局、勞工局、社會福利機構等單位的服務與資源，提供學生與家長未來畢業後可參考運用之相關資源。	輔導教師 特教班教師
	個別化轉銜會議	個別	另為綜職科未持有身障證明、考慮就學或需要就養之個案，辦理轉銜會議。	特教組長 特教班導師

表 7-2　集中式特教班一至三年級轉銜輔導與服務活動一覽表（續）

年級	會議／活動名稱	形式	辦理內容	辦理單位
高三 下學期	校外實習	個別	安排校外職場實習，依學生之能力、職業性向，以及考量跨職類之多元學習，進行校外職場實習安排，實際於業界進行工作與學習（高二每週 1 天、高三每週 3 天）。	特教組長 特教班導師 職場輔導教師 職業輔導員
	職場實習 檢討會議	團體	邀請廠商、家長、學生及職場輔導教師出席會議，分享及討論一年來學生實習之表現，感謝職場之協助外，建議事項也將作為未來努力之方向。	特教組長 特教班導師 職場輔導教師 職業輔導員

表 7-3　資源班一至三年級轉銜輔導與服務活動一覽表

年級	會議／活動名稱	形式	辦理內容	辦理單位
國中升高 一暑假	新生轉銜會議	個別	辦理當年度入學之身障生轉銜會議，邀請國中端老師、高職端導師與會，共同討論新生情況。	特教組長 資源班教師 資源班輔導員
高一 上學期	親師座談會	團體	由學務處辦理全校之親師座談會活動，活動包含專題演講及親師溝通時間等。	學務處 各班導師（含普教及特教）
	親師生涯輔導	團體	向家長、學生介紹未來升學管道，並鼓勵學生利用就學期間探索各職涯，以進行未來生涯規劃。	資源班教師資源班輔導員
	親師溝通 家訪或電訪	個別	視需要進行家訪或電訪，協助家長了解學生學習現況、職業教育課程學習內容，研討未來生涯轉銜發展可行方向。	資源班教師
高二 上學期	生涯輔導	團體	向家長、學生介紹未來升學管道，並鼓勵學生利用就學期間探索各職涯，以進行未來生涯規劃。	資源班教師資源班輔導員 各班導師
高二 下學期	生涯輔導	團體	協助調查學生升學意願及職涯性向，共同討論學生所需的協助與準備。	班級導師 資源班教師 資源班輔導員
高三 上學期	生涯輔導	團體	協助學生進行升學考試報名及職涯轉銜，以提供學生適切的服務。	教務處 資源班教師 資源班輔導員
高三 下學期	生涯輔導	個別	與學生進行個別晤談，了解其升學目標、協助學生認識科系概況及職涯規劃，以提供學生適切的服務。	資源班教師資源班輔導員
	轉銜會議	個別	協助已確定升學動向或有就業需求之學生進行轉銜會議，讓學生能盡速適應下一階段之生活，並延續相關服務。	特教組長 資源班教師 各任課教師 大學端資源教室 職業輔導員

237

第五項執行步驟為：成效評估。若以學生畢業後的流向調查結果作為教育的成效評估，此兩所實驗學校 105 學年度的畢業生升學或就業的結果如表 7-4 所示。若以畢業學生的離校後發展來看此兩校實施轉銜輔導與服務的成效，兩所技術型高中的教學績效乃非常值得肯定，甲校的身心障礙學生人數眾多，雖然最後賦閒在家的學生比例，分別為特教班有 13%、資源班有 14%，但實際整體的高中三年教育成效仍然值得肯定。從此資料分析中亦可發現，學生畢業後發展介於就業和無法就業而賦閒在家者，應有接受職業訓練的選擇，但實際接受職業訓練或職業試探的學生人數卻非常少，依據學校老師們的意見，乃是由於職業訓練機構所提供的機會一方面數量不多，再搭配學生的本身能力及生活獨立能力的適配性，因此畢業後先接受職業訓練再就業的學生比一直不高。

表 7-4　兩所實驗學校 105 學年度畢業生流向調查彙整表

學校類型／畢業生流向		就業	升學	職業訓練	賦閒在家
甲校	特教班（人數＝ 39）	32	2	0	5
	資源班（人數＝ 72）	31	31	0	10
乙校	特教班（人數＝ 12）	11	1	0	0
	資源班（人數＝ 9）	2	7	0	0

第六項執行步驟為：追蹤輔導。依據我國轉銜輔導的相關規定，高中畢業生畢業後至少追蹤 6 個月，兩所實驗學校皆能由特殊教育教師和資源班輔導員等相關人員，針對畢業生進行動向追蹤，了解其就學、就業或就養動態。

本文彙整我國近二十年來身心障礙學生高中職階段轉銜的相關研究趨勢，以了解我國轉銜議題的發展，再整合我國相關法規要求和行動研究成

效，發展出高中階段學校本位之轉銜輔導模式，本文再依據上述甲、乙兩所實驗學校，從高一到高三至離校後六個月的追蹤輔導轉銜歷程，擬以 Wehman（2013）的實務上成功轉銜服務之六項內容，以及 Kohler 等人（2016）的「轉銜方案向度 2.0 版」轉銜方案類別 2.0 版的五個教育指標向度，評析現階段我國高中階段學校本位之轉銜輔導與服務的發展現況，並且期能提出具體之建議。

　　先以 Wehman（2013）所提出的成功轉銜服務的六項內容觀之，甲、乙兩所實驗學校的集中式特教班在學生的職業能力、對就業的想法與準備，以及父母的參與其子女的轉銜規劃上，確實有其具體成效；然而在學生的社交能力、自我決策與自我倡權，以及社區的融合經驗上，學校所提供的學習經驗確實仍較為缺乏。另一方面資源班的轉銜輔導似乎偏向學生高中畢業後持續升學大專校院的選擇與發展，比較不強調學生的職業能力以及對就業的想法與準備；依據學校教育人員的經驗，上述現象主要乃是受到我國家長對其子女的期待之影響。

　　若以 Kohler 等人（2016）的的五個向度內容上來看，此兩所學校應該都有做到下列三個向度的主要內容：(1)考量學生的發展（含評估、基本學科能力、職業技能和就業能力、學生所需的支持、教學上的需求）；(2)整合相關單位的合作（含合作的機制、相關服務的銜接）；(3)家庭的參與（含家庭的參與、家庭的賦權）。

　　再者，比較集中式特教班（綜合職能科）和資源班兩種教育安置型態，可以發現現階段技術型高中身心障礙學生的轉銜輔導與服務在每個年級有不同的活動內容，但是分散式資源班和集中式特教班之間則有明顯落差。整體而言，現階段和集中式特教班的身心障礙學生所得到的轉銜輔導協助顯著優於資源班的學生，此現象乃和兩種安置型態的特殊教育教師數量和學生人數比例有關，目前依照法規規定集中式特殊教育班的教師編制，一個班級至少有兩位老師，但是一所高中職學校的全校資源班（教室）僅有一至三名的資源教師可以協助身心障礙學生的輔導，所以學生所得到的轉銜與輔導的服務相對非常有限；此外，目前我國相關辦法要求每一所學校的就業輔導員也僅提供綜合職能科學生的轉銜就業協助，並未包

含資源班（教室）的學生，此規定對於安置於資源班（教室）的身心障礙學生確實有所不公平。簡言之，針對資源（班）教室學生的轉銜輔導與服務，需要普通班教師、資源教師、資源教室輔導員和就業輔導員共同合作，將每一位身心障礙學生的轉銜輔導與服務，皆納入個別化教育計畫或生涯轉銜計畫規劃和實施，而高中資源教室輔導員確實可以承擔轉銜輔導與服務之個案輔導員職責。

伍、我國高中階段轉銜輔導與服務之展望

我國於 2019 年 8 月起，已全面實施十二年國民基本教育之特殊教育課程綱要，亦即是除了普通教育八大基本學習領域的課程調整外，基於特殊教育學生的學習需求，學校也應提供特殊教育的特殊需求領域課程，本文乃以 2016 年 Kohler 等人所提出的「轉銜方案向度 2.0 版」內容，並依據本文所提出臺灣高中階段學校本位的轉銜輔導與服務模式，提出配合十二年國民基本教育之特殊教育課程實施的具體建議，以落實我國在高中階段實施轉銜輔導與服務之成效。

一、考量學生的轉銜需求評估

目前，國內技術型高中基本上都會關注學生的基本學科能力或職業性向或職能評估，然而對於轉銜的整體需求評估以及未來成人生活能力的教學議題觸及較少；成人生活能力上的教學需求，除了調整普通教育的基本課程內容外，未來學校可藉由生活管理、社會技巧、輔助科技運用等特殊需求評估，以了解學生畢業後就業、升學或獨立生活所需能力的教學需求程度。目前我們轉銜需求的評估則受限於評量工具的不足，學校人員較少整體性進行轉銜的需求評估，因此轉銜評估工具的研發和推廣，乃有待相關人員一起努力。我國因為有技術型高中的設置，對於身心障礙學生的生涯轉銜發展非常有利，學生可以透過三年的學習時間強化職業知能，學校也有專門課程和專職單位實施學生的職場實習和就業輔導，此乃我國身心

障礙學生轉銜規劃之優勢資源；若在普通型高中，學校則可以透過特殊需求領域課程之職業教育等課程，協助學生了解並發展其職業性向或特定職業技能等。

二、以學生為主規劃的個別化教育計畫或生涯轉銜計畫

目前我國各級學校基本上都會因應法規要求，針對在校生開學前召開學生的個別化教育計畫會議。針對個別化教育計畫和生涯轉銜計畫的整合規劃，我國《各教育階段身心障礙學生轉銜輔導及服務辦法》第3條也載明高級中等以下學校應將生涯轉銜計畫納入學生個別化教育計畫，亦即是個別化教育計畫內容的第五項：學生之轉銜輔導及服務，內容包括升學、輔導、生活、就業、心理輔導、福利服務及其他相關專業服務等項目。也就是從高中一年級開始，學校就要開始規劃及實施學生的轉銜，若學生準備要繼續升學高等教育，未來三年的教育即要協助其為下一階段的升學預作準備，若學生畢業後即要就業，也要開始做就業的準備，而不管學生高中畢業後要升學或就業或有其他的規劃，學校教育皆要引導學生學習面對成人獨立生活的相關能力，以及身心障礙者如何運用社會福利資源的能力等，此皆要從高中一年級開始，學校需要運用個別化教育計畫或生涯轉銜計畫，為身心障礙學生的個別需求逐步建構無接縫轉銜（seamless transition）能力。此外，現階段我國身心障礙高中學生參與擬定自己的計畫之情況仍偏低，或許未來教師和家長也可多鼓勵和引導學生參與自己的生涯抉擇之規劃。

三、整合校內和校外相關單位的合作與銜接

針對身心障礙學生的轉銜計畫執行，目前學校的主要參與人員仍以特殊教育老師為主，即使是資源教室輔導員也受限於法規限制，沒有參與學生的轉銜輔導與服務，而職業輔導員目前也僅協助集中式特教班學生的就業轉銜，尚未擴及資源班的學生；未來期待學校的輔導教師和實習輔導人員也能介入身心障礙學生的轉銜輔導工作。至於校外相關單位的銜接，若

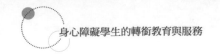

學生繼續升學大專校院,高中端和大專校院端的銜接成效較佳;而直接就業或無法就業的學生,在社政單位或勞工單位的銜接則較困難,這主要是受限於社政單位或勞工單位的人力資源不若學校單位充裕,另一方面也受限於學生的需求更多元性,執行上也更困難;然而如何強化非升學學生的轉銜銜接,仍有待相關單位再多發展因應策略。

四、家庭的參與、賦權與準備度

基於華人文化的傳統,身心障礙學生的父母傾向主導其子女的生涯規劃,林素貞等人(2016)對全國高中職資源教師和輔導員的問卷研究發現,我國高中職身心障礙學生的生涯抉擇最主要的決定者還是家長(家庭),第二順位是學生本人,第三順位才是學校老師等;由此可見,臺灣的家庭或父母大都積極參與身心障礙學生的生涯抉擇,但是是否有充分了解其子女的生涯興趣、優勢和偏好,則仍有待學校教師以親職教育多進行親師溝通。誠如本研究之實驗學校會不斷地與家長溝通,或是舉辦實習場所業主、職場員工和家長與學生的座談會,以及職場參訪,讓家長和學生了解不同職場的要求、就業環境的現況等,以提升家長對其子女就業轉銜的準備度。

五、學校有系統地規劃轉銜相關活動

目前,我國高中職特殊教育教師和輔導員基本上會遵循轉銜的相關法規要求,有擬訂生涯轉銜計畫、在特殊教育通報網上填寫學生的轉銜資料,但是針對系統性的規劃和實施轉銜活動仍覺得有困難。首先是對轉銜議題尚缺乏相關專業知能,也缺乏轉銜評估工具,亦即是目前從認知層次到執行層次,學校相關行政人員、教師和輔導員仍需要更多專業訓練和支援的配套措施,方能建構有系統且完整的校園氛圍,以落實執行高中階段身心障礙學生的轉銜輔導與服務。

教師在執行轉銜課程與教學過程中,最困擾的莫過於如何調整普通教育課程成為實用性或功能性課程內容,Wehman 與 Kregel(2012)以及 Polloway、Patton、Serna 與 Bailey（2018b）都曾經提出如何在普通教育課程當中，融入實用性課程的教學建議，除此之外，特殊需求領域當中的職業教育、生活管理、社會技巧、輔助科技運用等科目亦需要列入學生的轉銜課程，轉銜是一個整體性和系統性課程教學與活動的整合，教育工作人員和相關勞政單位人員需要攜手合作，方能讓學生在畢業離開學校之前，學習到足夠的相關經驗，具備基本的能力，以無接縫銜接至生涯的下一個成人階段。

▌陸、結語

綜論之，以學生高中畢業後的成果論述身心障礙學生的教育成效，應是我們檢視特殊教育長達十六年以上對身心障礙學生長期介入成果的具體指標之一，研究或實務都指出，學校提供多元、整體和系列的轉銜相關學習經驗，方能造就學生畢業後成功地適應成人的社會。現階段我國高中階段身心障礙學生的轉銜輔導與服務議題，確實已經在集中式特教班的職業技能養成和就業部分建立了正向的成效，但是整體而言，協助學生面對升學、就業和獨立生活的轉銜輔導仍處於方興未艾，尤其針對所有身心障礙學生的升學和獨立生活的能力養成，更是我們需要透過相關課程和活動，幫助學生建構的能力。

針對我國高中階段轉銜教育與服務的展望，期待相關法規可以定義更明確且具體、詳細的內容，導引學校可以整體性且系統化方式進行轉銜需求評估、擬定計畫、分工執行到追蹤輔導的歷程，而學校相關人員則需要更深入充實對轉銜的完整概念和實施的專業知能，加強與家長的溝通；臺灣的家長對其子女的升學或就業之生涯抉擇主導性較高，但是準備度並不見得相對足夠，因此如何透過不同形式的活動和溝通，讓家長可以了解其子女對職業的興趣、優勢和偏好，從而和學校教師共同合作，方能落實執行對每一位學生的轉銜輔導。

跨機構的合作是學生轉銜成功的重要關鍵，針對升學大專校院的身心障礙學生，目前各高中和大專校院資源教室單位的轉銜合作關係已臻穩定

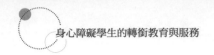

且有一定的制度模式，值得肯定。然而針對就業或是無法就業的學生，學校單位與勞工局的就業輔導或職業重建單位尚需要加強合作關係，方能協助有就業或參加職業訓練需求的身心障礙學生。特殊教育的最終目標，乃為培養身心障礙學生成為獨立自足的個體，身心障礙學生在高中畢業後，是否可以無接縫轉銜到就業職場或繼續升學高等教育，以及是否有足夠的生活自理能力，乃檢視著特殊教育的整體成效，更是身心障礙學生人生最重要的轉捩點，攸關著其成人的生活品質與福祉，也因此我們必須一起為身心障礙學生的轉銜輔導與服務而努力。

參考文獻

中文部分

尤淑君（2008）。高職特教班教師及就業服務人員在就業轉銜服務中專業角色之探討（未出版之碩士論文）。國立臺灣師範大學，臺北市。

石筱郁（2007）。高職綜合職能科智障學生家長參與子女轉銜規劃及未來生活照顧選擇之研究（未出版之碩士論文）。國立嘉義大學，嘉義縣。

吳季純（2008）。高職階段特殊教育學校（班）教師轉銜服務素養（未出版之碩士論文）。國立彰化師範大學，彰化市。

吳明燕（2015）。教師與家長攜手轉銜服務方案促進特殊學校綜合職能科自閉症學生生涯轉銜之行動研究（未出版之碩士論文）。國立臺南大學，臺南市。

吳宣鋒（2009）。特殊教育學校高職部實施智能障礙學生就業轉銜狀況之調查研究（未出版之碩士論文）。國立彰化師範大學，彰化市。

吳政寰（2019）。中部地區高級中等職業學校特殊教育教師實施就業轉銜服務之調查研究（未出版之碩士論文）。國立彰化師範大學，彰化市。

宋采霓（2016）。高中職特教班學生生涯轉銜動機及其相關影響因素之調查研究（未出版之碩士論文）。中原大學，桃園縣。

李玉錦（2014）。高職特教班自閉症學生自我決策就業轉銜教學方案之行動研究（未出版之博士論文）。國立臺灣師範大學，臺北市。

李建德（2012）。就業轉銜方案以改善高職學習障礙學生求職自我效能低落之行動研究（未出版之碩士論文）。國立彰化師範大學，彰化市。

李淑君（2003）。女性智能障礙高職學生就業轉銜之研究（未出版之碩士論文）。國立彰化師範大學，彰化市。

李雯琪（2010）。特殊教育學校智能障礙高職畢業生家長對其子女離校準備之研究（未出版之碩士論文）。朝陽科技大學，臺中市。

周玫君（2018）。特殊教育學校高職部就業轉銜學生性別意識：身體自主權培力成效之研究（未出版之博士論文）。國立彰化師範大學，彰化市。

林宏熾（1999）。身心障礙者生涯規劃與轉銜教育。臺北市：五南。

林和姻（2003）。高中職階段身心障礙學生升學轉銜服務之研究（未出版之碩士論文）。國立彰化師範大學，彰化市。

林幸台（2019）。身心障礙者生涯輔導與轉銜服務（第二版）。新北市：心理。

林炯承（2011）。高中職學習障礙學生轉銜服務需求度、滿意度、符合度及其相關因素之研究（未出版之碩士論文）。國立彰化師範大學，彰化市。

林素貞（2007）。個別化教育計畫之實施。臺北市：五南。

林素貞（2014）。資源教室方案與經營。臺北市：五南。

林素貞、詹孟琦、陳玉娸（2016）。我國高中職轉銜輔導與服務運作模式之研究。教育部國民及學前教育署成果報告。臺北市：教育部。

邱志鴻（2013）。從職場實習到就業：親師合作支持高職特教班學生參與就業轉銜（未出版之碩士論文）。國立臺灣師範大學，臺北市。

胡曼莉（2013）。智能障礙學生大學升學之路探究（未出版之碩士論文）。國立臺灣師範大學，臺北市。

張嘉容（2016）。高職綜合職能科畢業生職場實習留用經驗探討（未出版之碩士論文）。國立高雄師範大學，高雄市。

教育部（2010）。各教育階段身心障礙學生轉銜輔導及服務辦法。臺北市：作者。

教育部（2019）。特殊教育法。臺北市：作者。

許明儀（2006）。臺北縣高職綜合職能科畢業生就業轉銜服務狀況調查研究（未出版之碩士論文）。中國文化大學，臺北市。

許芳瑜（2009）。家長參與智能障礙者轉銜歷程之研究：應用生態系統觀

點（未出版之碩士論文）。國立臺灣師範大學，臺北市。

許家璇（2003）。高職階段智能障礙學生休閒娛樂轉銜服務之研究（未出版之碩士論文）。國立彰化師範大學，彰化市。

許雅婷（2008）。中部地區特殊教育學校高職部智能障礙學生家長轉銜服務認知與參與轉銜服務之研究（未出版之碩士論文）。國立彰化師範大學，彰化市。

郭嫦燕（2014）。綜合職能科學生家長參與轉銜服務之研究：以雙北市為例（未出版之碩士論文）。國立臺灣師範大學，臺北市。

陳怡錦（2014）。特殊學校高職部智能障礙畢業生接受就業轉銜服務歷程之探究（未出版之碩士論文）。國立屏東科技大學，屏東縣。

陳冠伶（2011）。高職特教班教師對就業轉銜實施現況與需求之調查研究（未出版之碩士論文）。國立臺中教育大學，臺中市。

陳映如（2009）。高中職特教班推動校外職場實習轉銜服務之個案探討（未出版之碩士論文）。國立雲林科技大學，雲林縣。

陳維婷（2013）。從不可能到可能？兩名綜合職能科自閉症畢業生轉銜至就業歷程（未出版之碩士論文）。國立臺灣師範大學，臺北市。

陳靜江、鈕文英（2008）。高中職階段身心障礙者轉銜能力評量表之編製。特殊教育研究學刊，33（1），1-20。

陳靜怡（2006）。特殊教育學校高職部智能障礙學生家長轉銜服務期望及其相關因素之研究（未出版之碩士論文）。國立彰化師範大學，彰化市。

陳韻年（2013）。臺北市特殊教育教師及職業重建服務人員對高職學生社區化就業轉銜服務之了解與期待（未出版之碩士論文）。國立臺灣師範大學，臺北市。

黃小婷（2009）。就業轉銜服務現況與需求之研究：以臺北市公私立高職綜合職能科學生為例（未出版之碩士論文）。中國文化大學，臺北市。

黃蕙蓮（2006）。高職特教班就業轉銜服務現況與相關因素之探討（未出版之碩士論文）。國立臺灣師範大學，臺北市。

黃靜宜（2006）。高雄市高中職身心障礙畢業生就業轉銜服務現況之研究（未出版之碩士論文）。國立政治大學，臺北市。

黃璽璇（2005）。高職階段特殊教育（班）智能障礙學生生活轉銜之研究（未出版之碩士論文）。國立彰化師範大學，彰化市。

楊岱蓉（2016）。影響特殊教育青少年離校後轉銜之探討（未出版之碩士論文）。國防醫學院，臺北市。

楊純斐（2011）。高職階段特殊教育教師轉銜服務相關知能之研究（未出版之碩士論文）。中臺科技大學，臺中市。

楊琇雅（2011）。高中職階段教師實施與應用身心障礙學生轉銜評量之研究（未出版之碩士論文）。國立臺灣師範大學，臺北市。

葉盈均（2014）。新北市綜合職能科家長參與子女升高職階段的轉銜服務現況之研究（未出版之碩士論文）。國立臺北教育大學，臺北市。

劉玉婷（2001）。高職特殊學校（班）智能障礙學生轉銜服務之現況調查及其相關因素之探討（未出版之碩士論文）。國立高雄師範大學，高雄市

歐怡君（2003）。高雄市特殊學校高職部智能障礙學生家長對子女轉銜課程服務意見之研究（未出版之碩士論文）。國立臺灣師範大學，臺北市。

潘佳伶（2017）。臺東縣高中職綜合職能科畢業生生活品質調查研究（未出版之碩士論文）。國立高雄師範大學，高雄市。

蕭漢寧（2014）。雙北市高職綜合職能科學生家長對轉銜服務之參與現況與期望（未出版之碩士論文）。國立臺灣師範大學，臺北市。

鍾和村（2013）。高職階段特殊教育學校教師與家長轉銜合作之研究（未出版之碩士論文）。國立臺灣師範大學，臺北市。

簡美蘭（2010）。高雄市特殊學校高職部教師與家長對智能障礙學生轉銜能力表現與需求之評價（未出版之碩士論文）。國立高雄師範大學，高雄市。

蘇皇妃（2008）。高職階段特殊教育學校智能障礙學生生涯轉銜課程分析與課程模式之研究（未出版之博士論文）。國立彰化師範大學，彰化

市。

蘇盈宇（2003）。高職特教班智能障礙學生就業轉銜服務現況與需求之研究（未出版之碩士論文）。國立彰化師範大學，彰化市。

蘇湘甯（2014）。高職特教教師於就業轉銜服務提供時運用職業重建資源之現況探討（未出版之碩士論文）。國立彰化師範大學，彰化市。

蘇微真（2015）。高職特教班學生在新舊課綱中轉銜能力之差異（未出版之碩士論文）。國立高雄師範大學，高雄市。

龔瑀婷（2013）。綜合職能科智能障礙學生升大專校院轉銜技能準備度之研究（未出版之碩士論文）。臺北市立體育學院，臺北市。

英文部分

Brolin, D. E. (1995). *Career education: A functional life skills approach* (3rd ed.). Columbus, OH: Prentice-Hall.

Clark, G. M., Synatschk, K. O., Patton, J. R., & Steel, L. E. (2012). *Career Interests, Preferences, and Strengths Inventory (CIPSI)*. Austin, TX: Pro-ed.

Flexer, R. W., Baer, R. M, Luft, P., & Simmons, T. J. (2013). *Transition planning for secondary students with disabilities* (4th ed.). Upper Saddle River, NJ: Pearson.

Halpern, A. S. (1991). Transition: Old wine in new bottles. *Exceptional Children, 58* (3), 202-211.

Halpern, A. S., Yovanoff, P., Doren, B., & Benz, M. R. (1995). Predicting participation in postsecondary education for school leavers with disabilities. *Exceptional Children, 62*, 151-164.

Heal, L. W., & Rusch, F. R. (1995). Predicting employment for students who leave special education high school programs. *Exceptional Children, 61*, 472-487.

Individuals with Disabilities Education Act. (IDEA) (2004). *Section 300.43 transition services*. Retrieved from https://sites.ed.gov/idea/regs/b/a/300.43

Kohler, P. D. (1993). Best practices in transition: Substantiated or implied? *Career*

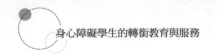

Development for Exceptional Individuals, 16, 107-121.

Kohler, P. D. (1996). *Taxonomy for transition programming: Linking research and practice*. Champaign, IL: University of Illinois at Urbana-Champaign, Transition Research Institute.

Kohler, P. D. (1998). Implementing a transition perspective of education: A comprehensive approach to planning and delivering secondary education and transition services. In F. R. Rusch & J. Chadsey (Eds.), *High school and beyond: Transition from school to work* (pp. 179- 205). Belmont, CA: Wadsworth.

Kohler, P. D., Gothberg, J. E., Fowler, C., & Coyle, J. (2016). *Taxonomy for transition programming 2.0: A model for planning, organizing, and evaluating transition education, services, and programs*. Retrieved from https://reurl.cc/xDv0jZ

Kohler, P., & Field, S. (2003). Transition-focused education: Foundation for the future. *Journal of Special Education, 37*(3), 174-184.

Levinson, E. (1998). *Transition: Facilitating the postschool adjustment of students with disabilities*. Boulder, Co: Westview Press.

Morgan, R. L., & Riesen, T. (2016). *Promoting successful transition to adulthood for students with disabilities*. New York, NY: The Guilford Press.

National Technical Assistance Center on Transition. [NTACT] (2019). *Predictors by outcome area*. Retrieved from https://reurl.cc/rlv8jr

Patton, J. R., & Clark, G. M. (2014). *Transition Planning Inventory (2nd ed.): Administration and resource guide*. Austin, TX: Pro-ed.

Polloway, E. A., Patton, J. R., Serna, L., & Bailey, J. W. (2018a). Career development and transition across school levels. In *Strategies for teaching learners with special needs* (11th ed.) (pp. 352-380). Boston, MA: Pearson.

Polloway, E. A., Patton, J. R., Serna, L., & Bailey, J. W. (2018b). Applied academics. In *Strategies for teaching learners with special needs* (11th ed.) (pp. 325-351). Boston, MA: Pearson.

Sitlington, P., Neubert, D. A., & Clark, G. (2010). *Transition education and services for students with disabilities* (5th ed.). Boston, MA: Pearson.

Test, D. W., Aspel, N. P., & Everson, J. M. (2006). *Transition methods for youth with disabilities*. Upper Saddle River, NJ: Pearson.

Test, D. W., Mazzotti, V. L., Mustian, A. L., Fowler, C. H., Kortering, L., & Kohler, P. (2009). Evidence-based secondary transition predictors for improving postschool outcomes for students with disabilities. *Career Development for Exceptional Individuals, 32*, 160-181.

Thomas, J. E. (2019). *Transition planning*. Salem Press Encyclopedia. Retrieved from https://reurl.cc/oDydoq

Trainor, A. A. (2017). *Transition by design: Improving equity and outcomes for adolescents with disabilities*. New York, NY: Teachers College Press.

Wehman, P. (2013). *Life beyond the classroom: Transition strategies for young adults with disabilities* (5th ed.). Baltimore, MD: Paul H. Brookes.

Wehman, P., & Kregel, J. (2012). *Functional curriculum for elementary, middle, and secondary age students with special needs* (3rd ed.). Austin, TX: Pro-ed.

第八章　學習障礙學生的生涯發展與轉銜

The Career Development and Transition of Students with Learning Disabilities

　　本章乃透過兩位學習障礙大學生從小到大的成長歷程,分享他們如何面對自己的學習障礙所造成的升學、生活和就業上的挑戰,本章的形成先由編輯給兩位個案的父親和輔導老師敘述架構:(1)我有哪些學習上的困難,我何時確定知道自己是學習障礙者,長期以來那些困難如何影響我的學習和生活,甚至成人後的就業?(2)我的學習障礙如何影響我的升學抉擇,例如:學校的選擇、科系的選擇,或是就業抉擇等,若是未就業者,可以描述未來就業抉擇的考量;(3)從我個人的成長經驗,我認為學習障礙者在面對學習、升學、就業準備與抉擇以及生活挑戰時,可以有哪些考量和準備?此兩篇經驗分享乃以學習障礙學生為主,父親與輔導老師為輔,共同完成學習障礙者的生涯轉銜故事。

壹、一位學習障礙大學生的故事：我有興趣又擅長的事
The Story of a College Student with Learning Disabilities: The Topic that I am Interested in and Good at it

余昌儒（Jimmy Yu）

　　昌儒目前就讀大學三年級，過去讀中小學時成績都是全班吊車尾，就讀大學後，大一到大二的學業成績都維持在全班前五名以內。本文第一部分是昌儒自己獨立打字完成的自我成長表述，沒有他人的協助或提示，爸爸和編輯只是做極少部分的字詞增減、錯字訂正和增減標點符號。第二部分是昌儒的爸爸肩負起孩子生涯發展協助者的角色，一路帶著孩子做升學和生活的抉擇與適應，從家長的角度提出學習障礙者的轉銜經驗分享。

一、昌儒說自己的故事

　　我從小學一年級開始課業就完全跟不上，只要有關閱讀和書寫的事情我都沒辦法，當時覺得上學就是折磨，上課幾乎都聽不懂，一直被老師罵、被同學搞、回家爸媽看到成績也不開心，每天就是罰抄和罰寫，其他同學期末時可能只寫完一本作業本，我光是罰抄就寫了三本以上，但就算寫了這麼多，考試我還是不會，尤其是國文、英文和數學。國文考試我只寫選擇題，因為改錯字我找不到錯字在哪裡？造句和接龍我只會寫注音，我看得懂國字，但要我寫字，我就是想不起來那些字長得怎樣。英文考試我只寫聽力測驗，因為我背不起一堆字母組成的單字，但聽力測驗我至少能猜得到答案，而且比較聽得懂。數學考試我就真的沒那個腦算，沒轍了。除了社會、自然我比較有興趣，而且考試都是選擇題，成績稍微高分一點外，不然，基本上我考試超過 30 分，同學們就覺得是我作弊，這種狀

態一直持續到國中畢業。我就讀附中國中部，大部分同學都是高材生，成績優異，還會鄙視我。每次考完試都會說我拉低班上成績，所以我乾脆擺爛，大家互相傷害，我上課會睡覺，拿美工刀切課本和畫畫等。我依然只對自然、歷史那些可以聽故事的課程，還有操作類型的家政課和電腦課等有興趣。

因為我的成績在全年級已經黑到發亮，於是老師們叫我去輔導室參加抽離課程和補救教學，還好我遇到一位很好的輔導老師，輔導老師一對一教我的東西，比原班還簡單、也慢許多，國文一句一起唸個好幾次，聽完一遍再看字，然後考試使用報讀，不會寫的字可以寫注音，這樣一來我每一項考試都進步了，雖然是用注音符號，但是證明了我也能默寫出課文與作文，同學們也許會覺得很可笑，不過我跟老師都很高興，之後我也更有自信。到了國二下學期時，輔導老師要我去做檢測，我去參加檢測後，才確認我是識字讀寫障礙學生，以後我參加考試、考證照都可以使用報讀等特殊考場服務，我的分數也不會比一般人差。

國中時期我整天在玩電腦和看電影，在學校時除了好玩的課程、下課打球，以及和同等級的同學混以外，我沒有別的地方能有成就感；當時我為了不想待在無聊的學校，所以國中時就去其他高職參加技藝班。我參加過兩次技藝班，一次是多媒體設計相關課程，一次是電機電子相關課程。我參加這兩次的技藝班，成績都是前幾名，還算不錯；由於我在多媒體這方面有更多興趣，而且多媒體著重操作，不像一般高中那麼強調讀、寫、背、考，這種是會讓人窒息的學習方式，所以升高中時，我就選擇讀高職的多媒體設計科。

我升上大學時也差不多，選擇影視設計科。因為我很清楚自己喜歡什麼、討厭什麼、無法做什麼、缺陷是什麼，所以我要進入能夠發揮自己專長，並且是自己有興趣的科系去發展。雖然上不了比較好的學校，不過我相信不管在哪裡，修行都是看個人。我覺得我的學習障礙情況會隨著年齡增長而變好，一開始我從無法理解文字、無法閱讀，到現在只剩下寫字方面的問題較嚴重而已。不過因為我在大學大部分是用電腦作業，或是需要動手操作的術科測驗，極少學科有需要手寫的部分。我跟老師解釋一下我

的困難，老師們也大多都能通融。我未來應該也會選擇相關行業，而且現在能夠使用的工具也比以前多很多，我相信我一樣能表現的比普通人好。

我在國二時才知道自己是學習障礙，最早從幼稚園開始到國二，我有長達八年的在學時間都過得非常辛苦。還好我運氣好，早點發現自己喜歡又擅長，並且值得精進的事物。我覺得在學期間不需要太在意成績和他人眼光，也不需要一直去跟別人做比較。多去探索尋找幾個自己既擅長又有熱情，甚至比別人優秀的事物，再鎖定一條不後悔的路，一直堅持下去就好了。

二、爸爸說昌儒的故事

誠如昌儒的自述，他其實是一位被鑑定具有讀寫障礙（dyslexia）及疑似亞斯伯格症輕微情緒困擾的孩子，直到國二時，輔導老師建議我們去做鑑定診斷，我們才確切知道昌儒是學習障礙學生。整整快九年的時間裡，在國中小學強調大量書寫文字訓練的教育階段裡，真的是難為他了！但是在那幾年之中，他會自創「圖像文字」來應付書寫問題，頗讓老師與同學們笑到噴飯，而老師們也會臭罵他一頓；事實上，他自創的「圖像文字」連我都看不懂。但這些文字或符號本身卻是具有系統性的編碼規則，即使事隔多日後我再問他每個符號的意義，他也都能夠一致性地回答我，顯然，這些圖像文字在他腦海中是對應到某個有意義、有系統、有連貫、有一致性的表徵，是一套可以用來表達他的概念及想法的代碼。同學們都幫他取個外號：「道士畫符」！他雖有讀寫障礙，但卻也能「倉頡造字」，連我都佩服！

昌儒經過縣市鑑輔會確定為讀寫障礙的特殊教育學生後，此後他的考試，我都為他申請報讀及電腦打字書寫服務。但是在學校模擬考試仍要求手寫下，他的作文成績只能得 1 級分；後來在升學高中職的國中會考作文考試裡，由於事先有申請特教生考場報讀服務，現場可用電腦打字，他的作文成績就可以得到 5 級分。我十分感謝教育部對特殊教育學生所提供的考場服務，讓他的潛能得以有發揮的機會！

　　昌儒的學習歷程真的很辛苦，小學一共就轉讀了四所學校。昌儒就讀的第一所小學是私立小學，每次要上英文課的前一堂課，昌儒的體溫就會自動升高到 38 度、39 度，連老師都害怕，趕緊把他送到保健室，到了保健室後，他的體溫就會慢慢恢復正常。所以，他的小一上學期的英文課，幾乎都在保健室度過。我發現這個問題時，已經太晚了。所以小一上學期中途，不得不幫他轉學到公立學校，這是他的第二所小學，昌儒一直讀到小二結束，學習才正慢慢地要上軌道。

　　到了昌儒升上三年級時，學校重新編班換導師，卻遇到一位求好心切、緊張過頭又有焦慮症的導師，把全班孩子逼到有人每天作惡夢、磨牙、說夢話罵人、啃指甲、拔頭髮或有人撕聯絡簿等不良行為的出現；而昌儒因為讀寫障礙的關係，老師指派 30 分鐘可以完成的作業，他卻可以寫兩個半小時以上，所以每天作業都寫到半夜。後來全班家長聯合起來要求校長更換導師，不然就要轉班或轉校，我個人認為家長與學校對抗，會不利於孩子的正常學習，所以我立即決定幫他轉學到一所新北市山區公立的鄉村型小學，也因此我每天早晚要各花 40 分鐘，開車送他上山去學校，這是昌儒的第三所小學。

　　第三所學校與臺北市的公立小學比較起來，是一所放牛吃草的學校，但是非常適合昌儒的胃口；這所小學的老師們和臺北市公立小學比較起來，工作和精神壓力相對比較低，中午時刻，我還觀察到有老師居然有空和有閒情逸致玩電動遊戲。在這所學校裡，昌儒不僅曬得比較黑、過敏症狀也沒了、體力與免疫力都變好了，不僅學會游泳，也敢徒手抓昆蟲，玩優人神鼓、舞龍舞獅、扯鈴等才藝活動，身高也快速抽高，體重也加重。他的班級導師十分了解昌儒的狀況，竟然允許他的作業可以分期付款，週一的作業週四前再交即可，週二的作業週五前再交即可，依此類推。我第一次碰到老師出的作業可以「分期付款」繳交！不會寫的中文字他可以使用注音符號代替，甚至使用自創的圖像文字也行，不過導師會問他每個符號的意思為何。這讓我覺得這所學校很適合昌儒的生存，很對他的胃口！可惜好景不常，因為搬家和我疲於接送他上下學的緣故，他在該校只讀了將近兩年，升五年級時，只好又把他轉學到新家門口前的臺北市公立小

學，這是他就讀的第四所小學。

第四所學校學區內比較多勞工階層及新移民家長，因此對孩子課業的要求，比較是順其自然發展，沒有像一般公立明星學校那麼強調學業競爭。我向昌儒分析選擇「就近就讀」的利弊得失後，他同意轉學。自此，從五年級讀到小學六年級畢業，他每天睡到 7：40 起床，趕在 7：50 前到校。因為睡得夠飽，吃得夠好，運動得夠，所以他在小學最後這兩年裡長高約 10 公分。我認為孩子長高一點，長壯一點，同學們也比較不敢對他肢體霸凌！尤其像昌儒這樣課業墊底、個性溫和的孩子，如果在學校長期飽受霸凌，其實是很容易塑造出將來會危害社會的反社會人格與行為；幸好，我應該有即時幫忙消除這個潛在的危機！

昌儒升學到附中的國中部後，遇到一位很棒的導師，他有很正確的教育哲學理念，認為孩子的成就是多元的，十分鼓勵學生去探索自己的性向。雖然附中的學生家長們多半是我的同事，與我的社經地位都相當，但校園氛圍比較重視與強調課業競爭的重要性，因此昌儒的同學也常常因為學業問題而瞧不起他、貶損他。幸好，他的導師會鼓勵與強調其他才藝活動的重要性，這讓昌儒有機會在班上同學面前一展長才。昌儒自學 RPG 軟體程式，設計一個闖關遊戲，在期末才藝表演時秀給全班同學看。他的這項才藝表演打垮全班同學，自此同學們開始對他另眼相看，昌儒也從此開始建立起對學習的信心，更加努力去探索自己喜歡的是什麼等。他開始探索自己生涯發展的問題，更加上輔導老師對他的了解與幫助，細心與耐心地對他進行補救教學，也鼓勵我們去申請特殊教育的鑑定，以確認了他的特殊教育學生的身分與接受特殊教育服務。從此之後，昌儒的升學高中，我讓他自己決定，選讀什麼科系，也是他自己決定，我只是協助分析每一所學校及科系的優劣點給他參考而已。國中畢業後，他最後自己決定選讀離家近的高職多媒體設計科，大學也是選讀離家近的科技大學影視設計系，這都是他自己的決定，我充分地支持和尊重他！

身為一位學習障礙孩子的父親，這十幾年來，我也真的改變不少！這就好比一位健康的人，平時是不太容易體會健康的涵意，直到失去健康或遇到健康有問題，才會有機會重新審視、體會與定義什麼叫做健康。我也是

一樣！我是一位從小就頗具自我效能、時間管理、學習方法和學術性向很高的學生，任何學習都難不倒我，也一路順順利利成為大學教授。直到碰到自己的孩子是學習障礙時，才讓我有機會重新去審視在「學習光譜」另一端的學習不利者，他們的學習到底有多大的困難？

根據我自己的學術研究心得，「學習成就與有效投入學習的時間是成正比的」。因此，把時間專注地投入在一件事情上，對學習而言是一件很重要的事。而該如何讓人專心於一件事，其背後的動力來源即是「興趣」。心理學上，不是就有學習的「快樂原則」說法嘛！因為有趣，才能讓學習持久！而要讓學習持久，就必須能夠經驗過「積小勝成大勝」的學習歷程，也就是，從小小的學習成果有趣，獲得情緒的正向回饋，如果還能受到來自家長、老師或同儕的鼓勵，情緒的正向回饋會慢慢自動化成一種良性習慣，學習者只要再給予足夠的學習時間，就一定可以達成令人滿意的結果。因此，興趣很重要，也就是說，學習的內在動機──「興趣」，才是促進學習能夠持久的動力所在！

一個人很擅長做某一件事，即表示這個人很有信心、有把握可以把該事情做得很好，而這樣的動力來源，通常也是來自於個人過去曾經累積出來的成就感。隨著做同一件事情的成就感愈累積愈高，即可將事情愈做愈熟練，甚至可以達到成為一種「習慣性」的境界，個人絲毫不花心力地，即可把一件事情駕輕就熟地做好。因此，把一件事情做到成為習慣化，自然而然地一件事情即可不必多花力氣、心思與時間去自動完成它，這就是最具效率與效能的一種正向心理素質！我個人的自我效能就是這樣建立起來的！

因此，從昌儒小時候開始，我就一直鼓勵他，需要花時間去探索與了解什麼是自己真正喜歡的事務？什麼又是自己真正所擅長的領域？人如果能夠把這兩者結合起來，甚至作為生涯抉擇的依據，那就準沒錯了！一位能夠從事既喜歡又擅長工作的人，做完工作後又能獲得老闆給的薪水，這就是「幸福」的工作，這個人即是「幸福的人」。看來，到目前為止，昌儒似乎是有聽進去我的話，正往此方向邁進中！

身為學習障礙生的家長，我的個人體會是：對孩子提供長期且無盡的

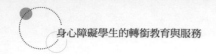

關懷，給孩子支持與鼓勵的力量，這是孩子成長所必要之認知能力與良好行為的基礎。就像一棵小幼苗一樣，如果人類對它提供無盡地關懷與照顧，小幼苗才有機會長成一棵大樹，大樹反過來也會提供人類遮風避雨的保護作用。所以你能說細心呵護孩子不重要嗎？

▶貳、一位學習障礙大學生的學習歷程：
　　成長是找到自己想要的未來
The Story of a Student with Learning Disabilities:
The Growth is Finding What I Want to Be

林靜如（Ching-Ju Lin）、**王小語**（Lisa Wong）

　　學習障礙者如何在大學生活中發展出適應策略，以克服他們的學習上的挑戰，並能為下一階段的升學或就業做準備？以下將從一位學習障礙大學生的個人訪談、個案管理老師的回饋，以及高中與大學階段的轉銜和學習歷程，梳理其在經歷挫折逃避後，又開始嘗試行動，並在自省中調適與再行動，繼而產生職涯目標的成長歷程。冀望此學習故事能為未來預備就讀大學，或同樣正在為自身生涯發展努力的人提供參考。

一、從懵懂走向覺察

　　小語現就讀私立科技大學觀光休閒系二年級，雖從國小時就自覺自身在英文與數學方面都跟不上班上同學，然而因為父親早逝，需由不識字的母親獨力工作負擔家計，使得小語的生活與學習困難難以獲得家庭的充分關心，所以她一直到九年級時才被鑑定為學習障礙學生，當時她的學習障礙鑑定為書寫合併數學障礙。

　　小語從國小時隱約感受到自己學習比別人慢，到九年級時被老師告知有「學習障礙」。直到大學小語雖然仍不能具體說明「學習障礙是什麼」，以及當時如何獲得這個特殊教育資格的過程，然而她能覺察有學習障礙對自身帶來的影響：自己「學習的會比較慢」、「動作比較慢」、「要花更多的時間與精力去學習」，清楚地知道自己在數學、語言方面的劣勢，以及在地理、歷史領域上的興趣與優勢，這些自我能力的了解將影響其對學業與未來生／職涯發展的自我決策與行動。

　　雖然書寫能力弱，而且有顯著的數學學習困難，小語在不清楚自身興

趣與性向的情況下，以一種「當初不知道怎麼想的，就想去讀讀看」的懵懂狀態，在升高中時選擇某國立高商商業經營科就讀。然而，因為不希望被同儕發現自己是特殊教育學生，小語在當時並未接受任何特殊教育的補救教學服務，所以學業表現普遍不佳，且自覺學習得非常痛苦。在選擇升上大學時，小語從先前經驗中習得教訓，知道自己數學能力不佳，就先排除與商業相關的科系，再依據自身對「地理」、「歷史」的興趣，並且事先上網查詢系科相關資料後，選擇了「觀光休閒」。在這次讀大學的抉擇時，小語已經知道自己「要學什麼」，而且能符合能力優弱勢的科系就讀。進入大學就讀後，小語也逐漸改變以往拒絕使用特殊教育資源，以避免被標籤的態度，在資源教室輔導員的協助下，針對自己弱勢的語言科目申請課業輔導。

二、從實作邁向生涯定向

大學二年級是小語的重要轉捩點，大一時雖然選擇了覺得有興趣且與專長相符的科系，但是大學裡需要個人自行規劃與負責的學習環境，伴隨著不佳的學業能力，使得小語缺乏學習動機，上課出席率低落，自陳自己「不常來學校，都在家耍廢」。然而，也是在此時期，小語首度嘗試在校外打工。在嘗試連鎖藥妝店的門市、餐廳內場等工作後，小語發現自己「記憶力不佳」、「動作慢」、「不擅與他人應對」、「數學不佳，計算速度慢，容易計算錯誤」的特質，確認自己不適合需要快速度、計算能力，或與人溝通的工作。因此，餐廳工作中需要高效率與高速洗洗切切的內場、需要與人溝通的外場，乃至於需要計算能力，並回應客人不同即時問題的門市服務人員，都被小語列為不適合自己的工作。

升上大二後，由於感受到資源教室確實能協助自己的學業學習與生活適應，小語開始願意主動接觸特教資源，也在輔導員的鼓勵下，鼓起勇氣申請擔任資源教室的工讀生，每週於固定時間前來資源教室從事整理環境、傳遞公文、處理文書資料，甚至是協助其他身障同學等工作。資源教室的工作不太要求效率性，而且是提供教導與練習的環境。小語在經過近

一年的工讀生工作後，自覺找到適合且有興趣的未來工作——「文書行政」。她期待下一年能維持在資源教室的工讀工作，藉此訓練自己的能力，與嚮往的未來職業接軌。懷抱著對未來職業的嚮往，小語也因此產生需要學習如 Excel、Google 表單等文書軟體的具體學習目標，並具備堅定的信念與學習動機——這些技能雖然尚未習得，「可是我可以學」。

三、一段期盼自我實現的旅程

對許多學科能力弱但實作能力相對為強項的學習障礙學生而言，若能強化自己的優勢能力，並往自身的興趣領域發展，則未來前景可期。詢問小語對學弟妹的學習建議時，小語提出「在選科系時，應該先確認自己有沒有興趣」，而針對如何探索自身興趣，小語則建議可運用：「勤查資料」、「實際動手做」等方式進行。此外，她並根據自身經驗，鼓勵學弟妹在學校遇到困難時，應該「善用學校資源」，尋求資源教室老師的協助。歸納小語所提出的建議，面對升學與學習挑戰，學習障礙大學生可抱持勤奮、積極主動、能設定目標的學習態度，並發展能向外尋求協助與資源的自我決策能力。

藉著在不同職種的工作經驗，小語更加了解自己的優劣勢能力、擅長的和不適合做的工作。在一次一次校內外打工經驗的實作嘗試中，她從「不能」（I can't...）中，產生了「能做」（I can...），以及「嚮往去做」（I look forward to...）的領域，並配搭上自身的興趣，建構出未來的職涯目標。小語的敘說呈顯了一位學習障礙大學生，如何在實作中認識自我，並藉由學校／環境提供的支持性鷹架，建立自身生涯目標的藍圖。雖然，此份藍圖尚有許多模糊未清之處，然而這份將在行動中持續修正的藍圖，也正代表著成人學障者依然具備學習與發展的潛能。

藉由自身的自我覺知和不斷嘗試，以及周遭環境能對個人的實作探索提供有效的支持與資源，這些都有助於學習障礙學生從行動中邁向成功的未來成人世界。就像小語所言：「感覺未來很難達成某些目標，可是我也會盡我的能力去完成，在一定的時間點讓自己找到自己想要的東西，就是感覺自己長大了。」

NOTE

國家圖書館出版品預行編目（CIP）資料

身心障礙學生的轉銜教育與服務 / 林素貞、趙本強、
黃秋霞主編. -- 初版. -- 新北市：心理，2020.01
面；　公分. --（特殊教育系列；63160）
ISBN 978-986-191-896-9（平裝）

1.身心障礙教育 2.生涯規劃 3.教材 4.中等教育

529.54　　　　　　　　　　　　　108022854

特殊教育系列 63160

身心障礙學生的轉銜教育與服務

策　　　劃：台灣學障學會
主　　　編：林素貞、趙本強、黃秋霞
責任編輯：郭佳玲
總 編 輯：林敬堯
發 行 人：洪有義
出 版 者：心理出版社股份有限公司
地　　　址：231 新北市新店區光明街 288 號 7 樓
電　　　話：(02) 29150566
傳　　　真：(02) 29152928
郵撥帳號：19293172　心理出版社股份有限公司
網　　　址：http://www.psy.com.tw
電子信箱：psychoco@ms15.hinet.net
駐美代表：Lisa Wu（lisawu99@optonline.net）
排 版 者：辰皓國際出版製作有限公司
印 刷 者：辰皓國際出版製作有限公司
初版一刷：2020 年 1 月
Ｉ Ｓ Ｂ Ｎ：978-986-191-896-9
定　　　價：新台幣 320 元